CALIFAILURE

CALIFAILURE

Reversing the Ruin of America's Worst-Run State

STEVE HILTON

with Edward Ring

BROADSIDE BOOKS

HarperCollins books may be purchased for educational, business, or sales promotional use. For information, please email the Special Markets Department at SPsales@harpercollins.com.

Broadside Books™ and the Broadside logo are trademarks of HarperCollins Publishers.

FIRST EDITION

Library of Congress Cataloging-in-Publication Data
Names: Hilton, Steve, author.
Title: Califailure : reversing the ruin of
America's worst-run state / Steve Hilton.
Description: First edition. | New York : HarperCollins Publishers,
2025. | Includes bibliographical references and index.
Identifiers: LCCN 2024049814 (print) | LCCN
2024049815 (ebook) | ISBN 9780063390416
(hardcover) | ISBN 9780063390409 (ebook)
Subjects: LCSH: Administrative agencies—California—
Evaluation. | Executive departments—California—Evaluation. |
California—Politics and government—21st century.
Classification: LCC JK8741 .H558 2025 (print) | LCC
JK8741 (ebook) | DDC 351.794—dc23/eng/20241216
LC record available at https://lccn.loc.gov/2024049814
LC ebook record available at https://lccn.loc.gov/2024049815

25 26 27 28 29 LBC 5 4 3 2 1

To Rachel and the boys. Love you so much.

I'm not interested in funding failure any longer.
—*Gavin Newsom, April 18, 2024*

Neither are we, Governor. Neither are we.

CONTENTS

INTRODUCTION

California means to America what America means to the world. California has always represented the essence of the American Dream. Optimism, adventure, opportunity. We are the home of free spirits, rebels, people from all over the world who dream big and work hard. There's nowhere better than California. The beautiful Golden State has been an inspiration to so many, for so long. Still today, our innovation connects the world. Our creativity entertains the world. Our farmers feed the world. In California, we build the future. We shape the culture.

But everyone can see that things have gone off track. California is now as famous for dystopian scenes of public squalor as for our magnificent landscapes. Upward mobility—the foundation of the California Dream—has been crushed as it becomes increasingly difficult to buy a home or afford the basics of a good life. Crime is up. The quality of life is down. In 2022, for the first time in state history, California lost representation in the Congress thanks to the exodus of people and businesses to other states.

For over a century, there wasn't anything Californians couldn't do. People moved to the Golden State by the millions. There were good jobs, affordable homes, great schools and universities, beaches, mountains, the best weather on earth.

But something terrible has happened. California is not the welcoming place it used to be.

In recent years, California has been top of every list you'd want to be at the bottom of, and bottom of every list you'd want to be at the top of. For every essential—homes, rent, tuition, gasoline, electricity, and water—the highest prices in the United States. The worst business climate in the country. The highest taxes. The highest housing costs and lowest rate of home ownership. The highest unemployment and lowest income growth. Shamefully, despite the enormous concentration of wealth in places like Silicon Valley, California has America's highest rate of poverty. (Yes, *rate*—not just the highest number of people living in poverty.) According to a recent study, over one-third of Californians cannot meet their basic needs. Public schools are failing, crime is soaring, cities are overrun with tens of thousands of desperate homeless people, electricity is unreliable, water is rationed, and the mismanaged forests are burning like hell.[1]

Worse, while the fabric of daily life disintegrates into chaos and decay, the politicians and activists who are in charge spend their time—and taxpayers' money—pushing increasingly fringe race, gender, and "climate" extremism instead of attending to the basics of good governance. Who cares if homeless addicts die in the street, schools fail to teach, families can't afford homes, and businesses can't make a profit if you can ban plastic bags or AI parodies on the internet? It is only a slight exaggeration to say that California has become the place where jokes are criminalized and crime is legalized.

Nearly every news story you read, whether you realize it or not, has a connection to California: the rise of Elon Musk and Tesla, the "homeless industrial complex," the "censorship industrial complex," the professor who wouldn't cancel a test just for Black students, social media companies, shoplifting videos, banning gas cars, banning gas stoves, the "Green New Deal," reparations, lists of words and phrases you can't say anymore, Covid lockdowns, pioneering "rules for thee but not for me" at the French Laundry, Netflix, iPhones, Chat GPT, the housing crisis, high-speed rail (okay, high-speed fail).

California's wounds are self-inflicted, the result of an unchallenged political monopoly. Democrats have controlled the state legislature for over twenty-five years. They have had complete control of all statewide political offices for fifteen. In recent years they have had the benefit of a "supermajority" that allows them to impose laws, regulations, and tax increases without limit.

Califailure is what you get when Democrats get everything they want.

The purpose of this book is to help you understand how and, most importantly, why this happened. Of course we will need to review the disastrous policies that have brought working families in California to the edge of the abyss. But in the end, that's not as interesting as trying to explain the true drivers of this calamitous experiment. After all, it's hard to imagine that the people who did this to California did so on purpose. Something else has been going on, something that is not captured in the (by now) routine media coverage of the manifestations of Califailure on every front. What did the architects of Califailure think they were doing?

The best way to understand it is in the context of ideological pathologies. The elites who run California were infected with intellectual superbugs, dogma-driven "isms" that have addled their brains and poisoned their hearts. As a result, California became the Wuhan Lab of modern leftism, the incubator of a virus that went on to sicken the world.

We will examine these ideological pathologies: Elitism, Narcissism, Maoism, Climatism, Socialism, Bureaucratism, Compassionism, Cronyism, and Incompetism. Yes, it's true: incompetence can, in the right (wrong!) hands, become a full-blown ideology rather than mere ineptitude. For each pathology, we will investigate the origin and what the disease has done to our wonderful state.

It wasn't always this way. Millions of Californians still alive can remember when the state was a welcoming place to live, where jobs were plentiful and homes were affordable. Even as California's population exploded in the postwar 1950s and 1960s, average home prices here were less than in the rest of the United States. In 1950, adjusting for inflation, a median-priced home only cost $121,336. In 1960, in 2023 dollars, it was $154,520. Even by 1970, a median-priced home in California in today's dollars cost only $180,335. These seem like giveaway prices today, and back then, people in the rest of the nation took notice. Drawn by a booming economy, great weather, and affordable homes, new residents arrived by the millions. In 1950 the state's population was 10.7 million, by 1960 it had risen to 15.9 million, and by 1970 it hit 20 million. Life was good.

It was a vision that appealed to me long before we moved to California in 2012. In my imagination, California had always represented the best of everything that was good, desirable, exciting. The word itself, expressive and beautiful: "California!" You just had to say it and immediately your mind was in a place that was positive and aspirational. Optimism, energy, opportunity: that was California, the very best of America. California means to America what America means to the world.

In February 2009, the British political magazine the *Spectator* published a cover story titled "California Dreaming." It referenced the fact that while I was working as senior advisor to David Cameron, I spent a year in California for family reasons before moving here full-time. This is from the opening paragraph of the article:

"Once every fortnight or so, David Cameron's chief strategist lands at San Francisco airport and returns to his own version of Paradise. Steve Hilton has spent just six months living in this self-imposed exile—but his friends joke that, inside his head, he has always been in California. . . . [I]t is here, to an extent that is greatly underestimated, that the Conservative government-in-waiting is looking to find a new blueprint for Britain."

Is there a single advisor to a political leader anywhere in the world who would look to California as a "blueprint" today?

Why would anyone want to emulate a state whose residents are leaving in the hundreds of thousands every year—driven out by falling quality of life combined with the rising cost of living? Top of the list is housing. The exorbitant cost of buying or renting a home is making it impossible for normal working people to achieve the California

Dream. Housing costs are the number one reason people are leaving California. You see ludicrous examples like the Orange County firefighter who kept his job in California but moved his family to Tennessee, where life is affordable. He commutes on a two-week cycle.[2] What have we come to that that kind of arrangement makes sense?

Today, thanks to exorbitant fees, artificially inflated land prices, ridiculously overwrought building codes, needlessly expensive building materials (since almost nothing can be sourced in-state), and punishing delays in acquiring permits from a Byzantine array of hostile agencies, it is impossible to profitably build most types of housing at prices most people can afford. The median price of a home in California in 2024 was $904,210, over twice the national average of $410,000. The median rent in California is 55 percent higher than in the rest of the U.S. And it's not just homes that are unaffordable. Compared to the U.S. average, utility bills are 22 percent higher, and even food, in the agricultural superpower that is California, costs 10 percent more than in the rest of the country. Overall the cost of living in California is 39 percent higher. California has gone off the deep end with far-left extremism, making it impossible for working families to survive.

How exactly it came to be that far-left Democrats turned the California Dream into a nightmare is a process that Americans in other states must not ignore. The trends that start in California almost always end up affecting the rest of the nation.

In almost every category of far-left "progressive" power, the epicenter is in California. To begin with, the sheer size of California, with nearly 40 million residents, gives it immense political and cultural influence. California has the largest congressional caucus and the highest number of politicians with national influence—former Speaker of the House Nancy Pelosi, governor and aspiring presidential candidate Gavin Newsom, vice president and presidential candidate Kamala Harris, the late senator Dianne Feinstein, veteran congressman and incoming U.S. senator Adam Schiff, and many others.

California's progressive power is further enhanced by its GDP of nearly $4 trillion, which makes it the fifth-largest economy in the world. Moreover, California's economic power includes leadership in high technology, the sector that is driving innovation all over the world, most recently with the AI revolution and the world's first $2 trillion company, Nvidia. And before AI, California became home to Facebook, Google, X, Snapchat, and Apple, making it the birthplace and ongoing host of the social media and smartphone phenomenon that is transforming culture and shaping opinion in ways we are still just beginning to understand. Even earlier, innovators in California gave the semiconductor revolution to the world, building companies that to this day remain powerhouses in high tech, and universally recognized brands: Intel, Hewlett-Packard, Oracle, Adobe, Cisco, and many others.

Not incidentally, where you have the fifth-largest GDP in the world, you have billionaires—an estimated 180 billionaires at last count, including dozens of far-left "progressive" billionaires willing to spend hundreds of millions on national political campaigns. If that weren't enough, California is also the center of the entertainment industry. Hollywood and Disneyland may have more competition these days than they used to, but Southern California is still America's biggest producer of music and films.

California's "progressive" elites use their power to elect like-minded Democrats and push far-left policies throughout the United States. They use their power in media and social media to shape public opinion throughout the country. But they also use their total control of the state legislature to enact far-left, extremist policies that become the model for Democrats to emulate in other states. It is a daunting list, and it's coming to your state.

You see it in the approach to building things. Excessive fees, costly materials, ludicrously complicated building codes, bureaucratic delays . . . all this and more have made the cost of building housing, along with everything else, unaffordable in California. Now this has become, in Governor Newsom's favorite—and unintentionally hilarious—phrase, "a model for the nation." On top of exorbitant construction costs, land costs are artificially inflated by a shortage of land that is driven in turn by two interrelated obsessions: so-called New Urbanism and extreme environmentalism.

The fundamental principle of New Urbanism is that towns, cities, and suburbs must not be allowed to expand geographically and must instead develop via "infill." The positive part of New Urbanism celebrates innovative home design and encourages "walkable," "pedestrian-friendly" cities, great for those who choose that lifestyle. In practice, however, it limits new construction to ultra-high-density neighborhoods, denying people and families who want any other kind of lifestyle their choice. It also has led to an acute housing shortage, since it simply isn't possible to compress all of California's housing demand into the same amount of space. Nonetheless, New Urbanist philosophy is furthest along in California, offering support to copycat state and local governments all over America.

New Urbanism's interrelated counterpart is extreme environmentalism, which also views the expansion of cities and suburbs as causing unsustainable "sprawl" and unacceptable damage to the natural world. Extreme environmentalist legislation in California has held back development across all industries: not just housing, but energy, water, transportation, and all the industries that require these essential inputs in order to remain competitive and provide affordable products and services. Legislation passed by extreme environmentalists in California has now become the model for their federal counterparts and for legislation and litigation in states across the U.S.

For example, California's Global Warming Solutions Act of 2006 became the model for national legislation, including the Green New Deal. California's decision to ban sales of cars using internal combustion engines by 2035 was the model for the Biden administration's executive order that aimed to do the same thing. The California Endangered Species Act was a model for similar federal legislation. The

California Environmental Quality Act (CEQA) was passed in 1970, the same year as the National Environmental Policy Act (NEPA), and since then, the continuous expansion of requirements under CEQA has influenced the administration of NEPA. The list goes on:

The installation of smart meters not only for electricity but also for water is rolling out in California with eager corporate participation around the U.S. While smart meters are necessary installations on homes with solar panels, in all cases they enable utilities to monitor and micromanage all use of electricity, water, and gas. The Western Climate Initiative, composed of far-western U.S. states, Mexico, and Canada, has its origins in California. Although this collaboration shares a laudable goal to reduce CO_2 emissions, it is applying this mandate in ways that are harming the working class while failing to address some of the most obvious causes of climate change.

While environmental extremism is destroying California's middle-class prosperity, rendering housing, energy, and other basic essentials unaffordable, other far-left "progressive" mandates emanating from California promise to destroy people's quality of life, starting with public education.

California's schools, laboring under the yoke of the radical teachers union, have failed. Only 33 percent of K–12 students meet state math standards, and only 47 percent meet state English language standards.[3] Instead of punishing or expelling disruptive students, "restorative justice" is now practiced in California's schools, eliminating accountability and encouraging more disturbances. California's new math instruction "framework" denies advanced instruction to gifted students and infuses the textbooks with rejecting "whiteness" and injecting social indoctrination into the coursework. Astonishingly, public school teachers are granted lifetime tenure after just sixteen months, making it all but impossible to remove those that underperform.

Along with the failure to recognize how progressive extremism has created a punitive cost of living and undermined public education, California's political leadership has supported and implemented policies on crime that have only encouraged more criminal behavior. For example, several major cities in California no longer require cash bail, eliminating the primary tool to ensure criminals and victims have their day in court. California's Proposition 47, sold to voters in 2014 through a massively funded and deceptive campaign, has downgraded penalties for property and drug crimes.[4] The result is an explosion in crime, an epidemic of drug-induced mental illness, and homelessness.

All of these supposedly "enlightened" policies are being implemented in California, then marketed and sold to voters around the country through ad campaigns, social media algorithms, and donor-controlled politicians, with the money, the algorithms, and the legislative language all coming from California.

Kamala Harris has spoken of how California "is a role model of what can be done around the country." Gavin Newsom says California is a model for other states. "California is always in the lead," Nancy Pelosi told talk-show host Bill Maher in 2024. These California Democrats, who have come to dominate the national political scene, all brag that California is a model for the nation. That's true. It's a model of what not to do.

Progressive leadership in California is dominated by billionaires, while the most vocal progressive grassroots activists are often members of affluent communities. They are immune to the consequences of the extreme policies they support. Their neighborhoods are not challenged by high crime. Their income is sufficient to render California's soaring costs for household essentials an annoyance, but not a crisis. They are able to hold what the author and commentator Rob Henderson first described as "luxury beliefs." These are sometimes well-intentioned but always unrealistic ideological schemes that make leftist elites feel virtuous without any real cost to them while inflicting grievous pain on California's working class—pain that is unmitigated by any actual virtue. Upward mobility, something that could be taken for granted fifty years ago, is now denied to California's new arrivals and aspiring communities.

Many Californians have given up and fled to other states. The latest estimates in mid-2023 are that California's population has declined by over 600,000 people in the last three years. The scale of this exodus is understated, however, because California remains a magnet for foreign immigrants as well as tens of thousands of Americans who find the weather, the benefits, and the lax law enforcement an inducement to live on California's streets. For example, just in 2020, an estimated 725,000 Californians moved to other states: over 105,000 to Texas, 63,000 to Arizona, 55,000 to Nevada, 46,000 to Washington, and 41,000 all the way to Florida. Not one state in the U.S. had net migration into California in 2020.[5]

Why on earth would anyone leave such a beautiful, amazing place as California? How did this happen? That is the question we will answer in Part I of this book.

PART I: CALIFAILURE

ONE-PARTY RULE

What caused California's decline? What changed, turning a state that created so much wealth and abundance, celebrated freedom and prosperity, enabled millions of people to buy homes and give quality education to their children, into a state that now denies those opportunities to all but a few most fortunate?

Answering this question first requires identifying the enabling milestones along the way. What created the conditions in which California's leftist elites felt empowered to strip away the broad-based prosperity and opportunity that defined California through most of the twentieth century? As it turns out, there are a few key turning points that made all the difference. The first requires going all the way back to 1968, when California was still a solidly Republican state, with Ronald Reagan serving as governor.

Reagan has gone down in history as a conservative, and during the turbulent 1960s he was regarded as a reliable conservative governor. But Reagan also signed the Meyers-Milias-Brown Act, which granted collective-bargaining rights to local government employees.[1] The expected impact of this legislation at the time was to solidify the political allegiance of California's police and firefighters, who were almost all committed Republicans during an era when police were routinely demonized by demonstrators protesting the Vietnam War.

For this reason, the harmful consequences of allowing government employees to unionize was considered an acceptable trade-off for their partisan support (at that time) for Republican politicians in California.

But a generation earlier, even Democrat superstar and four-term U.S. president Franklin Delano Roosevelt denounced public sector unions as incompatible with good governance, stating in 1937 that "all government employees should realize that the process of collective bargaining as usually understood cannot be transplanted into the public service."[2]

A further step in the unionization of California's public sector employees came in the 1970s. By this time the political pendulum in California had swung in favor of the Democrats, with ultraliberal Jerry Brown serving his first term as governor. Brown signed the Rodda Act in 1974, granting the right to unionize to all public school employees, and three years later in 1977 he signed the Ralph C. Dills Act, which extended that right to all state employees.[3]

With these pieces of legislation, passed a half century ago, the stage was set for one of California's biggest structural impediments to responsible governance—total domination of state and local government by public employee unions. The mechanics of their control are straightforward: taxpayers fund the government, which pays public employees, who then pay dues to the unions, and those unions use that money to make campaign contributions to politicians who then owe their allegiance to these unions.

In California today, public sector unions collect and spend roughly $1 billion per year.[4] About one-third of that money is explicitly used for politics—lobbying and campaign contributions. Approximately another third is used for public information campaigns that do not have to be reported as political spending but are designed to influence public opinion to support policies that the union is promoting. There is no special interest, anywhere, that has perennial clout at anything close to this scale. Every election cycle, California's public sector unions spend hundreds of millions of dollars to promote their political agenda and their chosen candidates, from the Governor's Mansion all the way to every city council, school board, and special district in the state.

Because their leftist ideologies were in basic alignment, and because Democrats were generally much less likely ever to call for fiscal restraint, the power of government unions in California was applied almost exclusively to supporting Democratic politicians. As a result, over time California went from being a battleground state to turning solidly Democratic, and Republicans became less and less able to influence public policy. But because the state budget had historically required a two-thirds majority of both houses to gain approval, the Republicans were able to retain some influence and relevance despite being in the minority for nearly twenty years.[5] This final structural obstacle to complete domination by Democrats was removed in 2010 with Proposition 25, which changed the requirement to pass the state budget from two-thirds to a simple majority vote.[6] It was sold to voters who were fed up with all politicians by cleverly adding a clause "requiring legislators to forfeit pay when they do not pass a state budget on time."

Voters approved Proposition 25 by a margin of 55 percent to 45 percent in 2010, but the Democrats didn't need it for long. Democrats achieved supermajority status in both the State Senate and the State Assembly in 2012 and have held it ever since. For over a dozen years, there has been no check on one-party rule in California. Business interests recognize the difficulties taking on the Democratic legislature and their union backers and typically reserve their political opposition to situations where they face existential threats.

Here again, there are structural barriers. Business interests, unlike public sector unions, for the most part have narrow operational priorities that divert their attention and resources from vital structural reforms that are broader in nature. Taking on California's public sector, which essentially governs itself for its own benefit, would require a commitment at the same scale and duration as the opposition—that's over a billion dollars per election cycle, forever. The strategy that California's business community has adopted in lieu of such costly long-term political engagement is accommodation whenever possible.

Democratic structural dominance in California received yet another decisive advantage with supposedly "nonpartisan" redistricting reforms approved in 2008 and first implemented in 2010. The California Citizens Redistricting Commission was formed to redraw the boundaries of the districts for the State Senate, the State Assembly, and the U.S. Congress every decade, adjusting for shifts in the state's population to ensure that each district has about the same number of residents.[7]

This process ought to be straightforward, and the commission got off to a good start. The fourteen members included five Democrats, five Republicans, and four people not affiliated with either party.[8] In the initial meetings the commissioners all agreed that the primary criteria would be to respect the borders of cities and counties. From there, maps could have been produced using the latest data to develop a set of district boundaries while maintaining equal populations. The commission could have used the centers of cities and county seats to specify the initial geographic centers of each district, and geographically logical district maps would have been produced.

That's not what happened. Instead, the commission had to deal with "expert" staff from the California State Bureau of Auditors, all of them union members. In line with pressure from the left-wing group Common Cause, redistricting commissioners and the people making recommendations to the commission were instructed to present boundary suggestions that took into account "communities of interest." This threw the entire process into entirely subjective territory, leaving the ultimate set of boundaries almost impossibly convoluted.[9] The true purpose of these blatantly gerrymandered new boundaries is easily verified merely by considering the results of recent elections.

There are eight elected offices in California where the entire state electorate votes together for partisan candidates: Governor, Lieutenant Governor, Attorney General, Secretary of State, Treasurer, Controller, Superintendent of Public Instruction, and Insurance

Commissioner.[10] In California's "top two" jungle primary system, Republicans managed to advance a candidate to the general election runoff in every one of these offices in 2022, and lost them all. But in every case, the Republican's share of the vote was over 40 percent—with one exception. The Republican candidate for secretary of state got 39.9 percent of the vote.

This has been the pattern for many election cycles, a performance that suggests that Republican candidates ought to attract 40 percent of the vote, and therefore around 40 percent of the seats—in the State Legislature (Senate and Assembly). But thanks to the insertion of "communities of interest" as cover for gerrymandering, Republicans only hold 22 percent of the seats in the State Assembly and 20 percent of the seats in the State Senate. For that matter, Republicans only hold 23 percent of California's 52 seats in the U.S. Congress, for which the "nonpartisan" redistricting commission also drew new boundaries in 2020. Republican voters in California receive only about half the representation that their performance in statewide—non-gerrymandered—elections indicate they should earn.

The structural advantages contributing to Democratic dominance in California are great indeed. And what is the result? Apart from the myriad policy failures, we see a creeping authoritarianism, a sense that the Democrat political monopoly cannot even be challenged; that any political alternative is illegitimate and must therefore be crushed. You see it in the contemptuous way Sacramento Democrats swoop in to overturn any election outcome they don't like, whether that's passing a bill overriding Huntington Beach voting for Voter ID or the state attorney general filing a lawsuit against a newly elected Chino Hills school board implementing a policy of parental notification for changes in their own children's gender identity.

Most of all, you also see it in the increasingly chaotic and cavalier behavior of the state legislature, whose 2023–24 session ended in a farcical meltdown of antidemocratic arrogance.

To begin with, by the time of the February 16 deadline for that year's legislative session, a staggering 2,124 bills had been introduced by state legislators. That is typical. The previous year, more than 2,600 bills were introduced, and 1,046 were passed and sent to Governor Newsom for his approval. He ended up signing 890 of them. What kind of a state, already choking on laws and regulations pursuant to those laws, needs to pass nearly 1,000 more, year after year?

In 2024, despite having had nearly seven months to deliberate on these bills, on August 31 the State Assembly still had 144 bills to either approve or reject. And so, in a special session on that last Saturday of the last month of their legislative year, they gathered bright and early, 2 p.m., in the Assembly chamber and got started. In the final hours of this final day, just to speed things along, they amended the Assembly's rules to limit debate on bills to just thirty seconds per person. Thirty seconds.

This didn't sit well with Bill Essayli, a Republican representing California's 63rd Assembly District in Southern California. As a former federal prosecutor and district attorney in Riverside County, Essayli is no lightweight. He understands the rules of the Assembly. But as someone serving his first term, he was also not yet numb to the corruption.

In a confrontation that was recorded on video and went viral, Essayli demanded the Assembly adhere to the existing rules. The presiding officer, Speaker Pro Tempore Jim Wood, was having none of it. The following dialogue ensued:

Wood: Mr. Essayli, you are using dilatory tactics, I will no longer recognize you.
Essayli: I have a right to debate.
Wood: You are no longer recognized, Mr. Essayli.
Essayli: Jim Wood, I'm talking to you. I have a goddamn right to speak.
Wood: You sacrificed that right earlier tonight.
Essayli: No I did not. You're a fucking liar. You lie.

Wood: You are out of order. Mr. Essayli, I've already told you, you will no longer be recognized tonight.

Essayli: I will debate this with or without you, I am allowed to debate every damn bill on this floor. You cannot stop me.

But they did stop him, and proceeded on that day to finish the session by passing 142 of the 144 bills that had been remaining. In a guest column published a few days later in the *Orange County Register*, "Authoritarianism Turned to Chaos at the Capitol," Essayli summed up what happened. "The message was clear: I was, for all intents and purposes, no longer a member of the Assembly, and the 478,000 Californians I represent were now voiceless—all because I dared to question the undemocratic actions of the self-proclaimed defenders of democracy. Sit down, shut up, and vote as you like, but we will do what we want with no regard for rules, civility, or respect. Any others who followed my lead would face the same silencing."

It is difficult to overstate how easy it is to send transformative legislation through a legislature that is captured by one party. Bills that will completely upend entire industries can sail through on the last day without even meaningful objections logged into the record by dissenting legislators. Once the 2023–24 session ended, Governor Newsom was left with 911 bills to either sign or veto, with 142 of them passed with little or no discussion on the last day.

Making matters worse is the fact that mad rushes to approve legislation before the close of the session is not the only way to enact laws without public scrutiny. An even more effective way to sneak game-changing legislation onto the books is via the so-called trailer bills. These are bills that are introduced when the state budget is being negotiated, and if they include even a token amount of financial appropriations in their language, they can be "attached" to the budget and automatically passed if the budget itself is approved. But when they are attached, they can be blank—devoid of any policy content. The bills are passed with zero scrutiny or debate. Pass it now, fill in the details later. Astonishing—but this is where one-party rule gets you.

Also available to legislators intent on circumventing the public vetting process is the "gut and amend" tactic. This is where a legislator takes an existing bill that has already made it through several committees and adds new, completely unrelated language. In some cases, the provisions of the original bill are completely removed.

This is not democracy. This is authoritarianism.

There is another structural factor enabling progressive fantasies to captivate California's elites and transmute into policies that rain misery down on the vast majority of Californians. It is what has been referred to in relation to dysfunctional petrostates as the "resource curse." A principality on the Persian Gulf can afford to descend into corruption and indolence because it is a spit of sand floating on a sea of petroleum. The weirdest and wildest excesses can be absorbed without fatal consequences, because they can always be patched up by a never-ending torrent of oil revenue. This is a curse, of course, because no reforms ever become necessary. The petrostate's incredible resource wealth makes all things possible.

California's resource curse, such as it is, derives from the fact that it is one of the most desirable places to live in the world. Scenic beauty and a Mediterranean climate give California's politicians latitude they would never enjoy in, say, Nebraska. When you have beaches to the west and alpine wonderlands to the east, with some of the world's finest farmland and wine-growing regions in between, businesses and billionaires alike are going to think twice before they relocate. There may indeed be an ongoing exodus from California by people and businesses that can't take it anymore, but if it were anywhere else but California, the state would already be pretty much empty!

The final factor enabling California's elites to indulge in policies that are failing everyone else is the truth that for so long, California actually worked. The state's growth during the second half of the twentieth century was remarkable and sustained. Fantastic infrastructure and world-class universities were built and expanded, and the state became the unrivaled, global epicenter of high-tech innovation and venture capital. California retains this status despite the policies that threaten to eventually take it away. There is a staggering amount of wealth concentrated in California. Wealth like that helps keep the state running. It also breeds arrogance and complacency.

Because this is a state with so many natural and preexisting advantages, the repercussions of bad policies are not always immediately felt. It may be that some of the most extreme of these failed policies, affecting the cost of living, the quality of public education, and the incidence of crime and homelessness, are finally coming to a head. But for decades these problems slowly festered and grew without voters demanding solutions. And in some ways, California's failures worsened the ability for California's politicians to be held accountable. Instead of confronting the deteriorating trends caused by their policies, they used them as a scapegoat to demand even higher taxes, more spending, and more laws and regulations. This is the Democrat Doom Loop:

1. Implement extremist policies that cause costs to rise.
2. Panic that rising costs will cost them votes.
3. Hand out cash to compensate for rising costs.
4. Raise taxes to pay for handouts.
5. Causing costs to rise.
6. Repeat . . .

California's politics moved from being idealistic and left-leaning, but still functional, into pathologically dysfunctional as California's elites—politicians and intellectuals, and the donors and patrons that sponsor their political campaigns and university endowments— turned away from the interests of the working- and middle-class people who live here. California's wealthiest citizens, with the recent tech booms adding dozens of multibillionaires to their ranks, began to smugly view their financial success as validating something much greater—the ability, even destiny, to define the future on their terms.

This hubris, backed up by a stupefying amount of money, brought California's economic elites into alignment with established special interests: extreme environmentalists and public sector unions.

Together they form what so far is an unassailable political bloc, maintaining a one-party state, serving their own agenda while systematically eliminating upward mobility and quality of life for the vast majority of Californians.

It was good while it lasted. California was the only state to have its own, proprietary version of the American Dream. With all due respect to those estimable states, our culture does not speak of a "Nebraska Dream" or even, despite its recent incarnation as the "Freedom State," a Florida variant.

Yet this priceless inheritance—the "California Dream"—has been, in just a few short years, destroyed by this generation of Democrat politicians and their backers. One-party rule has allowed their ideological pathologies to run rampant.

It starts with Elitism.

CHAPTER 2

ELITISM

On December 3, 2020, facing a Covid pandemic that continued to spread throughout California and around the world, Governor Gavin Newsom reluctantly issued a ban on all outdoor dining in the state. He and his advisors correctly foresaw January 2021 as having the most reported deaths in America for the whole pandemic. Already required not to serve diners indoors, California's restaurants were now restricted to filling takeout orders. With businesses barely able to operate and schools closed, residents braced themselves for another year of crippling lockdowns.

California was taking no chances with the Covid pandemic. Transmission rates were rising and the governor had just made another difficult decision, forced upon him by difficult times. It was one more step in a series of measures that were taken starting earlier that year.

In March 2020, Newsom was urging restaurants to enforce "social distancing" and urged public venues where people typically congregate in close proximity to each other—bars, nightclubs, wineries, and breweries—to shut down. In some counties, Newsom's suggestions quickly became local mandates. On March 15, Los Angeles mayor Eric Garcetti ordered bars in the city to close and ordered restaurants to cease indoor dining. Additional mandates quickly followed.

The next day, on March 16, we saw the nation's first "shelter-in-place" lockdown, led by Santa Clara County's public health officer Sara Cody. All seven San Francisco Bay Area counties jointly issued a lockdown order, shutting down festivals and even family gatherings, banning people from school, work, and church.[1] Within days, on March 19, Governor Newsom extended the lockdown across the state, including all public schools. For the most part, public schools didn't fully reopen for eighteen months, at the beginning of the 2021–22 school year.

California's response to Covid continued to escalate throughout 2020.[2] On April 15, Los Angeles County ordered all residents to wear "face coverings" whenever they left their own homes. This was consistent with similar orders that took effect in dozens of other cities and counties across the state.

By May 2020, the shutdown was affecting the entire supply chain. California was disproportionately impacted, due to the strict measures being applied to cope with the pandemic, and also because California's economy includes a huge agricultural sector. Farmers, truckers, along with restaurateurs and grocers, were all spiraling toward economic disaster. In response, in mid-May, the state allowed restaurants to resume indoor dining provided they adhere to new regulations, including requiring staff to wear face masks, and limited-capacity seating.

The summer of 2020 saw another surge in Covid cases and authorities quickly erased the limited reopening that had been permitted. On June 30, Newsom ordered seven counties to close all bars, breweries, and pubs and directed restaurants in nineteen counties to cease indoor dining. In Los Angeles County, affected by both state orders, officials authorized health inspectors to impose fines on any restaurants or bars that violated the new restrictions. By now countless restaurants had gone out of business across the state.

Throughout this period, California was praised for its strong leadership. Acting quickly and decisively, communicating transparently with the public, and putting public health professionals at the forefront of the state's response, California became the symbol of "following the science." At the start of 2021, the *New Yorker* ran a lengthy article whose title says it all: "What the San Francisco Bay Area Can Teach Us About Fighting the Pandemic." Governor Gavin Newsom took pride in, as he put it, "leading the nation" on the pandemic. (The article was published just as California posted its worst Covid death numbers, though defenders still made the case it would have been even worse without Newsom's actions.)

It is in this context that his announcement on December 3, 2020, shutting down outdoor dining, needs to be seen. Although there was a momentary decline in the rate of new Covid infections in September and October, by late fall the cases were increasing again. Newsom did not want California to fall behind.

And so it was that even outdoor dining was suspended.

...

That ban on outdoor dining prompted one of the most visceral moments of the entire pandemic, exemplified by what happened to the owner of a small restaurant in Los Angeles.

The Pineapple Hill Saloon & Grill sits in the heart of the San Fernando Valley in the city of Van Nuys. Populated mostly by working families, it is just a few blocks from Studio City, a few miles from Hollywood, with the northern entrances to the fabled Laurel Canyon and Beverly Glen Canyon within walking distance. With an eclectic clientele attracted by its all-natural Angus-beef "Hill Burgers," served with generous portions of fries or tater tots, it was a thriving business.[3]

That is, until Covid came along in 2020.

Angela Marsden, the youthful owner of the popular saloon, readily adapted to the crisis. Borrowing $80,000, she set up a spacious outdoor dining area in her parking lot in order to accommodate patrons, who were no longer permitted to dine indoors. For a time, her business continued to thrive.

But on November 25, 2020, Los Angeles County banned all outdoor dining. Just a week later, on December 3, Governor Newsom signed an order banning outdoor dining throughout the state.

With a business that would struggle to survive merely on takeout orders, Marsden knew she was in trouble. Financial assistance that had been promised to small businesses affected by the lockdowns had not arrived. She had just taken on new debt to pay for an outdoor dining area that she could no longer offer to her customers. The strict measures imposed to "stop the spread" were about to destroy everything she had worked for.

So imagine her surprise when a few days after the county and statewide ban on outdoor dining had taken effect, she saw a huge outdoor eating area set up to accommodate actors and crew who were filming on location, literally a few yards away from her own shut-down patio. Getting online, Marsden expressed her outrage in a video that quickly went viral.

"Everything I own is being taken away from me and they set up a movie company right next to my outdoor patio," Marsden said in the video. "They have not given us money and they have shut us down. We cannot survive. My staff cannot survive."[4]

We still hear that story. The governor claims he did what he had to do. But why, if the need to "stop the spread" was so desperately urgent, was it necessary to close down outdoor dining everywhere but make an exception for politically connected entertainment executives, whose Hollywood studios continued to conduct on-location shoots and continued to offer outdoor food service to their crew? *Because of Elitism.*

A core tenet of the modern left is their belief that some people have significantly superior morality and intellectual judgment, and that therefore they should make the decisions for the rest of us. How do you find such enlightened people? Easy: they are already at the top of liberal society. That is *how* they got to the top of liberal society.

California's elites believe their ideas are so good, they have to be made compulsory, ignoring the impact of those ideas on the working people they claim to defend. The "progressive" ideals that they insist on turning into policy almost never involve solving actual problems in real people's lives. When so many Californians struggle to balance a monthly budget for their family that will stretch to include rent, utilities, food, health insurance, and a car payment; when so many are anxious about their children's prospects in catastrophically failing government schools . . . or fearful as they go about daily life in their neighborhood thanks to the explosion of crime, the constant lectures about "climate," "gender," "race," and "equity" seem cruelly irrelevant, even decadent.

This elitist mindset drove California's pandemic response. It took nearly three years before things were back to normal. By contrast, California's elites—able to finagle exemptions to their own mandates, economically empowered to work around them, and indifferent to the impacts wreaked on working families—continued to live much as they had before the pandemic.

Over and over we heard the same justifications. This quote from state senator Richard Pan (D-Sacramento), who was an MD before entering politics, sums it up: "We're asking you to do really hard things," he said in March 2020, and "there's a science part of it. And then there's the 'getting everyone to go along.' Because we're going to ask people to do really hard things."[5]

The slogan "getting everyone to go along with hard things" summarizes the California left amazingly well.

The "science part of it" is how our elites routinely convince a majority of Californians that issues of major consequence to our quality of life and future prospects are "beyond debate." Senator Pan's quote was made during lockdowns that paralyzed the entire state for over a year. These lockdowns destroyed countless small businesses, drove millions of Californians into bankruptcy or near bankruptcy, and imposed devastating and prolonged interruptions in the opportunities for California's K–12 students to get an education.

Did any of these unprecedented efforts "stop the spread"? There's nothing like definitive proof they did, but we were told they were so obviously effective that it was evil to debate them. Their entire case—that they were smart and moral and everyone should obey— falls apart in retrospect.

This problem is not Covid-specific. It's just one well-known example of their believing themselves superior in every way to normal citizens.

At the time there were people—including me—who looked at the facts surrounding the virus and saw clearly that lockdowns, school closures, mask mandates, and most of the rest of the pandemic paraphernalia were hunches and superstitions rather than sound policy. As I put it on my Fox News show *The Next Revolution* in March 2020: "The cure is worse than the disease. In fact, the 'cure' is not even a cure!"

None of this deterred California's leaders from taking an extreme and unjustified approach. "Science" was how Covid lockdowns were sold to Californians, just as "science" is the rationale for other destructively misguided policy agendas in our state, from climate change to crime and homelessness.

From the legacy of hardship left by California's overwrought response to the Covid pandemic to the ongoing difficulties with crime, homelessness, affordability, and educational underachievement, policies that are justified on the basis of "the science" have routinely fooled Californians into acquiescence.

Genuine science is inseparable from skepticism. The scientific method begins by making a guess (the hypothesis), then running experiments either to verify or disprove the hypothesis, and only then drawing conclusions. And once there is enough data to point to a conclusion, the scientific method nonetheless embraces new information and welcomes challenges. But California's elites do not respect the scientific method. Instead they have misrepresented "science" in order to convince voters to support policies that are contrary to their own interests and contrary to the interests of the people these policies are supposedly designed to help.

Millions of Californians were convinced, thanks to politicized "science," that lockdowns were the only way to prevent the Covid pandemic from expanding into an apocalyptic catastrophe. Ignoring contrary evidence available at the time from the examples being set in other states and nations, our state went into a prolonged lockdown. While the elites were able to spare themselves hardship thanks to their spacious private estates, their ability to work virtually from home, and the private schools that stayed open for their children, millions of working families in California had their lives turned upside down.

The story of Raquel Lezama, a single mother of three who lives and works in Los Angeles, is testament to the fragility of working-class households in California.[6] An immigrant from Mexico who escaped a troubled marriage, she initially survived doing piecework in the downtown garment district. But after twenty years of hard work, Lezama had finally achieved a precarious measure of financial stability. She got a job at a luxury hotel and worked her way up to earning $17.76 per hour as a minibar attendant. Then came Covid, and as she told the *Los Angeles Times*, Lezama abruptly found herself laid off without severance and no longer eligible for health insurance for her and her children.[7] Even her life insurance plan, a benefit of employment, was canceled when she was laid off. Within days, the life she had worked so hard to attain was shattered.

The paychecks were gone but the bills still came due: $1,400 per month rent for a tiny duplex. A $300-per-month car payment; $140 per month for car insurance. Utility bills, medical bills, $35 per month for an internet connection that was a necessity for "distance learning." For Californians with savings or with jobs they could do remotely, Covid was an alarming financial drain and a serious annoyance. For members of the working class, for people like Raquel Lezama, and for people who had no savings, it was a catastrophe.

How Lezama tried to cope with the disaster exposed all of the weaknesses in a system designed by people who would never have to use it. Offering $450 per week, unemployment benefits could have helped. But the state's website was overwhelmed with applicants and repeatedly crashed. Once Lezama finally got an application submitted, working from a computer she was still making monthly payments on, it turned out she would have to wait ten days before getting a response. With late fees on rent assessed by her landlord at a rate of $10 per day of nonpayment, ten days is an eternity.

This is a world unrecognizable to—and unrecognized by—California's elites.

Along with only being permitted outside for "essential" errands, workers were only permitted to retain "essential" jobs. In California's hospitality industry, these Covid rules translated into massive lay-offs and hideous job conditions for those employees who remained. Another story that typifies what these workers went through is that of Cristina Velasquez, a hotel housekeeper in Hollywood who kept her job during the pandemic.[8] The conditions she encountered were appalling.

Because her hotel had made daily housekeeping optional during the Covid pandemic, based on the theory that regular room cleaning would create more opportunities to transmit the disease, Velazquez found herself most often cleaning rooms only once, after the guests had left. She encountered an astonishing level of filth and trash.

Examples of what Velazquez found in these rooms included multiple days' worth of trash, dirty towels, candy wrappers, takeout containers with rotting food still inside, spilled soft drinks, and mountains of dirty towels. The messes she found were at times gross in the extreme: dead animals, blood, maggots, hypodermic needles, feces smeared on a shower. But with most of the housekeepers laid off, Velaquez was under pressure to get these rooms ready under deadlines and quotas that had been set when room cleaning occurred every day.

Hotel housekeepers in Los Angeles, at least the ones who could keep their jobs, weren't just expected to try to perform the same number of cleanings per day despite the average room being much harder to clean. In many cases they were cleaning up after a new sort of client. During the pandemic, starting in April 2020, the Los Angeles Homeless Services Agency moved thousands of people off the street and into vacant hotel rooms.[9] It has been estimated that at least 80 percent of homeless people suffer from mental health problems, drug and alcohol addiction, or both. Herded into these rooms and under minimal supervision, the results were predictable, and hotel housekeepers were on the front lines.

Such was the heartbreaking cruelty of the lockdowns. But if you were a member of California's elite, the rules didn't apply. You met with family, friends, business partners, and political allies, going to exclusive restaurants and sporting events, and masks were optional. Your businesses stayed open. Unlike the public schools, the private school where you sent your children stayed open.

For example, on November 6, 2020, as documented in photos leaked to a Fox network affiliate in Los Angeles, Governor Newsom sat down for an intimate dinner with several of his associates at one of the most expensive restaurants in the world, the French Laundry in Napa Valley.[10] Newsom was photographed sitting at a crowded table with at least twelve people, part of a group that reportedly became so boisterous that the large sliding doors to one side of the "outdoor" room had to be closed to avoid creating a disturbance.

Newsom had been repeatedly warning Californians to avoid travel and family gatherings, and in fact less than a week after dining at the French Laundry had issued a "joint travel advisory" discouraging nonessential travel, including families getting together for Thanksgiving.[11] Weeks later he would shut down outdoor dining too. For everyone else, that is. Not for the elites.

Throughout 2021 Californians continued to reel under the pandemic and the lockdowns. And the hypocrisy from California's elites didn't stop. Just over a year after the French Laundry incident, in January 2022, in an elite private box at SoFi Stadium in Los Angeles, famous stars and powerful politicians were observed and photographed without their masks.[12] It was a who's who of celebrities, including then mayor of Los Angeles Eric Garcetti, San Francisco mayor London Breed, former NBA star Magic Johnson, and Governor Newsom.

For those of us who have thankfully forgotten the timeline of the Covid pandemic, January 2022 was one of the worst surges of the entire ordeal. On January 5, 2022, California had just extended its public health guidelines requiring people in all indoor public settings to wear masks regardless of their vaccination status until February 15.[13] There was no end in sight. But for Garcetti, Breed, Johnson, Newsom, and their elite entourages, none of that mattered.

These blatant violations of the rules set for everyone else aren't the exception. In the elitist world of Califailure, they *are* the rule. These examples define how California's elites ignored the lockdown protocols that were driving California's small businesses into bankruptcy and denying people the right to be with their loved ones, even to the point of prohibiting them to be present to comfort a dying relative. But apparently for members of California's ruling class, in the now-famous phrase, the rules are "for thee, but not for me."

Only a few months earlier, in September 2021, San Francisco's Mayor Breed was photographed "maskless" at a city nightclub.[14] She wasn't just maskless: she and her friends were laughing and dancing within inches of each other. My favorite part of this little hypocrisy vignette was the indignant press conference the mayor gave once the story came to light.

"We don't need the fun police to come in and micromanage and tell us what we should or shouldn't be doing. . . . My drink was sitting at the table," said Breed. "I got up and started dancing because I was feeling the spirit and I wasn't thinking about a mask."

Ah, yes, "feeling the spirit." Quite right too. And who could argue with Breed's point that we don't need the "fun police" bossing us around? Except: at that exact moment, Breed herself was presiding over precisely that kind of . . . what's the word? Micromanagement. Most hilarious was Breed's justification for breaking her own rules. The band playing that night was Oakland-based Tony! Toni! Toné! A reunion of the original members and a "monumental" moment, according to the spirit-feeling mayor. Now, as it happens I agree with her about Tony! Toni! Toné! I have in my record collection a vinyl edition of their classic "Oakland Stroke." But I'm pretty sure that had I, rather than the mayor of San Francisco, tried to use the "monumental" nature of a band reunion to get away with breaking Covid rules, I would not have gotten very far.

Neither would any of us have had much luck deploying London Breed's bravura declaration of common sense in the face of the mask policing that became so obnoxiously—and pointlessly familiar—to many of us at that time. Remember the endless instructions from flight attendants to replace your mask after taking a sip? Not for London Breed!

"No, I'm not going to sip, and put my mask on. Sip, and put my mask on. Sip and put my mask on. Eat and put my mask on. While I'm eating and drinking, I'm going to keep my mask off."

Good for you, London Breed. Way to stand up to the petty Covid tyrants with their utterly ineffective authoritarianism. There's just one problem. Why didn't London Breed apply the same kind of common sense she reserved for her personal life to public policy? Because of Elitism.

Indeed, the criticism Breed earned for ignoring the rules she was handing down to everyone else in San Francisco didn't stop her from going maskless at SoFi Stadium a few months later.

As for Los Angeles mayor Eric Garcetti, he was not the least bit chagrined after getting busted for going maskless at SoFi in January 2022. He actually claimed he was "holding his breath" during the photographs, in a stretch reminiscent of Bill Clinton's famous "but I didn't inhale" remark a few decades earlier.[15] Garcetti was photographed a few weeks later at the 2022 Super Bowl, in an indoor private luxury box, enjoying the game with mostly maskless celebrities.[16] Rules for thee, but not for me.

The Covid pandemic was also a time when rates of retail theft, from shoplifters to organized smash-and-grab gangs, already rising, sky-rocketed out of control. And yet in the aftermath of the worst of the Covid crisis, in 2023, California's legislature passed Senate Bill 553, which prohibited employers from "maintaining policies that require employees to confront active shooters or suspected shoplifters."[17] Remember that shopper who never made it to the register but instead just kept on circulating through the store, pretending to examine the produce or the canned goods, but actually keeping a watchful eye out for shoplifters? Thanks to SB 553, an employer better think twice before giving anyone that task.

What were these state legislators thinking? Have any of them ever tried to run a small retail business or, for that matter, a large retail chain? Have any of them had to work in a retail business and felt the anxiety of knowing that thieves are empowered to come in, threaten staff, and take whatever they want, because they know that nobody is going to try to stop them?

In January 2024 the governor himself, who actually signed SB 553, was witness to an incident that might not have happened if he had refused to approve that legislation. He was in a Target store and witnessed a shoplifting. The details of this encounter epitomize how big the divide is between California's elites and the rest of us.[18]

Newsom not only saw someone walking out of the store with stolen merchandise, but saw how when the shoplifter dropped one of the items, a Target employee picked it up and handed it back, helping the criminal leave with everything he had stolen. What happened next is a story that will be told for years to come.

"Why didn't you stop him?" Newsom asked a Target clerk.

"The governor lowered the threshold, there's no accountability," the employee replied, according to the governor himself, who claimed he then reminded the clerk that California's $950 limit on petty theft is low compared to other states. (What he didn't mention was that other states allow individual thefts to be "rolled up" so that serial offenders can be prosecuted and deterred.)

To that, the woman simply said, "Well, we don't stop them because of the governor."

Brazen, unchallenged theft in California is a constant occurrence and a reality that is forcing the closure of retail businesses in every major city in the state. In San Francisco, where Newsom was mayor, major retailers including Walgreens, Old Navy, Nordstrom, and Whole Foods all shut their doors in 2023, citing retail theft as a primary cause. In early 2024, after anchoring San Francisco's fabled Union Square for over a century, Macy's announced it was going to close this landmark store.

What Newsom witnessed at that Target store in January 2024 was a visceral indictment of an out-of-touch legislature that has failed to protect the law-abiding citizens of the state, much less the retail businesses that cannot operate in an unstable, lawless environment. This out-of-touch legislature also failed to protect the interests of California's six million students enrolled in K–12 public schools. During the Covid pandemic, in October 2020, when most California K–12 students remained at home, unable to attend public schools, Newsom's four children returned to in-person instruction at a private school.[19]

Newsom himself knew that remote learning was harming the vast majority of California's schoolchildren whose parents couldn't afford the private schools that mostly stayed open during the pandemic. In August 2021, as debate raged over whether California's public schools were going to stay closed for another school year, he said, "There's simply no substitute for that enrichment that comes from being in school, being with trusted friends and extraordinary leaders, particularly our teachers."

Yes, exactly. So why didn't he insist that public schools educating the majority of California's students open for in-person instruction, and not just the schools attended by his children and the other children of the elite?

When it comes to elitist privilege, it's useful to recognize that some of California's most prominent politicians are all connected by family ties going back generations. Newsom is an intimate member of what in earlier times would have been called an aristocracy. When Governor Jerry Brown left office and Newsom began his first term as governor in 2018, noted political columnist Dan Walters had this to say about his family connections:

> Newsom is succeeding someone who could be considered his quasi-uncle, since his inauguration continues the decades-long saga of four San Francisco families intertwined by blood, by marriage, by money, by culture and, of course, by politics—the Browns, the Newsoms, the Pelosis and the Gettys.[20]

This incestuous network goes all the way back to 1943, when Jerry Brown's father, Pat Brown, was elected on his second attempt to become the San Francisco district attorney. Helping the elder Brown launch his political career was a close friend, William Newsom, grandfather of Gavin Newsom. The families have been exchanging political favors and lucrative commercial deals ever since.

Newsom's connections to the Pelosi dynasty also run deep. When Pat Brown was governor, from 1959 to 1967, his administration gave the concession to operate the Sierra Nevada ski resort Squaw Valley for the 1960 Winter Olympics to William Newsom and his business partner, John Pelosi. One of Pelosi's sons married William Newsom's daughter, Barbara, although they were later divorced. Another of Pelosi's sons married Nancy D'Alesandro. Now serving her eighteenth consecutive term as a member of Congress, including serving twice as Speaker, she is known to the world as Nancy Pelosi.

When Jerry Brown took office as California's thirty-fourth governor in 1975, he was only thirty-six years old. Helping him ascend to such a high office in such a short time was his father's political machine, and one of the first acts of a grateful young governor was to appoint William Newsom Jr., son of William Newsom Sr. and father of Gavin Newsom, to a Placer County judgeship. Three years later, Brown appointed William Newsom Jr. to the state Court of Appeal.

But no modern aristocracy would be complete without super-wealthy grandees. Enter John Paul Getty, who at the time of his death in 1976 was reputed to be the richest man in the world.[21] One of J. Paul Getty's intimate business partners was none other than Gavin Newsom's father, William Newsom Jr., the man Getty trusted in 1973 to pay a $3 million ransom to the kidnappers of Getty's grandson. When William Newsom Jr. retired in 1995, he became the administrator of the trust set up for Gordon Getty, son of J. Paul Getty.

Which brings us to the Plump Jack Group, a portfolio of restaurants, wineries, and retail establishments founded in 1992 with seed money invested by, you guessed it, Gordon Getty's trust. While California languished under Newsom's lockdown in the summer of 2020, Plump Jack Winery in Napa County remained open.[22] At the time, comedian Andrew Schulz made this observation as to the apparent double standard:

> Gavin Newsom ordered wineries in 19 counties to close. You know what Gavin didn't order closed? His own fucking winery! Nothing says man of the people like owning a vineyard. There's a drought in California, and Gavin is hosing down his grapes like they're striving for civil rights in Selma.[23]

In deference to the fact that Napa County had fewer instances of Covid than other counties under lockdown, fact-checker Snopes only rated Schulz's comment "mostly true." Coming from the liberal-leaning Snopes, that's a strong statement. Snopes declined to opine on Schulz's other observation, that Gavin was hosing down his grapes in the midst of a drought.

This brings up another area of elitist indifference to the challenges facing most Californians: laws intended to show the unimpeachable morality of our ruling elite actually reveal their inability to imagine second-order effects.

A survey of laws that have just been passed, or were making their way through California's state legislature during the 2023–24 session, offers evidence of how far removed these leaders are from the day-to-day challenges of most Californians. Depending on how you look at it, this evidence is either hilarious or terrifying. Perhaps both. We will encounter many more of these laws and regulations, state and locally issued, throughout this book. Indeed, there are so many that even a very large book with a hefty sampling of these laws and regulations would nonetheless present only a small fraction of what's out there. Here are just a few:

In 2020 the California legislature passed the Racial Justice Act, something that on the surface reads as though it were eminently reasonable.[24] What decent person wouldn't support racial justice? But this law adds a perverse condition to any successful criminal prosecution: it allows anyone convicted of a felony in California to challenge their conviction on the grounds of "systemic racial bias."

In practice, this law creates an opportunity for defense lawyers to argue that if the convicted defendant—who was found guilty by a jury of peers—is a member of an ethnic group with a rate of convictions and sentencing lengths that exceed the rate of a different ethnic group, then "implicit bias" may have unfairly affected the outcome of their case. The result has been a flurry of appeals to reopen cases where a convicted criminal is in prison, and an avalanche of discovery requests going to district attorneys forcing them to compile and report years of data on conviction rates and sentencing durations by race.

California's Racial Justice Act is a gold mine for defense attorneys, a full employment act for "experts" on racial disparities, and a tool to overwhelm and intimidate prosecutors operating on limited budgets. It will result in fewer convictions and premature releases of potentially dangerous felons. But when you're one of California's elite "thought leaders," living in a gated community with private security, it's the idealistic thought that counts, not the havoc that thought has unleashed in the real world.

Passed by the legislature in August 2024 is Assembly Bill 1840, which would expand eligibility criteria for a state loan program to include undocumented migrants who are first-time buyers.[25] There are plenty of problems with this bill, none of which are of concern to an ideologically extreme ruling elite. It is a slap in the face to any naturalized citizen who went through the arduous process of obtaining citizenship status legally. It is a tone-deaf acknowledgment that illegal immigrants are passing across a cartel-controlled "border" and getting access to benefits that exceed those available to American citizens. It is yet another Band-Aid placed on a broken system that has destroyed the competitive home building market, making house prices out of reach for almost all Californians.

The leftist elite love to cloak their actions in "compassion," but I'm not sure there is anything more cruel and heartless than taking money in taxes from hardworking legal immigrants who can't afford to buy a home so that newly arrived illegal immigrants can. (Any normal person who complains is just proving the elite are the more enlightened, more moral ones. See how that works?)

Here's a pending law not being considered yet at the state level, but in Santa Clara County. Better known as Silicon Valley, Santa Clara County's electorate can be described as either very wealthy high-tech entrepreneurs and employees, or very poor people displaced from elsewhere in the Bay Area by the highest home prices in the state. The county is also very left-wing and very elitist—a degree of self-regard made easier every time another earthshaking tech innovation comes out of its corporate campuses. So how do they cope with unaffordable housing and rampant homelessness? Their enlightened activists intend to force anyone selling their single-family home to give the local housing "nonprofits" the first opportunity to purchase it. These are the organizations that have already squandered billions of dollars in taxpayer-funded subsidies to build expensive free housing in numbers insufficient to house more than a tiny fraction of the qualifying population. Meanwhile, home prices for everyone else just kept going up along with the number of unsheltered homeless.

Given a benevolent and benign name, the Community Opportunity to Purchase Act (COPA) "would give non-profits the first right to purchase rental properties and forbid sellers from listing their property on the open market."[26] Here's how it would work:

Any seller of a rental property must notify nonprofit housing groups of their intent to sell before placing their property on the market. If the nonprofit is interested, the seller must give the nonprofit the first right to make an offer and may not place the property on the market during that time. If the seller turns down the offer, then the seller can place the property on the open market. That's bad enough. But there's more!

If the seller receives an acceptable offer, they must go back to the nonprofit and give them the opportunity to match the price. If a nonprofit matches the price, then the nonprofit has the right to purchase the property for that price. But the timeline doesn't have to work; the nonprofit still has several months to obtain financing. At that point the negotiations end without the original potential buyer being able to counteroffer.

What could possibly go wrong? Imagine the effect this ordinance would have on any young family trying to buy their first home. They would be competing with nonprofits with budgets in the hundreds of millions, nonprofits that have already proven they are indifferent to costs. The entire project, which is gaining echoes in the activist-dominated city council of Los Angeles, is a crude usurpation of property rights. But can it be struck down in court? The greatest hope to stop schemes like COPA is grassroots opposition by what remains of San Jose's small business and individual home ownership communities. But the siren song of caring and compassion for the less fortunate can often delude voters. If any place is proof of that, it's California.

For California's elites to prioritize these abstract issues and unworkable schemes over practical solutions is a luxury. Just as the elites have their luxury goods, so too do they embrace these luxury policies. It may feel noble and "highly evolved" to them, but for the majority of working people what it really translates into is a cavalier indifference to the core challenges that make or break families and households. These airy aspirations, which we can refer to as luxury beliefs, are an accurate reflection of the groupthink of California's elite. They are so fixated on their lofty ideals, and so insulated from the consequences of implementing them, that they are unaware of the harmful impact of these beliefs on working families. Or maybe they just feel so strongly about their luxury beliefs that they believe any sacrifice is necessary to achieve them. But it's easier to take that position when the sacrifice is being made by someone else and you won't personally experience the hardship your policies will cause.

This is overwhelmingly the case, of course, when it comes to perhaps the defining luxury belief of California's elites, and that is extreme environmentalism, explored in more detail in chapter 5, "Climatism." Elitist politicians have passed laws that restrict almost every form of productive activity involving tangible materials. Farming, ranching, mining, logging, manufacturing, construction, home building, investment in practical infrastructure, operating small businesses— all of it and more has been throttled by extreme environmentalist laws, regulations, and the endless interference of a multiplicity of government agencies and bureaucracies all infected with the same dreary, negative, antihuman, antigrowth ideological mindset of scarcity and austerity.

The people who are hit are the working class. Working people and families in California are absolutely hammered by "climate" extremism. It's an example of how, on so many issues, the leftist ruling class in California have simply lost touch with working people, and only care about the ideological obsessions of the college-educated elite.

This is compounded by a smug, self-obsessed insularity. Those who wield power in California tend to live in wealthy coastal enclaves, sur-rounded by like-minded peers. The policies that are killing everyone else in California do not seem extreme or destructive if you live in an affluent bubble and rarely, if ever, encounter dissenting views.

Meanwhile, California's blue-collar workers are under assault, and endless burdens are placed on small businesses. Controlling a super-majority of politicians, California's elites suppress speech, shut down opposition, and dismiss disagreement with moralizing contempt. Elit-ists tend to think rules for others don't apply to them. The elites in California do not have to live with the consequences of the policies they enact. Their wealth and their privilege, the spectacular successes that defined California for so long, and maybe even the weather, insu-late them from the realities they create, and nurture their arrogance. Perhaps they view themselves as the new masters of the universe.[27]

Which brings us to Narcissism.

CHAPTER 3

NARCISSISM

My name is Governor Gavin Newsom, from the great state of Nancy Pelosi. . . . We believe the future happens in California first, and, Democrats, I've had the privilege for over twenty years to see that future taking shape, with a star in an Alameda courtroom by the name of Kamala Harris. I saw that star fighting for criminal justice, racial justice, economic justice, social justice. I saw that star get even brighter, as attorney general of California, as a United States senator, and as vice president of the United States of America. Kamala Harris has always done the right thing. A champion for voting rights, civil rights, LGBTQ rights. The rights for women and girls . . . It is time for us to do the right thing, and that is to elect Kamala Harris the next president of the United States of America.

August 2024, floor of the Democratic National Convention in Chicago. In that moment, Gavin Newsom, as he delivered the delegates that confirmed then–vice president Harris as the Democratic nominee, captured the sense of swagger and pride that characterizes the current generation of California Democratic leadership. Pelosi, Newsom, Harris—major figures bestriding the national stage, both in terms of personal impact and policy innovation, asserting California's leading role.

It was the same attitude that informed Gavin Newsom's approach to major policy issues.

"As governor, I will lead the effort to develop the 3.5 million new housing units we need by 2025 because our solutions must be as bold as the problem is big."

In October 2017, running for governor of California, Newsom made clear that he was not interested in half measures when it came to the state's twin, and interrelated, housing and homelessness crises. "I realize building 3.5 million new housing units is an audacious goal—but it's achievable. There is no silver bullet to solve this crisis. We need to attack the problem on multiple fronts. . . . We can't have a conversation about housing without addressing homelessness. . . . Homelessness drove the 'why' for me when I ran for mayor, and I'm going to take the issue on with equal intensity as governor. We've been 'managing' this problem for too long; it's time to solve it."[1]

These are huge challenges. They require bold leadership, just as bold leadership is required to address the "existential crisis" of climate change. Here, too, Newsom's leadership has been commensurate with a certain idea of California—as a global and not just national pioneer. In December 2022, the governor issued a flurry of executive orders that included bringing offshore wind power to the West Coast, providing funding for 90,000 new EV chargers across the state, approving a new solar policy that will make our grid more reliable and accelerate energy independence, and finalizing a plan to cut air pollution by more than 70 percent. Here's what he said at that moment:

"We are making history here in California, and today caps an amazing ten days for world-leading climate action. California is leading the world's most significant economic transformation since the Industrial Revolution—we're cutting pollution, turning the page on fossil fuels and creating millions of new jobs."

It's easy to criticize plans this big, designed to cope with problems this daunting, as grandiose posturing. But what is politics for, if not to set lofty goals? If we didn't have these grand aspirations, how would we accomplish anything?

We can do great things, things that would seem either miraculous or impossible prior to their achievement. We should have the confidence to believe that we truly can change the course of history. All great leaders and innovators have had a capacity for outsize confidence and wild ambition. The cynic might call it hubris, but without limitless faith and persistence, Lyndon Johnson wouldn't have gathered the political support needed to reach the moon before the end of the 1960s, Martin Luther King Jr. would not have inspired millions of Americans to embrace the civil rights movement, and Ronald Reagan would not have led us to victory in the Cold War without a shot being fired.

To solve intractable problems like homelessness, housing, crime, climate change . . . not to mention poverty, inequality, educational failure, chronic disease, racism, and all forms of discrimination: we must have bold ambition. We must believe that setting lofty goals and working hard to achieve them will ultimately change the course of history and set an example for generations ahead of us to emulate.

...

And so where are we today? Whatever happened to the grandiose plans to build houses in California? Did we get those "3.5 million new housing units by 2025"? Not exactly. Latest tally: less than a million. To be fair, Newsom in 2022 acknowledged falling short: "The biggest risk in life, however one defines risk, is not that we aim too high and miss it. It's that we aim too low and reach it. It was always a stretch goal."[2]

An unkind person might say: he's making a habit of this. In 2003, as newly elected mayor of San Francisco, he pledged to end chronic homelessness in ten years. Over two decades later, we're still waiting. "I recognize that I'm setting myself up. I'm not naïve to that," Newsom said at the time. "I don't want to overpromise, but I also don't want to underdeliver."[3] Looks like you managed to do both, Gavin. Twenty-one years after that speech, he would be found standing under a freeway overpass in Los Angeles, personally clearing a homeless encampment and saying: "People are done. If we don't deal with this, we don't deserve to be in office." One can only imagine what he might say after another twenty years of Democrat policies that continue to make this (and other) problems worse, not better.

As for Kamala Harris, that great champion of "racial justice . . . social justice . . . the rights of women and girls," her last-minute run for the presidency focused attention on her California record. Here the gulf between the noble self-portrait and the somewhat less virtuous reality was made plain for all to see. As San Francisco district attorney, she helped cover up child sex abuse, siding with perpetrators who could advance her political career rather than the victims who needed her help. As state attorney general she arranged a lenient plea deal for a political crony amid accusations that he was a serial sexual harasser.[4] And, as Tulsi Gabbard memorably pointed out on the presidential debate stage in 2020, Harris targeted and victimized young Black men to burnish her crime-fighting credentials.

How can politicians deceive themselves so completely? It seems to especially afflict those on the left, who are more prone to idealistic utopianism, perhaps. With Elitism comes Narcissism. People who want to run everything, with plans for everyone, tend to think a lot of themselves.

In February 2024, while visiting San Francisco, former NBA star and sports commentator Charles Barkley was brutally honest regarding what he saw on the streets. He referred to San Francisco's thousands of unhoused as "homeless crooks," and claimed they had taken over the city.[5] If Barkley's characterization of the problem is somewhat harsh, the fact that it is allowed to persist is surely a symptom of narcissistic compassion.

This disorder is characterized by people who reserve their empathy for the underdog while exhibiting no empathy for hardworking people who muster the self-discipline to be accountable and responsible. Does this sound familiar? Public displays of generosity (albeit with other people's money) help the narcissist maintain a positive self-image and gain personal benefits for themselves, allowing them to justify any negative consequences of their actions.

Clinical psychologist Seth Meyers, writing for *Psychology Today*, describes the narcissistic personality as follows: "When narcissists exercise their empathy, they often show it to individuals whom they perceive to be vulnerable or inferior in some way."[6] Continuing, Meyers observes that successful people "are seen as extreme threats to the narcissist's ego, as the narcissist operates from the scarcity mindset that says there simply isn't enough attention and admiration for everyone to go around."

California's rulers have created a state where crime is legal but protecting yourself from crime is criminal. They've created a state where purchasing a home or even renting an apartment is a barely endurable hardship for working people, if not an impossible dream, while at the same time they're offering luxury hotel rooms to homeless drug addicts. The cost of narcissistic political leadership is not merely cities that are collapsing into dystopian chaos, lawlessness, and squalor. It is also financially untenable, and the bills are coming due.

California's prominent politicians travel with assigned security, with "advance" people and bodyguards who work around the clock to protect them. But thanks to their narcissistic compassion, the laws, systems, and services that everyone else relies on for protection have been undermined, not strengthened. It's been going on for years in California.

For example, in 2015, Christina Voyles, a marketing executive who had just moved to San Francisco with her husband, was attacked by a troubled homeless person for making the impertinent decision to have lunch outdoors.[7] Instead of going back indoors to finish her workday, Voyles found herself being dragged down the street by her hair, and screamed for help. When two construction workers nearby rescued her and contacted the police, Voyles recalls being amazed that the police spent most of their time attempting to calm the homeless attacker down, instead of making certain she was okay.

Voyles ended up having to take drugs to prevent possible HIV infections that could have ensued when the attacker scratched her inside her mouth. The attack left her permanently traumatized, and within a few months after the attack, Voyles and her husband decided to leave San Francisco and move to a safer city.

One of the most troublingly typical things about this attack was how the police knew the assailant. He was well-known to them as a homeless person who had a history of escalating violence. But there was nothing the police could do. As Voyles described it, "Homeless folk are very enabled. If there is no repercussions to bad and aggressive behavior, why would they change? The city has been very lax."

The city has remained lax. In 2020, Leo Hainzl made the fatal mistake of taking his dog out for a walk. That was too much for a fifty-three-year-old homeless man who confronted Hainzl, who died soon after. As one witness put it, describing the assailant, "We've been hearing from neighbors, he's been out on the street threatening folks, they called police many, many times, older folks felt very threatened in particular, kids, he has been a challenge in the neighborhood for some time and the police have been out and talk to him and offered him services on many occasions and people knew he was suffering from mental illness, he was not taking his medication but the police were not able to get him services and nobody else was either."[8]

Hainzl, who was ninety-four, had lived in the neighborhood for over fifty years. Two years later, the alleged assailant, Peter Rocha, was acquitted, because prosecutors couldn't establish beyond reasonable doubt that he had actually hit Hainzl with his walking stick. The defense claimed Rocha merely swung his stick in the air and that Hainzl, even though not struck, then tripped and fell, hitting his head and later dying from his injuries. But why was this man on the street to begin with? Why wasn't this man, who had a history of menacing behavior, not taken off the streets? As a spokesperson for the San Francisco Public Defender's Office said in a press release at the time of Rocha's acquittal, "We live in a state where mental healthcare is so severely underfunded, that many of our most vulnerable community members end up unnecessarily incarcerated, and even the courts can't guarantee access to the care they may need when there is a supply deficit of beds and services."[9] This is of little comfort to the victim or his family.

Criminals. The mentally ill. Drug addicts and alcoholics. According to a 2022 study of San Francisco's homeless, 65 percent of them either have a "substance use disorder" or a "mental health disorder."[10] The study didn't assess how many of San Francisco's homeless committed crimes apart from drunk and disorderly conduct, which evidently in San Francisco is not much of a crime.

During the Covid pandemic, the city of San Francisco decided to move thousands of homeless people into empty hotels to "slow the spread." Initially, the Federal Emergency Management Agency (FEMA) approved of the plan and agreed to reimburse 75 percent of the costs. FEMA later committed to paying 100 percent of the costs until July 1, 2022, then 90 percent after that until May 2023. But FEMA ultimately reneged and announced that in most cases it would not cover hotel stays of longer than twenty days. That left the city having to pay an estimated $190 million that they had originally thought would be covered by the federal government.[11]

San Francisco is a big city that was already sinking into the red. The budget deficit over the city's next two fiscal years (through June 2026) could exceed $1 billion.[12] According to the *San Francisco Chronicle*, the city spent over $423 million paying for more than 5,000 homeless people to stay in hotels during the pandemic.[13] There were alternatives. For the past several years, San Francisco could have been building congregate shelters where thousands of homeless can safely and cost-effectively receive housing and services. Instead the city's strategy has been to pay politically connected developers to build homeless housing at prices that typically exceed half a million dollars per unit. More to the point, San Francisco could have enforced laws governing public drug use, possession of hard drugs, petty theft, and disorderly conduct; if they'd done that, the city would not have attracted so many homeless residents in the first place.

California politicians, including Gavin Newsom and San Francisco mayor London Breed, jumped on a 2024 Supreme Court ruling, *Grant's Pass v. Oregon*, to claim that it removed a major barrier to enforcing the law on homeless encampments. But that's just an excuse for years of inaction. The previous ruling that the court overturned in *Grant's Pass*, and which these leaders cited in defense of their passivity, was *Martin v. Boise* in the Ninth Circuit. It simply stated that jurisdictions could only enforce anticamping ordinances if they provided sufficient shelter beds for their homeless population. It is possible to provide shelter that is cheaper than half a million dollars per bed. California leaders, however, gave in to the demands of homelessness nonprofits and their allied developers (the "homeless-industrial complex," as it has been dubbed) and made no effort to deliver shelter on the scale needed.

True compassion carries with it obligations. Sometimes the best thing that a person suffering from substance use disorder needs is to be taken somewhere and sobered up. In the old days, people arrested for public intoxication were thrown into the so-called drunk tank, where they would spend a grim night incarcerated, then they would have to appear in court and, depending on the severity of the offense, might have to spend a few weeks or even a few months in the county jail. This was a powerful deterrent to public intoxication. It was harsh, but how many individuals who might have succumbed to substance abuse instead found that the certainty of unpleasant consequences provided just enough additional motivation to stay clean?

A similar logic applies to property crimes. The certainty of punishment is a deterrent to would-be thieves. And conversely, without deterrence, crime spirals. Here again this story has played itself out in San Francisco. More than thirty major retailers have abandoned their downtown San Francisco locations in just the past two years. In February 2024 San Francisco officials reluctantly announced that Macy's was leaving. This was Macy's flagship store, located on the iconic Union Square. The loss of this store is a devastating blow to San Francisco.

It's fair to attribute some of San Francisco's retail store flight to difficulties recovering from the Covid pandemic (which shut down in-store shopping for months on end), as well as to ongoing difficulties in coping with the rise of online commerce. But Macy's on Union Square, just like the five-story Nordstrom in the prestigious downtown Westfield San Francisco Centre mall, were places that locals and tourists went to precisely because of their downtown cachet. These iconic stores, and stores like them, still thrive in cities where crime and homelessness are under control. The owners of the Westfield mall were blunt when describing Nordstrom's primary reason for leaving. They cited a lack of enforcement against criminal activity.

But the obligations of true compassion are not relevant to a narcissist. For them, compassion is a way to publicly elevate themselves above the morally inferior. To keep the hustle of narcissistic compassion going, narcissists need victims to rescue. If they run out of the downtrodden, they will create more. This is why they suddenly need to explain criminal behavior as a consequence of oppression.

San Francisco's district attorney from 2011 through most of 2018 was the disastrous George Gascón, elected in 2011 by promising to move away from cash bail, deemphasize incarceration for nonviolent offenders, reintegrate prisoners into society, push for funds to be invested in mental health services instead of jails, expunge marijuana convictions, and advocate for undocumented immigrants.[14] Was it the same narcissistic passion that grips the far-left politicians they routinely elect that drove a majority of San Franciscans to vote for Gascón? Or did they actually believe his plan would work? Either way: it didn't.

During Gascón's tenure, billions were spent to help homeless people, over $300 million in 2018 alone, his last year in office.[15] But the population of homeless only grew, to nearly 10,000 by the time he left office. During that same period, California voters approved Proposition 47, which downgraded penalties for property and drug crime. The initiative, as is now well-known, was cynically mis-sold to the voters by then–attorney general Kamala Harris.

When the proposition qualified as an initiative to be put before the state's voters in 2014, Harris as state AG was responsible for writing the so-called title and summary that would appear on the ballot. Often this brief description of the bill is all that voters will see. For what has become one of the most disastrous "reforms" California voters have ever been conned into supporting, here's how that title and summary read:

> Criminal Sentences. Misdemeanor Penalties. Initiative Statute.
> Requires misdemeanor sentence instead of felony for certain drug and property offenses. Inapplicable to persons with prior conviction for serious or violent crime and registered sex offenders. Fiscal Impact: State and county criminal justice savings potentially in the high hundreds of millions of dollars annually. State savings spent on school truancy and dropout prevention, mental health and substance abuse treatment, and victim services.

That's fairly innocuous. "Inapplicable" to anyone with a prior conviction for serious or violent crimes, or sex offenders. And it will save hundreds of millions of dollars that can be used to help at-risk youth, or people struggling with mental health and substance use disorder. What's not to like? In addition, voters who took the time to read the voter guide were treated to the name favored by proponents: the Safe Neighborhoods and Schools Act. All of this language was approved by Kamala Harris. Never mind the actual consequences of Prop. 47, which has made large sections of California cities virtually ungovernable.

Two years later, Harris landed Californians with another pro-crime disaster. Proposition 57 was intended to relieve state prison over-crowding by reducing sentences for "nonviolent" crimes. But while it was approved by California voters in 2016, opponents of the ini-tiative warned that it also "authorized state government bureaucrats to reduce many sentences for 'good behavior,' even for inmates con-victed of murder, rape, child molestation and human trafficking." As the *Sacramento Bee* reported in 2022, Proposition 57 "gave California Department of Corrections and Rehabilitation the power to increase the amount of [early release] credits all prisoners can earn, including violent offenders. The agency has done this for both violent and non-violent offenders since the measure passed, through policy updates in 2017 and 2021."

As a result, Prop. 57 has released thousands of dangerous criminals into California's cities. The list of crimes these people committed, yet still earned early release under Prop. 57, includes human trafficking of a child, felony domestic violence, rape of an unconscious person or by intoxication, drive-by shooting at inhabited dwelling or vehicle, assault with a firearm or deadly weapon, assault on a police officer, serial arson, exploding a bomb to injure people, solicitation to commit murder, and assault from a caregiver to a child under eight years old that could result in a coma or death.

Where was Kamala Harris? As California's attorney general in 2016, Harris's office wrote the official "title and summary" for the ballot initiative. What they came up with was cynically innocuous: "Criminal Sentences. Parole. Juvenile Criminal Proceedings and Sentencing." That is followed up by a bullet point that is highly mis-leading: "Authorizes Department of Corrections and Rehabilitation to award sentence credits for rehabilitation, good behavior, or edu-cational achievements." Nowhere in this title and summary does the voter learn that these early-release sentence credits can be earned by violent criminals including murderers, rapists, child molesters, and human traffickers. Harris as AG had an opportunity to accurately present to voters what Prop. 57 was going to inflict on the state's law-abiding citizens. She chose to ignore that opportunity.

These dramatic changes in the criminal justice framework, all on Kamala Harris's watch, led to a dramatic change in the character of San Francisco's homeless population, with open drug use and rampant theft becoming the norm. Between 2011 and 2018, property crimes increased by nearly 50 percent in the city.[16]

Narcissistic personality disorder is characterized by exaggerated achievements and talents. Narcissists expect to be recognized as superior without superior accomplishments. A normal person might readily anticipate that decriminalizing crime, effectively legalizing possession and use of hard drugs, eliminating bail, and releasing prisoners would have a detrimental impact on society. But to a narcissist, a utopian outcome is to be expected simply because they say so. When a narcissist fails, they simply insist they succeeded.

In October 2019, Gascón decided he would not seek reelection to the office of district attorney in San Francisco, because he had set his sights on the DA position in Los Angeles County. More on that later. But San Franciscans had not yet had enough. In November 2019, they elected Chesa Boudin. If not a narcissistic twin to George Gascón, Boudin was perhaps an even more narcissistic, overachieving sibling. And he came from a family of narcissistic psychopaths.

Boudin was born in 1980 in New York City to parents who were members of the notorious, murderous Weather Underground, a Marxist domestic terror organization that during the late 1960s through the mid-1970s carried out dozens of bombings across the country. Targets included banks and government buildings, such as the U.S. Capitol in 1971 and the Pentagon in 1972. After the end of the Vietnam War, the Weather Underground's terrorist activities dwindled, but their criminal activities continued. Both of Boudin's parents were convicted in 1981 of robbing a Brink's armored car in New York, stealing $1.6 million. During the heist and the ensuing manhunt, a Brink's guard was killed along with two Nyack, New York, police officers.

Although his terrorist parents were in jail, the infant Chesa Boudin did not escape a childhood of Marxist terrorist indoctrination. He was adopted by fellow Weather Underground members Bill Ayers and Bernardine Dohrn. These two were not mere members of that terrorist network. Ayers was cofounder of the group and, as he acknowledges in his own writings, participated in at least three bombings. Dohrn, for her part, was at times the leader of the Weather Underground.[17] Improbably, both of these terrorists escaped lengthy prison sentences—Dohrn by pleading guilty to lesser charges, with Ayers's case dismissed due to alleged FBI misconduct.

Given who raised him, it shouldn't take too much imagination to conclude that Chesa Boudin assimilated a hardcore Marxist worldview. And as his parents were not only remarkably immune to prosecution proportional to their crimes, but also well-connected and evidently well-off financially, Boudin attended an elite private, and very progressive, K–12 school: the University of Chicago Laboratory Schools. After high school graduation, he went on to earn his undergraduate degree at Yale, a master's degree at Oxford, and a law degree at Yale Law School. Before entering law school, Boudin worked as a translator in Venezuela for, you guessed it, Hugo Chavez. After his illustrious academic career, Boudin moved to San Francisco, where he got a job as a public defender.

It should come as no surprise that under Boudin's progressive reign, perpetuating the policies first implemented by Gascón, the city continued to go downhill. But instead of holding him accountable for his evident failures, California elite media, shaping public opinion, egged him on. In June 2022, the *Los Angeles Times* published an op-ed defending Boudin.[18] The writer, Miriam Pawel, actually framed opposition to Boudin's criminal-friendly policies as an orchestrated fraud, as she put it, "a case study in the power of millionaires to set a political agenda."

Pawel's op-ed was timely. San Franciscans had finally had enough, and despite the efforts of her and other journalists, despite support from the press and despite support from other progressive politicians, Boudin was recalled from office in a special election a week after Pawel's op-ed appeared. A solid majority, 55 percent, supported his removal. Chesa Boudin, for all the brilliant rhetoric and manipulative skills of a classic narcissist, overplayed his hand and lost. Even in San Francisco. But the delusional policies of Narcissism continue to underlie California's ongoing struggles with crime and homelessness.

Narcissism in California politics also drives climate activism and climate policies. Obviously, none of the environmental changes we have observed under the broad heading of "climate change" literally signify the "end of the world." The endless, grating use of the term *existential threat*, however, imbues the climate activist with a genuine feeling that they are, literally, "saving the world." What more could a far-left narcissist want? In an influential essay published in 2022, "The Narcissism of the Apocalypse," writer Michael Shellenberger exposes the psychology of the typical climate activist.[19] "Since the seventies," he writes, "the narcissism of the Left has become significantly more outer-directed, status-oriented, and focused on the coming apocalypse. Apocalyptic environmentalism is exhibitionist to the point of Messianic. Adherents demand to be recognized for their supposedly unique insight into the 'climate emergency.' They demand to be rewarded with cultural, economic, and political power to save the planet. Such exhibitionist Narcissism captures one's need to be the center of attention, often at the expense of others; this includes expecting greater attention be given to one's issues, opinions and values."

Social media, delivered through smartphones, has only thrown gasoline onto this fire. Distilling their most meaningful reality into the hours each day spent staring into a small screen, this is a generation that has lost the interactive, ego-shrinking therapy of outdoor activities, actual face-to-face personal relationships, and authentic physical accountability in the real world. As they stare into the tiny screen, it stares back at them, inviting them to click their way down into infinite and very manipulative rabbit holes only partially of their own choosing, reinforcing pathologies, indulging every fantasy or paranoia. And into this fragile and compromised reality of today's affluent youth is poured an incessant message: "the Climate Crisis will destroy the world, and you must rise to stop it."

We might excuse the young climate activists, given the circumstances of their upbringing combined with the fact that almost every content option pouring out of their smartphones in some way adheres to the same narrative—the climate apocalypse is upon us! Less forgivable are California's political elites who share the same narcissistic impulse to save the world from the "Climate Crisis" but also recognize the movement as an opportunity to grow their own political power and the power of the bureaucracies they control. All the while, as they enhance their own power at our expense, they make sure everyone knows that they are the ones "saving the world."

So it is that California leads the world in pushing extremist policies to "save us all from a climate apocalypse." Every time there is a wildfire that spreads out of control (usually caused by decades of neglect and poor forest management), or a severe storm that blows in off the Pacific, or just a really hot day, nearly every state and local official takes that opportunity to remind us all of the "existential threat" we face, and announce the latest round of laws, regulations, and executive orders with which they will "save us."

Climate extremism, and the climate industrial complex it enables, were made for narcissists. And narcissists answered the call, as we will see in chapter 5.

Califailure is often the result of the narcissistic elite finding a real problem and designing a terrible solution. It is absolutely true that earlier periods of mass incarceration led to far too many people—in particular young Black men—being in jail for crimes that would have been better dealt with through noncustodial means, and that police officers and police departments should be transparent, accountable, and just as tough on wrongdoing if it occurs inside their ranks as when it does in wider society. We do need commonsense action on climate change, and on environmental challenges more broadly. What we don't need are sensible policy positions that could command widespread support jacked up into extremist dogma to feed the ego of narcissist politicians and activists acting out some salvationist fantasy.

The real problems confronting working families in California are not solved when narcissistic "criminal justice reform" extremists and "progressive DAs" convince themselves and their acolytes that "decarceration"—the widespread and experimental release of criminals—is somehow going to reduce crime. Working families are not helped when narcissistic "climate" extremists take over California's institutions and implement policies that make energy and housing unaffordable, because they've convinced themselves that they alone can "save the world."

California is broken. The education system (as we will see) needs a complete overhaul, the criminal justice system has been inverted to prosecute law-abiding citizens, and the astronomical cost of living has made it almost impossible for working- and middle-class households to survive. These fundamental failures require dramatic shifts in policy. They are the priorities that ought to be keeping the lights on in Sacramento late into the evenings. Our best minds should be working on fixing these problems. But that's not what's happening.

The Narcissism that informs California's policies on crime and the "climate crisis" are part of an even larger narcissistic pathology. California's elites—as evidenced by Gavin Newsom's remarks at the nomination of Kamala Harris—seem to believe they are engineering a new utopia, a perfect society where nobody will ever feel offended, nobody will ever feel unsafe, a society where even the most hypersensitive among us will be respected and protected. They believe they are engineering a perfect economy where everyone will not only be treated equally, but everyone will enjoy precisely the same economic status as everyone else, which they call "equity." No more oppression. No more exploitation. A perfected society.

Who could be against that? Unfortunately, history teaches us that the attempt to achieve a perfect society—rather than steady steps toward the "more perfect Union" envisaged by America's Founders, tends to produce much more harm than good.

In the modern era, achieving utopian dreams has been the siren song of narcissistic Pied Pipers since the publication of *The Communist Manifesto* in 1848.[20] Over the nearly two centuries since then, the pages of history are red with the blood of millions who were killed in the battles to create a workers' paradise. For the survivors of communist violence, lives of poverty and cowed obedience to a brutal regime was their fate.

My own family experienced this. My father, mother, stepfather—all are Hungarian and lived under the oppression of a communist regime. It wasn't the worst in Eastern Europe, it wasn't the Soviet Union, Mao's China, or North Korea today. But it was bad. It wasn't free. And California is, if it is anything, a bastion of freedom. California: follow your dream, live how you want to live, love who you want to love, be who you want to be.

That's not the mentality of the far-left narcissistic elite. It's not "follow your dream," but follow theirs. Not "live how you want to live" but how they tell you to live. You will be exactly what they want you to be—or else.

It's Narcissism that enables all this. California's elites don't look in the mirror and acknowledge where their policies are taking working families. They're not sitting around a conference table like the pigs in Orwell's masterpiece *Animal Farm*, suddenly indistinguishable from the human oppressors they have overthrown, proclaiming that "all animals are equal, but some animals are more equal than others."[21] They are too narcissistic to be that self-aware. But as they drive millions of working families into lives of chaos and poverty while exempting themselves from the consequences of their failed policies, that is exactly what they are doing.

The pathology of Narcissism is tailor-made for an elite class that believes its own utopian fantasies can replace the mundane reality of how to fight crime or produce adequate energy to power our economy. These narcissists, however, extend their fantasies into every aspect of society. And like Nero, who fiddled as fires swept through ancient Rome, their attention has fiddled its way into abstract causes and faux crises about which people trying to figure out how to pay their bills or manage their small private businesses can only shake their heads in disbelief.

California's legislature is fully engaged in the narcissistic quest to turn California into utopia and in their zealotry have enacted countless laws that reach down into the minutest details of our private lives. A recent example, mercifully shelved in committee during the 2023–24 legislative session but likely to resurface, was Assembly Bill 2751, introduced by San Francisco assemblyman Matt Haney, which "would require employers to identify specific work hours for their employees and prohibit them from demanding workers respond to communications outside those hours, except for emergencies and scheduling changes."[22]

In response to AB 2751, California businesses had to rally their resources and point out the obvious pitfalls of this intrusive proposal.[23] How would it affect salaried employees who are exempt from overtime laws and often work long hours? How would it affect contractors whose bosses are also their clients, who work on assigned projects at their own pace, choosing randomly what hours they will work? How would this affect any employee who works flexible hours? And aren't hourly employees already mostly protected by overtime laws? Compliance with AB 2751 would have been a nightmare, although it would have been a lucrative delight for California's burgeoning human resources industry.[24] For now the "right to disconnect" bill is dormant. Expect it to return in the next session, festooned with "mitigating" exemptions and new complexities.

The example of AB 2751 is one in which a law was proposed that in isolation might be considered to be a relatively minor nuisance. As such, it was something the business community could quickly respond to and muster enough clout to stop, or at least postpone. But there are two obvious problems with this win. First, it is another case of the business community playing defense instead of offense. Second, it highlights the scale of the true fight that is needed. It is one thing to win a successful defense against a minor onslaught, but what all working Californians face, whether they're employers or employees, is an unending and overwhelming cascade of laws and regulations that cripple the economy and destroy quality of life. This is the price of narcissistic progressive dreams infecting the leadership of nearly every major institution in the state.

Micromanaging businesses is just one aspect of narcissistic over-reach in California. How the far-left elites impose their fantasies on the rest of society is a case of end-to-end Narcissism. A perfect example of this is their determination to get everyone to start saying Latinx instead of Latino or Latina.

Latinx, pronounced "Latin-ex," is a concocted word being pushed on Latinos by far-left white extremists. These are people who think they're entitled to decide what everyone is supposed to think, how they're supposed to talk, what they're permitted to talk about, which nouns, verbs, adjectives, prepositions, etc., are permissible, and which are forbidden.

Fewer than 3 percent of Latinos have any interest in using the word *Latinx*.[25] For the vast majority of Latinos, this word is recognized for what it really is—cultural imperialism foisted on them by left-wing whites with a savior complex.

Narcissists.

You may think: Who cares? How much harm does any of this do, really? Well, first of all, put yourself in the position of the people being told to change how they describe their identity. Latinos are now the largest demographic group in California: 40 percent, compared to 35 percent white, 15 percent Asian, 5 percent Black, and 5 percent Native American and other. On top of that, Latinos are becoming more dominant. Fifty-six percent of the students in California's public schools today are Latino. In the words of the title of a report sponsored by my California policy organization, Golden Together, "El Futuro Es Latino." Yet a tiny group of extremist white people are telling the largest demographic group in California what to call themselves? How dare they!

The type of person who invents a word like *Latinx*—leftist activists and academics, or compliant bureaucrats—is the same type of person who comes up with such abominations as *accompliceship, androcentric, cisheteropatriarchy, conscientization, herstory, hxrstory, hybridities, womanism, xdisciplinary*, and much, much more.[26]

Most people see all of this for what it is: gibberish. But the narcissistic leftist word warriors have bitten off more than they can chew when they decided to take on Spanish, a "gendered" language. While they're deciding whether or not to demand we replace *Latino* and *Latina* with *Latinx/a/o* or move everyone straight to the new *Latinx*, they're forgetting that every noun in the Spanish language is either masculine or feminine. *Latinx* is the tip of an iceberg that runs deep into the linguistic ocean.

To truly appreciate how utterly futile the imposition of the gender-neutral *Latinx* is on the Spanish language, consider how Spanish handles its gendered nouns. It is not simply necessary to change the definite articles preceding these nouns. For example, you must say "el gato" because *gato*, which means "cat," is a masculine noun. But you must say "la mujer," because, naturally, *mujer*, which means "woman," is a feminine noun. *El* is masculine and *la* is feminine. And if it's plural, you have to go with *los* instead of *el*, and *las* instead of *la*. In English, all of that is merely *the*. But you're still just scratching the surface of this linguistic iceberg called Spanish.

If you want to say "the cat is pretty," you say "el gato es bonito." But if you want to say "the woman is pretty," you say "la mujer es bonita." Depending on the gender of the noun, not only the definite article, but the adjective is also altered: *bonito* versus *bonita*. Shall we go with *bonitx*? Why not?

It gets messier and messier. In Spanish, the pronouns affect how you conjugate a verb. For example, in English you'll say, "I eat," "you eat," "they eat," and "we eat." Not in Spanish. Instead it goes "yo como," "tu comes," "ellos comen," and "nosotros comemos." And it just goes on and on. This is just the present tense. Want to conjugate the indicative present, preterit, imperfect, conditional, or the subjunctive present, imperfect, second imperfect, or future? What about the various forms of the imperative, progressive, perfect, or perfect subjunctive tenses?

In English, regardless of the tense, there are four ways to conjugate the verb *eat*. You can say "eat," "eats," "eaten," or "ate." The conjugations of *eat* in Spanish, on the other hand, include, but are not limited to, the following words: "Coma, comiera, comiese, comiere, comas, comieras, comieses, comieres, comamos, comiéramos, comiésemos, comiéramos, comáis, comierais, comieses, comiereis, coman, comieran, comiesen, comiendo, and comido."[27]

The dictionary that catalogs just 501 of the most common Spanish verb conjugations is 681 pages of small type. Nobody has ever published an English verb dictionary. There is no such thing. It's too simple.

Don't think this is all merely offensive. It has tangible costs too. I was talking with a Mexican restaurant owner in Orange County about the endless nuisance lawsuits he has to deal with (a massive issue for most small businesses in California, and one that has been supercharged by Democrat policies that have made it easier and easier to sue over more and more trivial things). He told me a story that I had to check repeatedly with him to make sure it was real and not satire. One of the recent lawsuits faced by this particular restaurant was over gender discrimination. Not in relation to employment, as you might expect. But in relation to the menu. The section on the menu devoted to egg dishes (it was a breakfast and lunch place) was titled "Los Huevos." Masculine. Therefore, in the worldview of the far-left narcissist asserting their right to tell Latinos how to speak Spanish . . . discriminatory.

"But that's the actual word," I said. "That's what it is in Spanish—
los huevos. What did this person want instead?" "Les Huevos," replied
the restaurant owner. "Les Huevos isn't a thing," I pointed out. "It's
made up!" "Yes," agreed the poor guy, "of course it's ridiculous, but it
still cost us thousands of dollars to make it go away."

None of this matters to the narcissists who have decided *Latinx*
is the only equitable way to describe a Latino or Latina. By virtue
of their pathology, they think nothing of projecting their utopian
fantasies onto the rest of us. And it serves a pragmatic end as well,
since there is a cadre of activists they need as foot soldiers who will
recognize the power in demanding these verbal gymnastics. It feeds
the narrative of oppressor versus oppressed, in this case, the exclusion
of the female, the inherent structural racism of a gendered language.
But as we have seen, erasing gender from Spanish would require upending its entire grammatical architecture. It's impossible. Which
does not matter to the far-left white narcissist.

One of Mexico's early cinema heroes is Pedro Infante.[28] His films
mixed comedy, drama, and music, and they remain popular more
than sixty years after his death. In one of his movies, he is asked to
name the "ten fingers of Mexican culture." They are "religion, homeland, family, honor, work, and a horse, gun, drink, guitar, and cards."

Does this sound familiar? It should. Because the first five of the traits
he lists—religion, homeland, family, honor, and work—are awfully
similar to the "white traits" or "whiteness" the left so disparages, and
which, according to a famously derided poster from the Smithsonian's
National Museum of African American History & Culture, include
individualism, hard work, objectivity, the nuclear family, progress, respect for authority, and delayed gratification.[29] These are outer-directed
values, providing a framework for individuals to become productive
members of a community, with a personal character that is oriented to
serving others with integrity and humility. These traits that are shared
by Latino culture and "white" culture alike are antithetical to Narcissism, and hence represent a threat to narcissists.

Fundamentally changing how we speak, demanding we declare our pronouns on résumés and in emails, or even on the name tags we wear at social and professional gatherings, is a goal that could only be promulgated by individuals with powerful narcissistic delusions. Perhaps the pronoun mania is all just a huge distraction, calculated to preoccupy our emotions and divert us from responding to greater threats. That might be giving it too much credit, but it would explain why California's narcissistic elites have embraced it with all their might. It keeps us focused elsewhere while the even more transformative expressions of their narcissistic visions proceed apace—decriminalizing crime and citing a "climate crisis" to justify government micromanagement of every aspect of our lives.

CHAPTER 4

MAOISM

In December 2022, Stanford University's information technology (IT) department produced the Elimination of Harmful Language Initiative, a guide designed to promote more inclusive and sensitive communication within the university.[1] Created by Stanford's CIO Council, the thirteen-page guide identified over 150 words and phrases that could be potentially harmful or offensive. These problematic words were sorted into categories such as "ableism," "ageism," "colonialism," "culturally appropriative," "gender-based," "institutionalized racist," "person first," "violent language," and others. The purpose of the guide was not only to offer a list of words to avoid but to promote understanding of how language affects people, and encourage more thoughtful and respectful communication.

The language guide was part of an ongoing effort at Stanford to become a place where all individuals feel valued and respected. The words we use shape our perceptions and interactions. The words we choose can either bring us closer together or push us further apart. Raising awareness about the harm that certain words can cause was a way to encourage more "intentional and inclusive" language use.

One of the reasons the guide was considered necessary is that it attempted to explain the unconscious ways that language can exclude or harm others. The promoters of the guide would contend, for example, that "ableist" language perpetuates negative stereotypes about people with disabilities, or that using "gendered" words can reinforce notions of gender roles that they believe have become obsolete. By encouraging the use of more neutral or inclusive alternatives, they hoped to promote a more equitable and welcoming environment for everyone.

The guide was also designed to help members of the Stanford community understand the historical and cultural context behind certain terms. This understanding is considered crucial for fostering empathy and encouraging more thoughtful communication. When individuals are aware of the impact of their words, they are more likely to choose language that respects the dignity of others. The guide was not just about changing language, but about changing how we view ourselves and others and promoting a culture of respect and inclusion.

The people who produced Stanford's language guide weren't just thinking about campus culture. They understood that training people to make more sensitive language choices will extend beyond the university. They recognize that in today's increasingly diverse world, where everyone is connected, communicating in ways that respect others is a prerequisite for building inclusive and harmonious communities. Language shapes our reality. Using language that reflects the values of diversity, equity, and inclusion contributes to creating a society where all individuals feel valued and understood.

The ability to communicate with empathy and respect is more important than ever. Inclusive language fosters dialogue and understanding. It creates opportunities for connection and collaboration across lines of difference. It encourages us to see others not as "other" but as individuals with their own unique experiences and perspectives. Language can and should be a tool for building a more inclusive and harmonious society, where all individuals are recognized and respected for who they are. This is not a political agenda, but a human one. In the end it is no more complicated—and should be no more controversial—than the idea that we should be kind and respectful to one another.

...

But the Stanford Elimination of Harmful Language Initiative *was* controversial. It triggered a backlash, the tenor of which was best captured by a *Wall Street Journal* editorial that included the following examples from the initiative:[2]

> Call yourself an "American"? Please don't. Better to say "U.S. citizen," per the bias hunters, lest you slight the rest of the Americas. "Immigrant" is also out, with "person who has immigrated" as the approved alternative. It's the iron law of academic writing: Why use one word when four will do. You can't "master" your subject at Stanford any longer; in case you hadn't heard, the school instructs that "historically, masters enslaved people." And don't dare design a "blind study," which "unintentionally perpetuates that disability is somehow abnormal or negative, furthering an ableist culture." Blind studies are good and useful, but never mind; "masked study" is to be preferred. Follow the science. "Gangbusters" is banned because the index says it "invokes the notion of police action against 'gangs' in a positive light, which may have racial undertones." Not to beat a dead horse (a phrase that the index says "normalizes violence against animals"), but you used to have to get a graduate degree in the humanities to write something that stupid.

Within just a few weeks the Stanford document was taken offline. After all, eliminating words such as *American, immigrant,* and *grandfather* from polite conversation was too much to accept. But the institutionalization of hypersensitive, politically correct discourse, and ritual condemnation and cancellation of the noncompliant, proceeds undiminished. As we will see, with or without their harmful language guide, Stanford University remains in the vanguard of the far-left takeover of California, and it is part of a much bigger movement. Words define reality, and from the halls of academia to corporate conference rooms and public forums, reality is being redefined. But what have we gained?

For decades California's academic, political, and media elite have been in the vanguard of the diversity, equity, and inclusion movement. Has anything improved? Are we more united? Have we erased income inequality? Have disproportionate outcomes diminished? Real-world experiences tell a different story.

Lecturer Gordon Klein of the University of California, Los Angeles, was preparing final exams for his students in May 2020 when, on the other side of the country, George Floyd died while in the process of being arrested by four Minneapolis police officers. As protests, then riots, began to engulf the nation, one of Klein's white students sent him an email requesting he cancel the final exams—but only for Black students—in recognition of the emotional trauma they were experiencing in empathy with the Floyd tragedy. Klein refused to grant this request.

By the time the dogpile that ensued had run its course, Klein found himself suspended from his job and so hounded and threatened by outraged students that he was placed under police protection. The swift and massive fury that descended upon Klein for his refusal to agree to what in earlier times would have never been asked is just one example of the Maoist madness that has descended on California's universities, and from there spreads onward into every facet of American life.

What do I mean by Maoism? The history of China in the twentieth century is dominated by Mao Zedong, who was the chairman of the Communist Party of China from 1943 until his death in 1976. He is the founder of the People's Republic of China and is credited with leading the fight against Japanese occupation during World War II, then driving the nationalist (anti-communist) forces out of mainland China in 1949. His vision for China, which his supporters dubbed Maoism, was a variant of Marxism where the proletariat were agrarian peasants, whereas in Marxist theory the proletariat was the industrial working class. But both of these communist ideologies shared a rejection of individual rights and a demand that everyone share the same collective political opinions.

This intolerance for dissent reached its brutal zenith during the so-called Cultural Revolution, which convulsed China from 1966 until Mao's death in 1976. Launched by Mao to purge the government and society of "bourgeois elements" that he alleged were attempting to bring back capitalism, the foot soldiers in the Cultural Revolution were the nation's youth. Within months of Mao's call to revolution, young Chinese students and activists were forming militant cadres known as the Red Guards that violently took control of local governments, schools, and party offices.

One of the goals of the Red Guards was to destroy what Mao called the "Four Olds": old habits, customs, culture, and ideas. In pursuit of these goals the Red Guards targeted anyone they considered to be representative of the Four Olds, and they destroyed historical sites and artifacts. By the time the Cultural Revolution finally ended, the nation had endured over a decade of violence and bloodshed, and millions of people had been killed.

Gordon Klein's antagonists were also demanding that old habits, customs, culture, and ideas be discarded.

To be fair, the tone of Klein's response displayed an impertinent lack of sensitivity and emotional intelligence with respect to this student, who characterized himself as a white "ally" of his Black classmates.[3]

"Are there any students that may be of mixed parentage, such as half black-half Asian?" Klein wrote. "What do you suggest I do with respect to them? A full concession or just half? Also, do you have any idea if any students are from Minneapolis? I assume that they probably are especially devastated as well. I am thinking that a white student from there might be possibly even more devastated by this, especially because some might think that they're racist even if they are not."

Within days, the outraged students had launched a petition on Change.org and gathered more than twenty thousand signatures demanding the university fire him.[4] But for what? Refusing to practice racial discrimination? Adhering to the California state constitution, which prohibits race-based preferences in public education?[5]

. Within days, UCLA's dean suspended Klein, barred him from campus, and monitored his email account.[6] Thanks to student activists publicly condemning Klein, he became the victim of repeated death threats and the recipient of emails blistering with hatred. While Klein was reinstated later that year, the damage to his reputation was lasting. Klein's primary income was not from his work as a lecturer at UCLA, even though he'd logged forty years of unblemished service to that university. Most of his income came from consulting contracts with law firms and other corporations, and when Klein was suspended because he was an alleged racist bigot, he lost that business.[7] Finally, in September 2021, Klein sued UCLA for compensatory and punitive damages.[8]

The dynamics of Klein's experience may have been unique in the degree of national attention it gathered, but the culture he confronted is everywhere. In the spring of 2023, a renowned psychology professor, Yoel Inbar, then teaching at the University of Toronto, was reportedly all but a shoo-in to gain a faculty appointment at UCLA. But Inbar's reputation in his field didn't protect him when a few dozen graduate students scoured his online history and discovered a podcast where, nearly five years earlier, he criticized the need for "diversity statements" as a condition of faculty appointments.[9] How foolish of him!

Thankfully, at least before Inbar had completely uprooted himself from Toronto in order to move to Los Angeles and buy a house, the department chair told him that he would not get the job after all. According to the concerned students, allowing Inbar onto the university faculty "would threaten ongoing efforts to protect and uplift individuals of marginalized backgrounds."[10] Prior to searching Inbar's background for anything they might use against him, apparently these students felt Inbar's conduct was "less than satisfactory" during a meeting he had had with graduate students earlier in 2023. They concluded that "Dr. Inbar would not enter the Social Area as a member committed to creating a safe, welcoming, and inclusive environment, and that his hiring would threaten ongoing efforts to protect and uplift individuals of marginalized backgrounds."[11]

But was Inbar right? Should applicants have to fill out "diversity statements" as a condition for being considered for a faculty appointment? It turns out this requirement, now common in California and elsewhere, offers very little in terms of assessing a prospective faculty member's grasp of the topic they're hoping they will be able to teach. But it has everything to do with how well they conform to the great and growing ideology of diversity, equity, and inclusion, which is but one damaging facet of what we may call the new Maoism, California-style.

So watch out, aspiring professors. If you want to teach at the University of California, you'd better know how to fill out a diversity statement. Here are some guidelines to "crafting your diversity statement," taken from UCLA's form:

Demonstrate your COMMITMENT to use your position to be a force of enlightenment and change by opening up opportunities to first-generation and underrepresented students.

Describe how you have CREATED programs that provide access and establish a pipeline for students in traditionally underrepresented groups.

Show how you ENRICH the classroom environment through exposure to new perspectives on cultures, beliefs, practices, tolerance, acceptance, and a welcoming climate.

Demonstrate how your research provides EXPOSURE for individuals historically excluded from disciplines on the basis of their gender or ethnic identity.

Speak to your LEADERSHIP in any capacity that tangibly promotes an environment where diversity is welcomed, fostered, and celebrated.

Discuss MENTORING students from traditionally underrepresented groups and at-risk students.

Describe your OUTREACH to members of student clubs, organizations, or community groups whose mission includes service, education, or extending opportunity to disadvantaged people.

Show RECOGNITION of the challenges members of society face when they are members of underrepresented groups; or because of their religious, ethnic, or gender identities or orientation.

Detail SERVICE that promotes inclusion by striving to dismantle barriers to people historically excluded from the opportunities that all have a right to enjoy.[12]

Commitment, creation, enrichment, exposure, leadership, mentoring, outreach, recognition, and service. For each of these imperatives, applicants had better lay it on THICK, or else forget about getting that job they've worked for their whole lives. As for other qualifications? Nobel Prize laureate? Fulbright scholar? MacArthur Genius Grant recipient? That's all great, but you'd better ace that diversity statement, or it won't matter if you discovered a cure for malaria or even the secret to commercializing cold fusion power in a coffee cup. It won't matter.

Ironically, for an approach that is, superficially at least, so obsessed with helping "underrepresented groups," UCLA's diversity, equity, and inclusion guidelines come at a time when the actual cost of attending the university for children of regular working families has ballooned to a degree that can only be described as exclusionary. When the University of California system was renowned as the best in the world, in-state tuition (in 2024 dollars) was $3,681 per year. Today it is $16,608. A major reason for the massive inflation is the cost of the burgeoning administrative bloat churning out time-wasting nonsense like "diversity statements."

A surprisingly balanced examination of diversity, equity, and inclusion statements was published in the *New York Times* in the wake of UCLA rejecting Dr. Inbar. The article reported that nearly half of America's universities now require DEI statements from job applicants, and that the University of California now requires it as a condition of promotions or granting tenure.[13] The article quotes UC Berkeley history professor Daniel Sargent, who neatly expresses the farce that DEI statements have become, saying, "Professions of fealty to DEI ideology are so ubiquitous as to be meaningless. We are institutionalizing a performative dishonesty."

The definition of a farce is something that is supposed to be serious but has become ridiculous. That definition applies to diversity, equity, and inclusion ideology, at least insofar as it has become ubiquitous and meaningless. But they are deadly serious. It is part of what has been labeled a broader "woke" movement that also includes gender ideology, "social justice," "environmental justice," reparation payments to Black Americans, and active discrimination against anyone who isn't BIPOC (Black, Indigenous, and People of Color) or LGBTQ (Lesbian, Gay, Bisexual, Transgender, or Queer).

As noted previously, it is the extremism that is the problem. For example, of course it's true that California—like the rest of America—has a severe racial wealth gap, much of it the result of past discrimination. That's why I have argued in the past for "asset reparations": not handing out cash like some enhanced form of welfare, but policies that will help close the racial wealth gap in a lasting way: for example, help for Black people to own homes and start businesses. The most significant policy move that would help close the racial wealth gap in California would probably be school choice, considering the absolutely obscene failure of the union-run public school system to educate Black students properly. A recent study by the National Assessment of Education Progress (NAEP) found that Black students in California public schools are on average four years' worth of education behind their white peers.[14] However, the Maoist elite seem not to be interested in actual, practical steps that would move us toward "racial justice" in the real world. They adamantly oppose school choice, just as they oppose policies that would make housing more affordable or small businesses easier to start and grow.

No, this movement, born in academia, is resolutely determined to remain purely ideological. Common sense and positive, practical policies to address its stated objectives are almost entirely absent from its discourse. Instead it assigns primary responsibility for the ongoing challenges of poverty, inequality, oppression, war, and environmental degradation on Europeans and Americans of European descent, and classifies all of humanity into two categories: victims and oppressors. It is absolutist, authoritarian, intolerant, and fanatical.

We've seen this before. It's called Maoism.

Someone with firsthand experience of the legacy of Maoism is Habi Zhang, born and raised in a small village in Sichuan Province, China. Zhang grew up in the 1990s and 2000s, attending schools during an era when China, as she writes, "was ruled by a tiny group of oligarchs that constitutes an extremely opaque organization called the Politburo Standing Committee of the Chinese Communist Party. They find ideologies such as Maoism or Marxism to be only transparent propaganda schemes."[15]

In two sentences Zhang has characterized Maoism as it exists today in China and as it is rising in America. The propaganda is powerful: Equality. Fighting oppression. But behind the propaganda is a ruthless elite, micromanaging society and centralizing in its hands all economic and political power. And the facade? Performative dishonesty, with life-changing consequences for anyone whose performance falls short.

One of the rituals that characterized Mao's Cultural Revolution was what they called "struggle sessions," where people suspected of dissent were publicly shamed. Victims were often made to stand in front of a mob, sometimes forced to wear a pointed dunce cap or other humiliating attire, while their alleged thought crimes were announced to the crowd. They were forced to repeatedly apologize for their alleged transgressions, usually while being physically abused.

In countless cases, these struggle sessions would end with the person getting beaten to death.

Habi Zhang, whose parents were forced to participate in rallies and witness struggle sessions during the Cultural Revolution, made her way to the United States in 2015. Arriving in California and attending Pepperdine University, her initial impression of the campus environment there was that she had "died and gone to heaven." But then she began to see troubling evidence that campus culture in the United States was drifting increasingly toward the intolerant insistence on thought conformity that dominated China under Maoism and ever since. Her observations came in quick succession, which she now warns Americans about in her writings and lectures.

What first got Zhang's attention were the attacks that began in 2016 on Jordan Peterson's fight to preserve his right to free speech. Peterson, a Canadian psychologist, rose to prominence in that year by virtue of his public refusal to obey a new law that he believed would "classify the failure to use preferred pronouns of transgender people as hate speech." But that was just the beginning. Zhang writes, "I was then stunned to see social justice warriors attack, sometimes physically attack, conservative speakers for alleged 'hate speech' (i.e., the speech they hate). The administration shut down events or disinvited speakers to placate the angry mob (or so they wished). Meanwhile, they aggressively inculcate a cult of narcissistic victimhood on campus."

By 2019, when Zhang was completing a doctoral program in political science, she noticed, as she put it, the "catchy phrase 'white supremacy' mushroom in media and on campus. Nobody offered a definition or supplied evidence, but all cultural elites were speaking the narrative to students and media consumers, presenting it as the biggest threat to America." She goes on to describe how additional buzzwords became common rallying points for radicalized American students, including *intersectionality, critical race theory*, and of course *diversity, equity, and inclusion*.

The similarities of this steady radicalization of American college students to the student militants in China during the Cultural Revolution were obvious to Zhang. As she put it, by 2020 "I was flabbergasted to see the American replication of the Chinese Cultural Revolution on full blast."

I see the similarities too. My own grandmother in Hungary, head teacher at a local school, was unceremoniously fired from her job for the ideological "crime" of "allowing" her daughter (my mother) to leave Hungary for a life of freedom in the West. Not only did she lose her cherished vocation, but she was humiliated by being required to spend the rest of her working life sitting all day on a chair in the corner of a room in the local museum. On top of that, she was paraded in front of her entire school—students and teachers alike—and denounced for being disloyal to the party.

Public humiliation over ideological transgressions, career advancement being affected by political stances . . . all of that happens routinely in California today. When I see these far-left authoritarian Democrats in action, I can safely say: I know the type.

This is the historical context with which to view the experience of Gordon Klein, who not only declined to excuse his Black students from final exams in the aftermath of George Floyd's death, but did so in a way that failed to convey the requisite deference. This is also the perspective from which one must judge Yoel Inbar's daring suggestion that "diversity statements" might not need to be a requirement for applicants to faculty positions. Nothing these men did would have done more than perhaps raise a few eyebrows in previous decades. But now the Maoists are in charge. They violated what Zhang calls "the Unanimity Imperative" and paid a severe price.

Maoism in all of its American forms may have been creeping its way into colleges and universities in every state for the past several years, but California remains ground zero. One of the latest groupthink mandates concerns protecting the rights of transgender people, including their right to compete in women's sports.

In April 2023, a world-class swimmer named Riley Gaines traveled to San Francisco State University. Invited by the SFSU chapter of the conservative organization Turning Point USA, Gaines attended and spoke about her opposition to trans women participating in women's sports, and shared her personal experiences. But after the event concluded, Gaines was ambushed by dozens of protesters and alleges that one of them, a trans woman, struck her twice in the face. Her police escorts deemed the crowd so dangerous that they hustled her away to an adjacent room where they barred and guarded the door to keep her safe inside. Meanwhile, as she remained confined for over three hours, campus officials "negotiated" the conditions under which the protesters would permit her release. Ultimately Gaines was able to exit the campus, but what happened next illustrates just how far down the Maoist rabbit hole SFSU has fallen.

A few days after the incident, San Francisco State University president Lynn Mahoney issued a public statement that included these nuggets: "Last Thursday, Turning Point USA hosted an event on campus that advocated for the exclusion of trans people in athletics. The event was deeply traumatic for many in our trans and LGBTQ+ communities, and the speaker's message outraged many members of the SF State community."

Notice how in this statement there is no acknowledgment of the trauma that Riley Gaines endured: being ambushed and forced into a room under police guard for her safety, and not before being screamed at by a militant mob and allegedly assaulted. Nor did Mahoney acknowledge that the event wasn't to "advocate" anything, but rather was organized merely to permit someone with a view that violated the prescribed groupthink to have an opportunity to make her argument. Mahoney went on:

"Last week was a hard one for San Francisco State. As we have seen here and at many universities, balancing these with dearly held commitments to inclusion and social justice is hard and painful. To our trans community, please know how welcome you are. We will turn this moment into an opportunity to listen and learn about how we can better support you." Mahoney then appeared to actually praise the militants, complimenting them because they "rallied quickly to host alternative inclusive events, protest peacefully and provide one another with support at a difficult moment."

Gaines, for her part, alleged that the police did nothing to stop the protesters and barely managed to protect her from being even more violently attacked. But rather than identify and prosecute the individuals who actually accosted Gaines, SFSU vice president Jamillah Moore added her voice to the chorus of groupthink, stating that the traumatized mob might reach out to the campus Equity and Community Inclusion office in order to "reflect, process, and begin to heal."[16]

Ten months later, the SFSU police announced they had suspended their investigation into the students who allegedly assaulted Gaines. No consequences.

As we saw with its IT department's preposterous Elimination of Harmful Language Initiative, the Maoist Unanimity Imperative is also on full display at Stanford. In March 2023, Stanford Law School, ranked in a tie with Yale as the top law school in the United States, joined in. The law school invited federal appeals court judge Kyle Duncan to give a speech and lead a discussion about the Fifth Circuit's recent jurisprudence.[17] But not just any jurisprudence. Duncan had been involved in a case involving transgender rights. Instead of being permitted to speak, he was repeatedly interrupted. Finally, after attempting for thirty minutes to deliver his speech, Duncan stopped his remarks and asked an administrator to help him handle the heckling from protesters.

Duncan, who is a judge in the U.S. Court of Appeals for the Fifth Circuit, which covers Texas, Mississippi, and Louisiana, must have known what he was getting himself into when he accepted an invitation to speak at a California law school. According to the *Stanford Daily*, in 2021 "Duncan had served as lead trial and appellate counsel in a case that stopped transgender people from using the bathroom of their choice at state institutions."

For the protesters at Stanford, what Duncan had done was unforgivable. For the law students who disrupted his speech, Duncan was a pariah, and was treated as such. What happened next, however, demonstrates that Maoist ideology, or at the least, craven deference to Maoist ideology, has also infected the university administration.

When Duncan asked the administrator present at his speech for assistance controlling the crowd, Stanford Law dean Jennifer Martinez got up and, speaking from notes she had prepared in advance, joined the protesters in chastising Duncan and praising the student protesters.

A few days later, perhaps realizing that in a *law school*, of all places, the right to free speech should be respected, Martinez issued a public apology to Judge Duncan. This enraged the protesters, who demanded she withdraw her apology and that from now on she monitor and censor communications from the Federalist Society, which had invited Duncan to the campus. The protesters even proposed that Martinez expel some of their conservative classmates.

To her credit, this time Martinez didn't yield. Within a week she responded with a ten-page memorandum to the entire law school student body, where she asserted the school's commitment to free speech, free inquiry, minority rights, and the freedom of unpopular speakers to discuss unpopular ideas without being subjected to the so-called heckler's veto.[18] She even directed the law students to attend a training seminar where they could develop an appreciation for these principles.

If there are red lines left that Maoists still can't cross—and in the case of the Stanford Law School, apparently there still are—it doesn't change what has happened to campus culture at Stanford. The Maoists won. In a few short years, the campus has been transformed. As recently as 2010, Stanford was a place that embraced eccentricity and individualism and tolerated, if not actually encouraged, the sort of wild, rogue behavior that nurtures the creativity and initiative of gifted young students.

A searing portrait of what Stanford has become was written in 2022 by Ginevra Davis, who entered the university in 2018, a time when the last vestiges of what Stanford once was were being erased by an administration that can only be described as Maoist. In her essay "Stanford's War on Social Life," she describes how one of the primary ways this administration inflicted its very own cultural revolution onto Stanford was by eliminating every residence house that had any sort of identity.[19] One by one, the fraternities were kicked out of their houses. For over a century, Friday nights on the campus, which anyone who went to or visited Stanford will recall, were always raucous, with on-campus parties everywhere, music pouring out of every window, celebrants spilling out onto front lawns. Now, according to Davis, they're silent. The campus is dead.

In the fall of 2017, as Stanford's fraternities were being evicted one after another, the administration formed the Committee on Residential Living (CORL), a three-person tribunal with the power to kick any social organization out of their on-campus housing. Not only fraternities fell to CORL. Four European language–themed international houses were next—French, Italian, German, and Slavic—all gone.

What happened to these houses further illustrates the soulless essence of Maoist conformity. Since renaming these fraternity houses and international houses might stimulate dissent, the administration came up with a new housing system that would create "community" and "fairness." The entire campus housing system was divided into eight "neighborhoods," and the names of the neighborhoods were S, T, A, N, F, O, R, and D. As for the international houses, their identity was stripped away, and they were given numbers.

Stanford's administration was so bent on destroying anything that might betray a shred of distinct identity, they even eliminated the Outdoor House, located on the edge of the campus near hiking trails. The administration claimed the Outdoor House theme did not sufficiently embrace "diversity, equity, and inclusion." It was added to the "T" neighborhood. Many of the finest fraternity houses have now been taken over by Stanford's swelling administrative bureaucracy. Kick out the kids, move in the commissars. History rhymes. Stanford is still one of the best universities in the world. But Maoism corroded its soul.

For a searing glimpse into where Maoism is taking California, look no further than the teachers unions, one of the most powerful special interests in the state. There are at least four major unions representing faculty and school employees in the state, but the California Teachers Association (CTA) is the biggest and most influential. And it's been a long time, if ever, since this union focused merely on negotiating pay and benefits for its membership.

In a typical expression of Maoist "action," the largest chapter of the CTA, the United Teachers of Los Angeles, staged a May Day demonstration in a downtown park. The online promotional graphic for the rally was a case study in Maoist design, using the colors red, white, and black.[20] Below the "May Day 2024," "Worker Power Worldwide" headlines, black silhouettes of raised fists and signs were depicted against a red sky. At the base of the graphic, depicted in the foreground, masked demonstrators were illustrated, holding up signs that read "Abolish Colonial Borders," "Stop US Intervention in Cuba, Venezuela, Nicaragua, Haiti," "Solidarity and Revolution," "Defend Workers Rights to Organize," "Universal Healthcare, Education, Housing for All," and, of course, "Free Palestine Now."

This is classic CTA rhetoric. It's also classic Maoist rhetoric. There isn't a leftist cause imaginable that the CTA isn't likely to be promoting in public, pressuring politicians to codify into new laws, and pushing onto impressionable students starting in kindergarten and lasting all the way through high school. The Maoist worldview adopted by the CTA has captured the minds of countless K–12 public school teachers in California, and intimidated countless others into acquiescence. The Maoist mania disrupting and destroying California's colleges and universities is undoubtedly a product of faculties and administrations that have been taken over by the far left, but the students they have recruited as foot soldiers have been prepared in advance. They spent their formative years attending California's public schools.

The depths to which CTA indoctrination reaches is in plain sight. An excursion through the CTA's sprawling website offers evidence aplenty. A look at their "social justice" page reveals the "Social Justice Issues We Care About (just to name a few!)."[21] These so-called few items seem awfully comprehensive: "Racial Justice, Ethnic Studies, Black Lives Matter at School, Ending the School to Prison Pipeline, Dreamers, Families Belong Together, Creating Safe Zones, Students' and Educators' Civil Rights, LGBTQ+ Students, Equity for Girls and Women, Stopping Hate and Bias, Confronting White Nationalism, Addressing the 'isms,' Restorative Justice Practices, Economic Justice, Mental Health and Self-Care." Behind each of these social justice issues is an agenda. Unpacking any one of them uncovers a revolutionary Maoist design to completely remake society. But has any of this ever worked? Can history provide any example of Maoism ever achieving a workers' paradise? Are the nations of "Cuba, Venezuela, Nicaragua or Haiti" places where the average Californian would prefer to live?

Digging into the CTA's detailed work on each of these social justice issues—each of them promoted through CTA literature and training to over 309,000 member teachers in California—invariably points to the same, predictable, Maoist principles, updated for the twenty-first century. Oppressor versus oppressed. The dangers of colonialism, capitalism, patriarchy, heteronormativity and "othering," climate denial, sexism, racism, and on and on. They've even got workshops on how to "fight white supremacy culture." On the CTA's page "Upcoming Racial & Social Justice Programming," they link to a resource called "White Supremacy Culture."[22] Here's the pitch:

Learn and share ideas on how to fight white supremacy culture as it comes up in your local chapter, create and build regular spaces for folx to come together to do the "work," develop and strengthen your equity/social justice team, and get strategies on how to connect to parents and your larger community.

To digress, note *folks* is spelled *folx*. Why? Apparently because it is a more inclusive version, specifically, the choice of using *x* is "signifying the inclusion of BIPOC [Black, Indigenous, People Of Color], queer, and other marginalized communities that have been historically excluded from mainstream usage of folks."[23] Did you know this? The CTA does. Upending language is part of the revolution.

Here, then, is a three-paragraph excerpt from the CTA's recommended resource on "white supremacy culture."[24] It provides a useful summary of how California's youth are being indoctrinated to evaluate reality through the lens of racial oppression:

As early settlers came to what would become the U.S. from Europe, those in leadership were male and Christian. They did not identify as white. They identified with their ethnic, national, and/or religious roots—they were English, French, Dutch and they were Protestant, Catholic, Puritan. They came with the desire to create a "new world" where they could profit and prosper. But once here, they faced a big problem. These ruling class elites and their families were outnumbered by the Indigenous people whose lives and land they were stealing and the Africans who they forcibly kidnapped for enslavement and forced labor.

Because the ruling class elite were outnumbered, they had to persuade newly arriving immigrants from Europe to cast aside their ethnic, national, and/or religious differences into a solidarity that could meet the challenge. And so they created the category of "white" and whiteness and consolidated the idea of white supremacy as a way to organize these very different immigrants into a singular and unifying racial category. They did this by requiring them to disconnect from their ethnic and national identities in order to gain access to the material, emotional, physical, intellectual, and spiritual benefits of a whiteness designed specifically and intentionally to pit them against and place them above Indigenous and enslaved peoples.

They wed racism, and I use the word "wed" purposefully, to the construction of race; they created racism as white supremacy's tool. Their goal was and is to undermine communal solidarity. Their goal was and is to create a hegemonic Christian society based on white supremacy ideology.

There's a lot baked into those three paragraphs. It expresses in plain English (uncharacteristic for California's Maoist intelligentsia) the Maoist concept of race. Instead of teaching assimilation, the American "melting pot," today's students are taught that "whiteness" is a manipulative social construct designed to unify Europeans against Black and Indigenous people. The tragedy of this doctrine being spread by Maoist organizations like the CTA today is its destructive, divisive, and demoralizing effect. It is training anyone who is not of European descent to view themselves as victims of "white supremacy" at the same time as it is training white students to despise their culture and their ancestors. From this divisive premise, the foundation is laid for a more detailed Maoist agenda, starting with what they have come up with to replace the holy trinity, the secular trio of diversity, equity, and inclusion.

Amid all this, the CTA has lost all interest in what you might suppose would be its priority—the actual education of students. To take one almost comically predictable example, the Los Angeles Teachers Union, in the face of parent demands to reopen schools after over a year of pandemic closures, announced its own demands for reopening. Among them were defunding the police, housing for the homeless, Medicare for All, and a statewide wealth tax.[25]

The narrative of oppressor and oppressed has morphed into an industry. And if the players in this industry weren't able to point to rising levels of oppression in America, then their specialty would no longer be a growth industry. Where there is no oppression, they must manufacture it. They must discover new forms of oppressive hatred and bias, often so subtle that we foolishly fail to recognize it without their assistance. One of the ways California's Maoists are ensuring we focus an inordinate amount of attention on their oppressor-versus-oppressed paradigm is by accusing the oppressors of perpetrating "hate" incidents.

This is a dangerous and divisive game. For hate to exist, you have to have a hater and a victim of hate. And who might they be? To provide a comprehensive answer to that question, the state of California's Civil Rights Department has set up a web page that offers "Community Specific Resources for People Targeted for Hate."[26] Virtually every imaginable group is listed as "people targeted for hate," including "Communities living at the intersection of multiple identities (Coming Soon)." Isn't that great? Resources for those who live "at the intersection of multiple identities" are "coming soon." They're awfully busy at the Civil Rights Department.

Not listed as victims of hate, of course, are heterosexual, "cisgender" white males who speak English and lack learning disabilities, physical disabilities, or mental health disabilities or are elders or students and don't belong to the "Muslim, Sikh, Hindu, and Jewish communities." Got that? If someone is a member of this rapidly disappearing fraction of California's population, there are no "community resources." Of course not: they are the haters.

The problem for California's Maoists, and every other hate-hyping demagogue in America, is that data doesn't validate the "hate" narrative. To keep the industry supplied with the fuel of hatred, the Civil Rights Department must differentiate between hate crimes, because they are thankfully so small in number, and "hate incidents," which appear in numbers proportional to the amount of money invested to procure them. Here is how the department describes a hate incident:

"a hostile expression or action that may be motivated by bias against another person's actual or perceived identity(ies)."[27]

If this seems vague, that's on purpose. When trolling for hate incidents, cast as wide a net as possible. A "hostile expression" that "may" be motivated by bias. That's enormously broad and wildly subjective. And to ensure California's epidemic of hate is fully documented, a "CA vs. Hate Portal" has been set up through the "Submit Hate Incident or Hate Crime Report" button, which is available twenty-four hours a day, seven days a week, on your desktop computer or mobile device.[28]

If you click through this online interface to the main screen, you will learn that the "Types of Crime or Incident" that qualify include "cyberbullying/internet harassment (text, email, or social media)," "verbal harassment," "hate literature/flyers," "hate mail," and several other categories offering an almost unlimited latitude of qualifying criteria.

California's far-left elites are indoctrinating people to believe that they live in an oppressive, racist society where every disparity in achievement between races is a product of white racism, and that white racists are to blame for any failures in anyone else's individual lives or within their communities. It is such a miserable, insulting, diminishing ideology. California is the most diverse state in the most diverse nation on earth. Of course racism persists, because bad people persist and evil persists. That is the human condition.

I have always believed that we must fight racism with vigor and commitment: one of the proudest achievements of my professional life was producing an antiracism campaign many years ago for the United Kingdom's Commission for Racial Equality (since subsumed into the Equality and Human Rights Commission). But while fighting racism, shouldn't we also tell the truth? That California's glorious diversity is a wonder to behold, that there is nowhere better than America for anyone from any racial background to live, work, and flourish. That's why so many people from around the world want to come here!

The motivation for the Maoist indoctrination is political and economic. California's ruling elites harvest power and profit by selling this narrative. It justifies expanding government, nurturing dependency, and building "social justice" and diversity bureaucracies. It creates a divided and fractious electorate that is incapable of recognizing this political betrayal and unifying to stop it. It is a recipe for thought control and micromanagement of behavior. It is inherently authoritarian. It is Maoism, California-style, adapted to the twenty-first century.

The real shame is how much effort goes into the empty ideas of Maoist thinking, which dictates that we must throw out all old ways and shame anyone who stands up for them. At the same time, in the real world, the people the California elite say they're fighting for— the poor, the weak, and the nonwhite—are actually doing worse in school, jobs, and housing. This is primarily the result not of racism or society's unfairness, but the far-left policies pushed by the Maoist leaders themselves.

CHAPTER 5

CLIMATISM

September 23, 2020. Mega-wildfires were ravaging the state of California. Before it was over, 3.6 million acres had burned. The August Complex fire in Northern California's Mendocino County, which began in mid-August and grew to over a million acres, was the largest in the state's history.[1] Throughout that summer, the smell of smoke and an eerie all-day orange glow in the sky became familiar in towns and cities from the San Francisco Bay Area to Greater Los Angeles.

Amid the chaos and heartache, and the emergency response coordination, Governor Gavin Newsom stood in front of a mini-fleet of electric vehicles and made a wildfire announcement that at first glance seemed incongruous.[2] It wasn't more resources for Cal Fire, the state's hard-pressed Department of Forestry and Fire Protection. In fact it wasn't an announcement directly about wildfires at all. But it did represent the kind of visionary long-term leadership Newsom wanted California to be known and respected for the world over.

"Mother Nature is physics, biology, and chemistry. She bats last and she bats a thousand. That's the reality," said Newsom. "The debate is over around climate change. Just come to the state of California. Observe it with your own eyes. Across the entire spectrum, our goals are inadequate."

Newsom took action to back up his words. From the hood of an all-electric Ford Mustang Mach-E, Newsom signed an executive order to ban sales of new gasoline-powered cars within fifteen years.

Newsom declared that California is facing "a climate damn emergency," explaining, "Our cars shouldn't make wildfires worse and create more days filled with smoky air. Cars shouldn't melt glaciers or raise sea levels threatening our cherished beaches and coastlines."[3]

Banning gasoline-powered cars is a radical move, to be sure, but one in keeping with a state, and a governor, consistently at the forefront of climate leadership. The thinking was clear—and bold. Transportation-related CO_2 emissions, mostly tailpipe emissions from cars, contributed an estimated 160 million metric tons in 2020, which was 52 percent of California's total emissions.[4]

While the market on its own was already producing the innovation that would take the automobile into a clean energy future—most notably California-based Tesla—the transition was not happening at nearly fast enough a pace. Per current trends, it would take until the end of the century for America's car fleet to be fully electrified and powered by clean fuel of one sort or another. The world could not wait that long. Gavin Newsom could not wait that long.

The governor played one of his favorite cards—first mover. Just as he acted unilaterally in 2004 as mayor of San Francisco to issue marriage licenses to gay couples, years before the U.S. Supreme Court legalized gay marriage nationwide in 2015, now he announced the phaseout of gas cars before any sort of federal plan was in place.[5]

His reasoning was simple. California is such a large market that if it moves, the rest of the country—and then the world—will simply have to follow. Newsom's announcement that day was in line with an overarching "climate crisis" narrative that California has become a national and world leader in promoting. It goes like this:

Is there anything more urgent than saving our planet from certain destruction? Why can't more of the population see that? As industries have mushroomed everywhere in the world, carbon dioxide from burning oil, gas, and coal has risen to dangerous levels, trapping the sun's heat, boiling the oceans, and burning the forests. Newsom and his allies believe we must act NOW.

Unless we lower our emissions of carbon dioxide, methane, and other greenhouse gases, we will suffer extreme weather. Floods, hurricanes, and tornadoes will destroy our cities and towns. Droughts and scorching temperatures will kill our crops and unleash catastrophic wildfires. Our forests will die, our crops will die, wildlife will die, ecosystems will collapse, and we will all die. Democrats are certain this is an existential threat.

Stopping an Armageddon would require us to reinvent every industry, reduce our consumption, lower our "carbon footprint," and accept a new era of reasonable limits through sustainable consumption. The lifestyle we have enjoyed to date has been powered by burning fossil fuel. This is not merely unsustainable—it is plunging us at stunning velocity straight into an extinction-level event. Even our livestock, which emit methane gas, must be culled dramatically, to prevent them from releasing this gas that is even more dangerous than CO_2.

Only the most corrupt and selfish, we are told, would hesitate to change everything we do.

...

Of all the ideologies that have captivated California's political elites, Climatism may have the most compelling and legitimate underlying motivations. The result of California's past leadership in environmental protection has yielded benefits, including improved water quality and air quality, higher standards governing industrial processes, preservation of wilderness, and the rescue and survival of endangered species. The evidence of these accomplishments is all around us.

Anyone who can remember the unhealthy air in Los Angeles before the introduction of catalytic converters and unleaded gas will appreciate the environmental movement. Anyone viewing a magnificent California condor soaring along the cliffs off Big Sur, using its ten-foot wingspan to ride the updrafts, is also appreciating the fruits of environmentalism. In 1987, with only twenty-two birds left,

California's condors were captured and placed in a protective captive breeding program. In 1992 they began to be reintroduced, and today over five hundred condors thrive in California.[6] It is hard to overstate the beauty of this accomplishment, and others like it.

Seen in this context, concerns about the climate are an outgrowth of environmentalism. And just like environmentalism, a concern for the climate can lead to inspiring innovation and adaptation. But sadly, it is turning out to drive policies that impose unreasonable costs on working-class families without even delivering the intended benefits. More and more laws and regulations designed to combat climate change fall into this category, and even before climate change became a huge concern, environmentalism was becoming unbalanced and extreme. But in the last twenty years in California, all balance has been lost. If environmental concerns and climate change alarmism had been present in the last century with the intensity that it has reached in this century, *nothing would have been built*. We wouldn't have freeways, housing subdivisions, nuclear power, hydroelectric power, or natural gas power plants. We wouldn't have the California State Water Project, because we wouldn't have any reservoirs. There would have been almost no economic growth, and California would have a much smaller population, all confined to dense cities. That is the state we would be living in if luxury beliefs on "climate," in the jargon now used by activists, had taken hold 120 years ago instead of just twenty.

There is a massive irony here. It was the investment of the past century that laid the economic foundation for the extraordinary wealth that California's elites currently enjoy. What changed? What historical and cultural shifts occurred to bring us to the point where California's elites are now doing everything in their power to destroy for future generations the wealth-creating engine that so lavishly rewarded them?

It began in California in the 1970s. For the first few decades, many of the changes were a necessary response to a new awareness of the genuine and vital need to protect our environment. But by the middle of the decade, an extremist ideological fervor had taken hold. On January 7, 1976, in his annual State of the State address, Governor Jerry Brown uttered a phrase that perfectly captured the changing consensus in Sacramento and among California's elites:

> We are entering an era of limits. In place of a manifest economic destiny, we face a sober reassessment of new economic realities; and we all have to get used to it. We can't ignore the demands of social and economic justice or the fragile environment on which we all depend. But, in meeting our responsibility, we are now forced to make difficult choices. Freeways, childcare, schools, income assistance, pensions, health programs, prisons, environmental protection—all must compete with one another and be subject to the careful scrutiny of the common purpose we all serve.[7]

These remarks, and the actions to follow, represented a seismic shift in California's political landscape. Between 1959 and 1967, Jerry Brown's father, Governor Edmund G. "Pat" Brown, expanded the state's public works projects to build new colleges and universities, freeways and expressways—and the California Water Project, which remains the most extensive system of water storage and distribution in the world.[8] To this day, Californians still benefit from these public assets. Pat Brown, however, was a product of his time. It was an era when Californians welcomed growth. All of that changed, starting in the 1970s.

The "era of limits" Jerry Brown talked about was partly economic. The first oil embargo by the Organization of the Petroleum Exporting Countries (OPEC) in 1973 caused shortages of gasoline. The deep recession and double-digit inflation during the Carter years shook the confidence of business entrepreneurs and working families. But also emerging in the 1970s was the modern environmentalist movement. It found widespread support among Californians who lived in coastal cities, hemmed in by mountains, where the smog from leaded gasoline created dangerously unhealthy air pollution. It resonated with residents in the San Francisco Bay Area, who mobilized to stop developments from filling in the shallow wetlands of the South Bay to build more homes.

But the environmentalist movement has transformed: from what back in the 1970s was a necessary and commonsense reaction to air pollution and land development in sensitive areas into a powerful political lobby that has made significant development of almost everything, everywhere in California impossible.

This is how California became Califailure. Other states also have their share of ruling elites intoxicated by their wealth and insulated from the consequences of left-wing policies in general, and environmental extremism in particular. But California's leftist elites think in even more recklessly extreme terms than Democrats in other states. That's because they have had such a uniquely prosperous and wealthy state to cannibalize. It's because the state has such fair and forgiving weather.

While environmentalists are usefully warning us that our consumption trends could be creating problems all over the earth, including extreme warming and cooling, climatists believe only they can see an actual apocalypse just years away. No matter how painful we make our lives, the climatists say, it will be worth it to avoid the end of the world. Even if it means causing other kinds of environmental damage.

So we end up with performative protests, performative political gestures, and most dangerous and destructive of all, performative policies that not only do more harm than good in the short term, but very often fail even to advance the ostensible goals they are supposed to. A pragmatic, nonideological response would be the thoughtful implementation of a natural, long-term energy transition, combined with measured adaptation that adheres to rational cost-benefit analysis. California can and should be at the forefront of that. But instead of a sensibly managed energy transition that allows emerging technologies to develop and compete in an organic manner, ideologically driven Climatism is trying to force that transition at a truly reckless pace, massively increasing both costs and risks.

For example, in the name of saving the planet and solving the "climate crisis," California's legislature is systematically eliminating all but the most limited and costly options for water, energy, housing, and transportation. When the costs for these essentials are increased by government regulation, no matter how well-intentioned, the financial impact ripples through the entire economy and afflicts other core industries. The biggest victims are California's working-class families, who have to pay more for everything they consume.

The state's regulatory assault on energy is an example of this, with attacks targeting every source of energy—nuclear power, oil and gas, and electricity. Ideologically driven laws have forced shutdowns across the board. The unnecessary closure of the San Onofre nuclear power plant, which could have been retrofitted for less money than its decommissioning is costing, cut California's (carbon-free!) nuclear powered electricity generation in half. Lower-emission natural gas power plants, already operating at less than one-third of their capacity, are now mostly restricted to covering the power deficit on the grid when the sun stops shining on solar panels or the wind stops blowing to turn wind turbines. Perhaps worst of all is the war on California's production of oil in favor of more expensive and much dirtier imports, a shift that actually increases rather than reduces carbon emissions. This is especially egregious when considering that petroleum products are still the source for nearly 50 percent of the total energy consumption of Californians.

As recently as 2012, California was the nation's third-largest producer of oil, only behind Texas and North Dakota. The peak year was 1985, when nearly 394 million barrels were extracted from California wells. At that time, nearly two-thirds of California's oil demand was fulfilled by in-state supply, with most of the rest coming from Alaska. Foreign imports were negligible.

California's oil production is now down to less than one-third of those earlier levels, with only 118 million barrels being produced in 2023.[9] Great news for the climate! Not exactly. We're not using a third of what we once used—we're just importing it instead. Demand is only slightly down, from 644 million barrels in 1985 to 529 million barrels in 2023. Our domestic California production is down by 70 percent since 1985, but our total state demand for oil is down by only 18 percent. Meanwhile, we have reduced imports from Alaska by 60 percent, and our imports from foreign nations have increased by 800 percent. We import 77 percent of the oil we consume, a majority from foreign suppliers, including some of the world's worst authoritarian regimes, like Iran and Venezuela.[10]

Reducing oil exploration and drilling in California does absolutely nothing to help the global environment if we simply source our oil from somewhere else. While reliable data on remaining oil reserves in California are not readily available, just within the Los Angeles basin lies an estimated 1.6 billion barrels of recoverable oil.[11] A 2011 analysis from the U.S. Environmental Information Agency estimates the state's recoverable reserves at 2.3 billion barrels, but industry experts have estimated California's commercially recoverable reserves are probably closer to 5 billion barrels.[12] If shale oil is taken into account, California's oil reserves increase substantially. A study commissioned by the EIA in 2011 estimated that "the largest shale oil formation is the Monterey/Santos play in southern California, which is estimated to hold 15.4 billion barrels."[13] Not incidentally, the report estimated the quantity of recoverable natural gas contained in shale formations in California at 41.4 trillion cubic feet.

The emissions from operating wells in California are far less—both in terms of volume and toxicity—than the emissions from tankers that linger offshore to supply crude oil to California's coastal refineries. Maritime transport still relies on bunker fuel, cheap bulk fuel that is the least refined and filthiest of all petroleum-based fuels.[14] The prevailing Pacific winds typically blow this pollution spewing from oil tankers directly onto the mainland. Moving crude oil from far-flung sources around the world to California's refineries released an estimated 1.7 million metric tons of CO_2 into the atmosphere in 2023. All of this could be avoided if California's legislators and regulators simply followed the facts and the science and met our continuing demand for oil from the cleanest and lowest-emission source—domestic California production—instead of imposing irrational, ideologically driven constraints.

Instead we find ourselves in the lunatic situation of destroying jobs and communities in California in order to look like we're tackling the "climate crisis" by "waging war on fossil fuels," all the while actually increasing carbon emissions by importing oil that props up authoritarian regimes, using the dirtiest and most carbon-intensive form of transportation on the planet. There is surely a better way to manage the "energy transition" than this.

But common sense and practicality are driven out by Climatism. Ideology takes over. Thus we have Senate Bill 12, passed in 2023, which raises the state's greenhouse gas reduction (GHG) goal from 40 percent of 1990 levels by 2030 to a 55 percent reduction by 2030.[15] The crippling cost of achieving even the 40 percent target by 2030 is already evident in California having the highest overall energy prices in America. Yet now the ruling elite, in the grip of climatist dogma, has decided that the punishment for California's working families must be ratcheted up still further.

After explicitly engineering the energy shortages that have led to higher prices, with Senate Bill 12 only one recent example of this relentless assault on energy production, Governor Newsom called a special legislative session to "hold the oil industry accountable for price gouging."[16] Ultimately, at Newsom's urging, the legislature then passed the oddly designated Senate Bill X1-2, which sets a cap on the amount of profit a refinery operating in California can earn.[17]

The irony is, the real price gouging is being carried out by California's government. California's regulatory environment is the reason energy in California is in short supply and costs so much. When demand exceeds supply, prices go up. In Denver, Colorado being a less regulated state, gasoline in the second quarter of 2024 was $3.02 per gallon.[18] At the same time in San Francisco, it was $5.73 per gallon.[19] California has the highest gas taxes of any state in America, and California imposes regulations so severe that between 2017 and 2023, over 20 percent of the state's refinery capacity was closed or converted to biofuel.[20]

Despite the obvious need for Californians to rely on oil and gas until an affordable and reliable transition to carbon-free energy is complete, the regulatory attacks on production continue. In February 2024, California's oil and gas regulators released their plan to ban all fracking, after already having banned new fracking permits.[21] Then in March, environmental groups began pressing CalGEM (California's state Geologic Energy Management Division) to also ban what is known as steam injection, a method of oil extraction that is widely used in the state.[22]

The global climate impact of supporting rather than crushing California's energy industry would be positive—not only because the massive shipping pollution would be eliminated, but because in California our drillers have adopted practices that are far cleaner than most overseas drilling operations. The economic and social impact would be transformative. Thousands of high-paying jobs in a revitalized energy industry, along with lower prices for fuel.

As the companies that deliver affordable energy to Californians are being systematically regulated into oblivion, California's high-tech industry is cashing in on Climatism. Based on the premise that energy use in all its forms must be reduced, gadgetry that no practical consumer would ever choose is now mandated. Filled with chipsets and guaranteed to conserve energy—and water, which after all requires energy to be treated, pumped, and heated—high-tech products that used to sell because they were always getting better and costing less are now being sold because they are mandated by law.

They sell not because they are faster but because they are engineered to operate according to a climatist agenda. They are most definitely not cheaper, and in fact they cost far more than they should. Across the product spectrum from high tech to low tech, Silicon Valley increasingly uses its political clout to support this new agenda.

This is no longer competitive innovation. It is the climatist variant of crony capitalism. Here are examples of mandated products that are little more than expensive annoyances:

- Light switches that don't simply turn on (up) or off (down), but instead require prolonged pressing in exactly the right spots to activate power to a light source—not intuitive at all—and then automatically turn off again after a brief interval in order to save energy.
- "Low-flow" faucets that have ¼" feed pipes instead of ⅜", which doubles the time required to fill a pot or get hot water flowing.
- Public restroom faucets that require absurd—and often futile—hand waving in order to turn on. Then, when they're activated, they squirt tiny jets of water that bounce off the skin. Then they turn off almost immediately, requiring additional hand waving.
- "Low-flow" showerheads, also with reduced-diameter feed pipes, which double the time required to rinse shampoo out of long hair.
- LED streetlights that turn night into glaring day and impart the ambience of a prison compound to what once were peaceful suburban neighborhoods.
- "Drought-tolerant" landscaping—requiring expensive "smart" drip irrigation systems—that robs families of a lawn where their children can play. These "xeriscapes" require far more maintenance than is generally acknowledged and often within a few years turn into nothing but weeds poking through decorative rocks and degraded plastic ground cover.
- Reusable grocery bags that are expensive magnets for bacteria, require frequent, time-consuming, and largely ineffective

cleaning, and are thrown away at a frequency that actually makes them create more total waste than the lower-mass disposables.

- "Smart" thermostats with complicated programs and settings that nobody uses, when a twenty-dollar unit with a bimetallic strip used to be perfectly sufficient to activate cooling or heating whenever a hot or cold temperature threshold was reached.

And this is just the start. The "internet of things" is still in its infancy. Once it has become fully established, nanny robots will abet the nanny state, ensuring that a corporate climatist vision of utopia is omnipresent to monitor and manage us all.

Occasionally there are steps in the direction of sanity and common sense. After the city of Berkeley became in 2019 the first city in the U.S. to ban natural gas hookups in new buildings (in keeping with the city council's 2018 declaration to become a "fossil fuel–free city"), several other California cities, including Los Angeles and San Francisco, followed suit. *But not so fast.*[23] In response to a lawsuit filed by the California Restaurant Association, in early 2024 the Ninth Circuit Court of Appeals ruled that "Berkeley's ordinance banning gas pipelines in new construction runs afoul of the federal Energy Policy and Conservation Act."

Anyone who has tried to cook on an electric induction stove will attest to the superiority of gas for controlling the temperature of a pan. And ask a Latino household how they feel about cooking tortillas on an electric stove! But the restaurateurs' victory may be short-lived. In a self-righteous display of hubris typical of California's climatist elites, San Francisco officials quickly announced that the city would ignore the Ninth Circuit's ruling and would *continue prohibiting gas hookups* in new housing and commercial construction.[24]

It's not just gas cooktops, or natural gas hookups for new buildings, that are being taken away by California's climatists. In 2023, the California Air Resources Board (CARB) voted to ban the sale of new gas furnaces and water heaters beginning in 2030.[25] A statewide ban on cooktops can't be far behind. As San Francisco supervisor Rafael Mandelman said in reference to the Ninth Circuit decision overturning the city's ban on natural gas hookups, "We will continue to enforce it, continue to implement it, consistent with this court decision in the Berkeley case. We think we can do that." They will find a way.

The obvious danger here that escapes California's climatists is the cold reality that they have no idea how they're going to generate enough electricity to replace natural gas used for space heating and water heating, or to replace natural gas currently used to fuel electricity-generating plants, or, of course, to replace gasoline currently used to fuel cars and trucks. To achieve "net zero" in California would require electricity generation to *triple*. Given a few decades, technological innovation in solar and nuclear power, along with much-improved battery storage, can make the transition possible. Difficult, but possible. The path we are on today: a headlong rush to embrace solar and wind (where technology is not improving efficiency as it is with solar) while shutting down everything else, including, bizarrely, carbon-free nuclear, is an unconscionable risk to take. And it would come at an incredible punitive cost, driving millions more Californian households into poverty and dependency.

The obvious irony here is that natural gas, despite being dubbed an "existential threat" by California's climatists, is responsible for only a fraction of the greenhouse gas emissions that activists rightly target.

For example, one of California's biggest sources of greenhouse gas comes from wildfires. Since the year 2000, according to the California Air Resources Board, wildfires have destroyed over 19 million acres, mostly forest and chaparral, over thirty thousand square miles.[26] At the same time, these wildfires exposed millions of Californians to smoke so thick and toxic that people were advised to stay indoors for weeks. Utility companies, attempting to prevent fires from starting, cut power during hot and windy summer days to millions more Californians, sometimes for several days in a row. During one of the worst fire seasons in recent years, in the summer and fall of 2020, it is estimated that wildfire smoke released 127 million tons of CO_2 into the atmosphere, more than California's entire electric utility, commercial, and residential sectors combined.[27]

A recent study by University of California researchers revealed that in 2020, wildfires produced more than double the amount of greenhouse gas emissions than all the reductions made in California between 2003 and 2019 combined.[28] As noted, in 2020 the wildfires were California's second-highest source of CO_2 emissions—behind transportation but ahead of the industrial sector, and ahead of all power plants put together.

The conventional explanation for these catastrophic wildfires is that climate change has led to longer, hotter, drier summers in the state, creating conditions where small fires can more easily turn into "megafires." In response, California's politicians and government agencies have enacted a series of measures designed to achieve "net zero," such that all economic activity in the state will either generate zero CO_2 emissions or that whatever emissions are generated will be offset by activities that sequester an equal quantity of CO_2.[29]

But current climate policy, and public debate, has an enormous, gaping hole. It fails to take into account that one of the biggest sources of California's carbon emissions—not cars, not electricity generation, but "mega" wildfires—results from outdated, ideologically driven forest management practices. This mismanagement centers around two policy decisions: First, to aggressively extinguish wildfires even though they are a natural, even restorative phenomenon that is essential to ensure forest thinning and the overall good health of the forest. Second, to regulate a robust timber industry nearly out of existence.

A century ago, in the 1920s, tactics to suppress forest fires were still in their infancy. But techniques and technologies steadily improved, along with firefighting budgets. By the second half of the twentieth century, an army of firefighters could cope effectively with California's wildfires. For a while, a combination of timber harvesting and natural fires prevented excess fuel buildup in the forests. But regulatory restrictions on logging that started in the 1990s, and increasingly aggressive fire suppression, laid the foundation for the problems we see today.

During the 1980s, Cal Fire spent an average of $28 million per year ($66 million in inflation-adjusted 2020 dollars) on fire suppression, and the average annual timber harvest in the state was 6 billion board feet.[30] In 2020, Cal Fire spent an astonishing $1.7 billion on fire suppression, nearly 10 times more than in the 1980s after adjusting for inflation, while the annual timber harvest had declined to just 1.5 billion board feet.

These two trends are of course directly related. The "megafires" of recent years are the result of excessive undergrowth, which not only creates fuel for fires that are vastly more difficult and costly to control, but competes with mature trees for the sunlight, water, and soil nutrients needed for healthy growth. This is why California's forests are not only tinderboxes but are also filled with dying trees. Now Californians confront nearly 20 million acres of overgrown forests.

In a speech before Congress in September 2020, Representative Tom McClintock (R-CA) summarized the series of policy mistakes that are destroying California's forests.[31] McClintock's sprawling Fourth Congressional District covers 12,800 square miles and encompasses most of the northern Sierra Nevada mountain range.[32] His constituency bears a disproportionate share of the consequences of forest policies emanating from Washington, D.C., and Sacramento.

"Excess timber comes out of the forest in only two ways," McClintock said.

It is either carried out or it burns out. For most of the 20th Century, we carried it out. It's called "logging." Every year, U.S. Forest Service foresters would mark off excess timber and then we auctioned it off to lumber companies who paid us to remove it, funding both local communities and the forest service. We auctioned grazing contracts on our grasslands. The result: healthy forests, fewer fires and a thriving economy. But . . . we began imposing environmental laws that have made the management of our lands all but impossible. Draconian restrictions on logging, grazing, prescribed burns and herbicide use on public lands have made modern land management endlessly time-consuming and ultimately cost-prohibitive. A single tree thinning plan typically takes four years and more than 800 pages of analysis. The costs of this process exceed the value of timber—turning land maintenance from a revenue-generating activity to a revenue-consuming one.

When it comes to carrying out timber, California used to do a pretty good job.[33] From the 1950s to the 1980s, as noted, the average timber harvest in California was around 6 billion board feet per year. The precipitous drop in harvest volume began in the 1990s. The industry started that decade taking out not quite 5 billion board feet. By 2000 the annual harvest had dropped to just over 2 billion board feet. Today only about 1.5 billion board feet per year come out of California's forests as harvested timber.

Wildlife biologists and forest ecologists who spend their lives studying and managing these timberlands now agree that tree density in California's forests has increased thanks to "non-climatic factors such as the prohibition of controlled burning, and legacies of fire suppression."

The increase in tree density in California's forests is not subtle. Without controlled and naturally occurring fires that clear underbrush and small trees, and without responsible logging, forests become overgrown. According to a study conducted in 2020 by the University of California, Davis, and the U.S. Department of Agriculture, California's mid-elevation Ponderosa pine and mixed conifer forests used to average 60 trees per acre but now average 170.[34]

This is not an isolated finding. Observations of excessive tree density are corroborated by numerous studies, testimony, and journalistic investigations.[35] Roughly tripling the density of trees across millions of acres of forest leaves them stressed and starved for soil nutrients, sunlight, and water. California's excessive forest density not only results in overgrown, dried-out, and fire-prone trees and brush. It also impacts California's water supply and aquatic ecosystems.

That's because excessive forest density also causes excessive evapotranspiration, the process through which tiny pores in plant leaves emit water. And in this case, what goes up does not come down. Water lost to evapotranspiration is water that does not percolate into the ground to recharge springs and feed streams. Scientists affiliated with the National Science Foundation's Southern Sierra Critical Zone Observatory have concluded that "forest thinning could increase water flow from Sierra Nevada watersheds by as much as 10 percent."[36]

No reasonable person doubts the sincerity and good intentions of the environmentalists and activists, or the experts and legislative staff, or the judges and legislators who have unwittingly turned California's forests into tinderboxes. But instead of recognizing overcrowded forests as the primary cause of catastrophic wildfires, California's politicians blamed the phenomenon almost exclusively on climate change.

In September 2020, as Californians endured a summer of devastating wildfires, the state's most prominent politicians were all quick to attribute the cause to climate change. U.S. Senator Kamala Harris, visiting the hard-hit community of Auberry in Fresno County, surveyed a landscape of wiped-out homes, where only the chimneys were left standing, and said, "Those chimneys remind me of tombstones." Elaborating, Harris said, "Sadly, these wildfires and the devastation they cause are utterly predictable. This is not a partisan issue. This is just a fact. We have to do better as a country."

Harris was joined on her visit to Fresno County by Governor Newsom, who wasted little time in reminding us all what has caused these superfires. As described in an article in the *San Francisco Chronicle* that reported on their visit, while these two political heavyweights "peered into the rubble of a home that burned down to its foundation and looked at a burned pickup truck nearby," Newsom addressed then-president Trump, saying, "If you don't believe in science, come to California and observe it with your own eyes. You cannot be in denial about this reality."[37]

Unfortunately, all too often this is the version of Climatism that informs public policy. Whether it's "atmospheric rivers" and "bomb cyclones," mudslides and floods, heat waves and droughts, or wildfires, it's always time for more restrictions on land development, more rules governing farming and logging, more rationing of energy and water, and higher prices for everything. And when it comes to this ideology of scarcity, with its endless restrictions, rules, and rationing, California leads the world. Our state legislature and activist courts may not have changed the climate, but from the far north of the state to the border with Mexico, and from the Pacific beaches to the High Sierra, they have made life harder for every business and every household.

Climatism may not be the only example of a hostile elite doing everything it can to drive people and businesses out of California, but it has the most reach. There is literally nothing that anyone does that the state legislature or a clever climate litigator cannot connect to the "climate crisis." And some of the most sweeping edicts issued in the name of fighting climate change are the most transparently absurd.

That's how we end up with Governor Newsom, after fires had ravaged the state, and immediately after appearing before the cameras amid the rubble in Auberry, issuing an executive order requiring sales of all new passenger vehicles to be zero-emission by 2035.[38] The irrelevance of this order to actually saving California's forests is stunning and ignores a tremendous missed opportunity to actually reduce greenhouse emissions while also improving the health of the forests and reviving local economies.

If California's timber industry could begin responsible logging again at a rate that roughly equals the rate of growth, once the forests are thinned to historically normal and much lower tree density, most of the smaller and less destructive wildfires that ignite every summer could be permitted to burn naturally. There are several huge benefits to this strategy. Millions of tons of CO_2 would no longer be emitted into the atmosphere every year from these supersize wildfires. The forest itself would be healthy again, with enormous benefits to wildlife and watersheds. The fire danger to rural communities near fire zones would be reduced—along with insurance costs. The billions spent each year on fire suppression could be saved. Thousands of good jobs would be created in logging and milling; forest products would no longer have to be imported and would be less expensive for consumers and contractors. Finally, these forest products themselves would sequester CO_2. What no longer went up in smoke could now be used in construction.

This solution, thinning the forests with a revitalized logging industry, and the many benefits of doing that, could represent a healthy version of environmentalism. For the most part, though, here in California that isn't what's happening.

California's ruling elites have recognized the power of Climatism and climatist rhetoric to bend entire populations to the passions of zealots and the aspirations of opportunists seeking wealth and power. For example, witness California attorney general Rob Bonta, who in September 2023 sued the oil companies that do business in California for "hiding from the public the existential threat that fossil fuels created in terms of climate change and extreme weather and damage to the environment."

Ignored in this lawsuit are several realities that reasonable people ought to consider. As it replaced even dirtier fuel—wood, and then coal—refined crude oil, at least so far, has done far more to uplift humanity than to harm humanity—including generating the wealth we've needed to fund projects that protect the environment from even worse pollution. Also, as Bonta surely knows, even today we are still nowhere near ready to completely replace fossil fuel with new energy technologies.

Why doesn't Rob Bonta also recognize that, for decades, California's biggest environmental advocacy groups engaged in public relations campaigns, political lobbying, and litigation that demonized loggers, ranchers, and private property owners, preventing them from performing the logging, grazing, mechanical thinning, and controlled burns that up until the 1990s kept California's forests from becoming dangerously overgrown? Doesn't Bonta realize that a century of fire suppression along with two to three decades of reduced timber harvests has left tree density in California's forests at five to ten times what is historically normal, and that is the reason they're dried out, unhealthy, and burn like hell?[39]

Any reasonable public policy must recognize that concern about the climate not only has to be balanced with concern for the economic welfare of working-class families. It also has to be balanced with concern about the rest of the environment. The fact that environmentalists have advocated for rapid and exclusive adoption of EVs has had the negative side effect of a catastrophic uptick in mining around the world, nearly all of it happening in nations where environmental and labor standards are almost nonexistent. These impacts must also be taken into consideration when adopting "climate-friendly" policies.

Peter Zeihan, an economist whose new book, *The End of the World Is Just the Beginning,* should be mandatory reading for anyone promoting renewables, had this to say about relying on wind and solar power, along with transmission lines and battery backup: "Such infrastructure would be on a scale and of a scope that humanity has not yet attempted."[40] That is profoundly understating what is happening.

All conventional power plant alternatives using gas, nuclear, and coal require one-tenth or less raw materials to generate an equivalent quantity of electricity as solar or wind. For modern natural gas combined-cycle generating plants, the ratio is closer to one-twentieth as much raw inputs as solar or wind. But when it comes to solar and wind power, which is distributed and intermittent, what about the transmission lines and the batteries? What about the service life of all this installed base, the solar panels and batteries and wind turbines that degrade after twenty years and have to be decommissioned, recycled, and replaced? What about the environmental costs of extending this resource-guzzling scheme to every nation on earth?

Solar power has huge potential. Costs are coming down and efficiency is going up. But there are still major questions to be answered, and simply ignoring them in the name of ideological certitude is not a sensible strategy.

When discussing the sustainability of renewables, of course, an honest analysis cannot focus exclusively on the production side. If the energy consumption of an entire economy is electrified, that would include the transportation sector, where in every significant case the goal of electrification is fraught with challenges. Ships at sea cannot recharge their batteries during a four-week voyage on the deep ocean. Can they use hydrogen fuel cells instead? Can they go back to relying on sails?

Farm equipment that is too expensive to leave idle during harvests must operate up to eighteen hours a day, so how will they recharge in only six hours, then provide eighteen hours of continuous discharge at full power? Will farmers swap the batteries on their tractors and combines in the middle of a shift? Perhaps solutions exist. But they are expensive and they squander resources.

It is the ubiquitous automobile, at last count numbering 291 million in the United States alone, where "renewable" technology is most readily exposed as wasteful and destructive to the environment. Zeihan explains what it takes to build an all-electric vehicle: "You think going to war for oil was bad? Materials inputs for just the drivetrain of an EV are six times what's required for an internal combustion engine. If we're truly serious about a green transition that will electrify everything, our consumption of all these materials must increase by more than an order of magnitude."

Not just the environmental but the human impact of replacing hundreds of millions of conventional automobiles with EVs is outlined in a scathing new book by Siddharth Kara, *Cobalt Red: How the Blood of the Congo Powers Our Lives*.[41] When every supply chain on earth has been furiously bulking up to source raw materials at ten times the rate it previously required, it is now forced to address the "climate crisis," and abuse is inevitable.

The tragedy playing out in the Democratic Republic of the Congo to feed cobalt to the "green" West is almost apocalyptic. Kara describes how private militias control mining areas with child slaves picking their way through toxic pits in subhuman conditions. Environmental regulations are nonexistent. Human rights are nonexistent. This horrific drama repeats itself around the world, at the same time as slick television commercials market electric vehicles to Americans as a virtuous choice.

Shortly after announcing his lawsuit, Rob Bonta told a PBS interviewer that if the fossil fuel companies had been, according to him, more honest back in the 1950s, "choices would have been different, like doubling down and investing on clean energy and phasing out of fossil fuel."[42] To put it charitably, this is tenuous speculation. Even now, the materials science that may someday result in sustainable, affordable, practical batteries for EVs is still in its infancy.[43]

Climatism turns ecological concerns from a science into a religion. You have either had the scales fall from your eyes or not.

It overlooks the undeniable benefits of fossil fuels, which have brought prosperity worldwide. It's like a faith where facts are ignored: fossil fuels power over 80 percent of our world, we still don't have a viable alternative, replacing them is incredibly challenging, and renewables can harm the environment too. Believers in Climatism treat these issues not as scientific challenges but as apostasy that must be rejected. You are a believer, or you are not.

The Climatism practiced by Bonta, Newsom, the faceless bureaucrats at CARB, and the entire "climate crisis" community that has taken over California's elite could be more easily tolerated if it weren't for the incredible hypocrisy of its most zealous enforcers. Not only the gigantic carbon footprint of the politicians and their billionaire donors whose consumption is many times that of the average Californian, but the preposterous notion that clamping down on all production of fossil fuel in California is somehow virtuous even though it is just being extracted elsewhere in the world and imported into California.

This is hypocrisy at its most pointless extreme. Not just the hypocrisy of someone using their privilege to live a lifestyle for which they're condemning everyone else. But when California's climatists outsource the state's emissions and environmental havoc to nations that lack even the most minimal of environmental safeguards and labor standards, their hypocrisy harms people and the environment even more than if they had just let Californians use our own resources to power our own economy.

Thanks to this hypocrisy, Climatism in California means unemployment for Californians, while unregulated mining and drilling operations from West Africa to South America employ workers in terrible conditions. The fruits of their labor routinely arrive off the coast of Long Beach Harbor, after crossing thousands of miles of ocean in a ship burning bunker fuel, the filthiest, most unregulated source of energy in the world.

The consequences of Climatism driving policy in California are a state where only the wealthy can afford to live a comfortable lifestyle. For the vast majority of Californian families, just surviving is a challenge. The median home price in California is nine times the median household income, and the prices of gasoline and utilities are the highest in the nation.[44] The reason for these high prices and shortages is Climatism. These hardships are the result of policy choices. According to the media, however, it's all thanks to climate change. The irony here is thick, because most of the time it isn't climate change, but rather the extreme and misguided policies being forced onto Californians to cope with climate change, that cause so much hardship.

An article published by the *Guardian* in the summer of 2023 illustrates this disconnect. The author interviews a Hispanic woman, who along with her husband is struggling to support themselves and their young children. The article opens by declaring that "Minerva Contreras can't pay her bills."[45] It goes on to report the following travails.

"Practically, about one week's paycheck goes toward rent, the next week's toward the electrical bill, and the third week's toward the gas and water bills and the remaining for everything else," said Contreras. "We just can't keep up." The author then states, "The climate emergency is driving up the cost of living. Extreme weather, drought and drastic swings in temperature, all fueled by global heating, are affecting utility costs and insurance premiums, exacerbating housing shortages and causing food prices to go up."

"The climate emergency." A phrase, like "the climate crisis," that we are conditioned to accept at face value. But whether or not these two phrases deserve to be taken at face value, attributing the economic travails of Minerva Contreras to climate change is misleading at best. Well-intentioned but misguided Climatism doesn't merely inform California's elites; it also guides the reporters, far and wide, who cover California.

Perhaps the dramatic urgency of these media reports, or their tone of indisputable certainty, or the fact that frequently exactly the opposite of what they say is true, somehow obscures the misinformation. The multiple hardships afflicting the Contreras family reported by the journalist—just like the hardships inflicted on millions of other working families in California—are the direct result not of climate change but instead the bad policies that have been advocated by publications like the *Guardian* and articles just like this one. Let's consider them one at a time:

Utility costs are rising because the state legislature and the California Air Resources Board have mandated production of "renewable" electricity instead of clean nuclear and natural gas–generated electricity. Across the state, natural gas power plants are being shut down, and in 2013 state regulators shut down the San Onofre nuclear plant, cutting California's production of clean nuclear power by 50 percent. To replace natural gas and nuclear power? Hundreds of square miles of solar panels, wind farms, and battery farms to store the intermittently produced electricity, since the sun doesn't shine all the time, nor does the wind blow all the time. These installations, and the grid upgrades necessary to accommodate them, have given Californians the highest electricity rates of any major state.

Housing shortages in California are perhaps the most cruel consequence of Climatism. The consensus among climatists is that suburbs create "sprawl," which in turn generates more "vehicle miles traveled" since they assume suburban residents will undertake long commutes in order to work in the city while living in a distant suburb. California's legislators, abetted by climatist activists who staff regional agencies along with city and county governments, have drawn "urban service boundaries" around California's cities to ensure that any significant new home construction is restricted to within the existing footprint of urban areas. But this war on the actual homes that Californians want to live in, underpinned by the claimed moral imperative of saving the planet, will not actually improve the climate in any way.

Jobs are created within suburbs, employers relocate to new suburbs, people work from home now more than ever, and vehicles are becoming either zero-emission or ultralow-emission. Restrictions on available land to build has raised the price of the limited supply of land where building is permitted, and the shortage of homes has caused demand-driven price increases. California's climatists have also mandated extreme building codes, such as requiring solar panels on all new homes, which further raises construction costs. No wonder California has the highest housing costs in the country.

Food prices as well are affected by climatist policies, as farmers throughout the state are denied their water allocations in favor of "unimpaired flow" from the state's rivers into the ocean, and water storage projects are consistently blocked by bogus "environmental" litigation—in practice, more often special interest extortion. California hasn't built a major reservoir in over fifty years. Instead of investing in water projects, the state legislature has turned to rationing. Thanks to Senate Bill 1157, signed into law in 2022, residential indoor water consumption is going to be limited to 42 gallons per person per day. The cost to implement this, estimated to exceed $7 billion, will mean water bills will go up, even as water use goes down. Shamefully, one million Californians—most of them low-income Latinos in the Central Valley—do not even have access to clean, reliable drinking water.[46]

With "solutions" like this, no wonder the Contreras family can't afford to pay their bills.

Extremist climate policies create rising levels of politically contrived scarcity by forcing us to use EVs and electric stoves and heaters, eliminating natural gas, prohibiting new oil and gas extraction, shutting down refineries, and closing down pipelines. Despite a few last-minute reprieves, they are determined to shut down California's last nuclear power plant at Diablo Canyon.

There are alternative strategies.

Californians could build water projects again, not only restoring abundant water to the state but generating clean hydroelectric power. Even new off-site reservoirs could store surplus solar and wind electricity by pumping water into the upper reservoir from a lower forebay when the sun is shining and the wind is blowing, then letting it back down to turn generators when electricity demand is peaking. Californians could sequester CO_2 from natural gas power plants in underground caverns, allowing them to *triple* their output with no CO_2 emissions whatsoever, and that could be done at a fraction of the cost of some major renewables projects such as the monstrous floating offshore wind farms planned for Morro Bay and Humboldt. Californians could even allow more cities to be built on open land, taking into account remote work and rooftop solar to deliver a minimal carbon footprint.

What Climatism in California today actually reflects may be surprising to its proponents. It reveals a *lack* of faith in technology and innovation. California's climate activists are demanding a precipitous conversion, at incredible expense, to energy and transportation technologies that will almost certainly be obsolete within a few decades, if not a few years. Consider the tantalizing future that California can and should pioneer, and compare it to the narrow path we're on today.

Advanced hybrid cars and passenger drones could deliver clean and high-speed transportation, making today's EVs and even high-speed rail obsolete. Advanced nuclear energy technologies will turn billion-dollar solar, wind, and battery farms into stranded assets, unable to compete. New carbon-neutral synthetic fuels and new internal-combustion technologies may make hybrid automobiles and trucks a far cleaner and cost-effective solution than all-electric propulsion systems.

California's ruling elite are indifferent to the pain that the policies they're enacting might inflict on people less wealthy and privileged than they are. So what if gasoline rises to seven dollars a gallon? So what if electricity and water utilities set rates so high that their customers can't afford to pay, at the same time as they're imposing periodic power brownouts and mandating water rationing? So what if millions of families of Mexican heritage are forced to abandon the way they cook a staple food? So what, when these policies centralize power in the bureaucracies the elites control, and concentrate wealth in the hands of the donors to their election campaigns? So what, when you can simultaneously erase the well-being of your constituents, enhance the well-being of your donors, and parade yourself in front of friendly television journalists as a "courageous climate warrior" standing up to the dangerous "climate deniers"?

Climatists can only imagine a future where we must drastically change or face doom. They overlook any solutions that could help us without hurting working families. True environmentalists, however, believe in science and ingenuity. We see a future in voluntarily limiting emissions and inventing alternatives. California should embrace this optimistic, problem-solving spirit instead of sticking to a narrow, pessimistic view. The future won't be ruled by scarcity and fear.

CHAPTER 6

SOCIALISM

In January 2020, a pivotal moment in the ongoing fight for racial justice took place in the heart of San Francisco. District 10 supervisor Shamann Walton, San Francisco School Board member Stevon Cook, City College of San Francisco trustee Shanell Williams, and former District 10 supervisor Sophie Maxwell, among others, announced the formation of an advisory committee to create a reparations plan for San Francisco's African American community.[1]

The creation of the Reparations Advisory Committee, and the Reparations Plan they released in 2023, were considered a vital step forward in the struggle for racial justice.[2] For centuries, Black people in America have been subjected to systemic discrimination, beginning with slavery and continuing through segregation, redlining, and other forms of institutional racism. The advocates for reparations believe that the effects of these injustices persist to this day through disparities in wealth, education, health, and housing. They view reparations as necessary to address these disparities and promote healing.

The work of San Francisco's Reparations Advisory Committee is just one example of how government programs can be used to tackle not only the lingering effects of past discrimination but many other serious challenges that we face. The same commitment to justice and equity that drives the reparations initiative can be applied to the housing shortage, the homelessness crisis, how we manage the transition to renewable energy, and the ongoing struggle for workers' rights.

Consider the housing shortage, a crisis that affects millions of Californians, particularly in urban areas like San Francisco. Government programs to incentivize the construction of affordable housing, regulate rent prices, and provide subsidies for low-income families are considered necessary to ensure that everyone has access to safe and stable housing. Similarly, many activists for the homeless believe that effective solutions must involve a coordinated effort by federal, state, and local governments to provide not only shelter but also mental health services and job training.

The ongoing struggle for workers' rights also can be said to depend on government intervention to protect employees from exploitation and ensure fair wages and working conditions. With millions of workers being displaced by automation or finding gig work to be their only employment option, government regulations that safeguard workers' rights are more important than ever. These government actions can include raising the minimum wage, guaranteeing paid family leave, and ensuring access to affordable health care.

The San Francisco African American Reparations Advisory Committee is an example of the broader role that the government can play in addressing the challenges facing our society. Whether it's unaffordable goods and services, or racial injustice, sexism, transphobia, disproportionate outcomes based on race or gender, inadequate access to health care, or environmental justice and environmental protection, for many, government intervention is considered to be the best and often the only option. They would argue that by giving more power to the government to regulate, raise taxes, and take over and run private enterprises, we give our country back to the people.

Millions of activists, politicians, academics, journalists, and voters have decided that by implementing major government programs to solve the most difficult challenges of our time, we can begin to create a society that is more just, equitable, and sustainable for all.

...

That's the pitch. Big Government is going to solve our problems. How's that working out?

If there is one through line in my career—the businesses I've started, the ideas I have advocated inside and outside government, on both sides of the Atlantic, it's this: Putting power in people's hands. Decentralizing power so it is closest to the people affected. The opposite of Big Government, if you like. Certainly the opposite of Socialism.

Socialism is sometimes defined as a mode of political and economic organization where the means of production are owned or regulated by "society as a whole." It is also identified with the slogan "From each according to his ability, to each according to his needs." Socialism is an ideology that puts equality above results, government intervention above personal responsibility or the natural, free exchange of people interacting in a market.

Products and services directly owned by California's state and local governments include the production of hydroelectric power and allocations of water from the state water project, wastewater treatment plants and government-run landfills, the means of transportation on state highways, government-owned trains and buses, and every prison, police station, fire station, or government building.

These assets, collectively worth trillions, only constitute the so-called brick-and-mortar portion of government-controlled enterprise in California. Then there are the services operated out of these facilities. Public education, public safety, hospitals and clinics, and tens of thousands of state, regional, and local government agencies and special districts. All of this activity is owned by the government.

To put this into proportion, California's state and local governments already directly control nearly one-fifth of the state's economy. In 2021, according to the U.S. Census Bureau, California's combined state and local direct general expenditures were $575 billion, which was 18.3 percent of the total gross domestic product of $3.1 trillion in that year.[3]

Of course it's true that we need government. Even doctrinaire libertarians, who favor as little government as possible, concede that some functions, such as national defense and a judiciary, are appropriately relegated to the government. The problems begin when the share of the economy that is owned by the government gets too big. The bigger the slice, the more socialist you get. And in California, the size of the government slice has greatly expanded.

In just the last ten years, after adjusting for inflation, the California State General Fund, the budget that allocates taxpayer dollars to state government programs and departments, has nearly doubled. In 2013 the state's general fund expenditures were $96.3 billion.[4] Expressed in inflation-adjusted 2023 dollars, that was $125.9 billion. Compare that to the state's general fund in 2023 of $226.0 billion.[5] Even adjusting for inflation, that is a 79 percent increase in just ten years.

With that statistic, we've already taken into account inflation. But the per capita increase in California's general-fund spending is also huge over the past decade, because California's population hasn't increased very much since 2013.[6] Back in 2013 it was 38.3 million, and in 2023 it was only up to 38.9 million, an increase of only 0.6 percent. Over the past three years, California's population has actually dropped by nearly 600,000 residents since reaching a high of 39.5 million in 2020.

Taking population into account, California's spending in 2023 dollars has gone from $3,291 per person in 2013 to $5,800 per person in 2023, an increase of 76 percent. And it's going up, just as the population continues to go down: the 2024–25 budget came in at nearly $300 billion. This dramatic growth in per-person spending corresponds directly to more government control of the economy in the form of more programs and more employees.

They've doubled the budget, but is everything twice as good? Hardly. By every objective standard, not one aspect of government services has improved. Public education is a prime example.

Spending has gone up massively, but the population served has gone down, as have the results of the spending. Compared to ten years ago, total enrollment is actually down at community colleges and in K–12 public schools.[7] In the California State University system, enrollment is down 14 percent compared to a decade ago.[8] Only in California's UC system is enrollment up, by 23 percent today compared to a decade ago.

But these enrollment trends, down in three out of four cases, do not bear any resemblance to overall spending increases. Per-student spending in just the last ten years increased (again, after adjusting for inflation) by 97 percent at the community colleges, 73 percent in the California State University system, 38 percent for the UC system, and 53 percent in the K–12 public schools.

The most egregious of these examples has to be the K–12 schools. By law they are guaranteed to receive approximately 38 percent of the state general fund every year, no matter how swollen the budget gets. Imagine the perverse incentive this creates. The powerful teachers unions will push for anything that increases the state budget, because no matter what the expenditure is for, they will get thirty-eight cents out of every dollar increase. With all this money, have educational outcomes improved? No. The results are as shockingly bad as they were a decade ago: more than half of students fail to meet basic standards in English, and, disgracefully in the state that claims to be the world's technology leader, two-thirds of students fail to meet basic standards in math. On top of that, the outcomes for Black and Latino students—the very people the teachers unions and their socialist acolytes claim to speak for—are even worse. Two-thirds of Latinos and 70 percent of Black students fail to meet basic standards in English; for math it is 80 percent of Latinos and 85 percent of Black kids. Utterly shameful. How dare these leftist union leaders and the Democrat politicians who indulge them lecture anyone about "racial justice"?

What about crime? The state prison system increased spending by $3.4 billion (after adjusting for inflation) over the last ten years, a 29 percent increase. But the inmate population in state prisons dropped during the same period, from 168,000 in 2009 to 96,000 in 2022.[9] The prison population almost halved but the budget went up by a third. During the 2022–23 fiscal year, California's state prison system spent an estimated $159,000 per prisoner. It's not as if all this spending is delivering one of the main aims of any effective prison system: rehabilitation. California's recidivism rate has barely moved in the years of the spending splurge, hovering just above the national average at around 42 percent. Furthermore, that probably overstates the system's effectiveness, since California no longer prosecutes many offenses that in most other states are still considered crimes that will earn prison sentences. Also, the reported rate would be still higher if it weren't for the state legislature passing AB 1050 in 2013, which changed the definition of recidivism from being arrested after release to being convicted after release.[10]

As for homelessness, is California better off today than it was ten years ago? Drive down any urban boulevard, or up any freeway on-ramp, and survey the expanse of tents and makeshift shacks. Did you see that ten years ago? The state's answer? Turn tens of billions of dollars over to developers and "nonprofits" to build "permanent supportive housing" at an average cost that exceeds $500,000 per unit.[11] The state auditor recently reported that in the five years between 2019 and 2024, California government spent $24 billion on homelessness with no idea where the money went, and no evidence of any positive impact. Indeed, the more money that is spent, the worse the problem seems to get. While the so-called homeless industrial complex scams taxpayers for additional billions, thousands of the most vulnerable people in our society are left as prey for drug dealers (many of them government-sanctioned in "safe injection sites") while living in squalor.

Despite spending tens of billions for government programs and subsidies to assist California's homeless, the unsheltered population grew from an estimated 73,000 people in 2013 to 123,423 people in 2023.[12] The official figure for 2024 is over 170,000 but unofficial estimates from organizations working with the homeless population say it could be ten times higher.

The biggest growth in California's government, however, is in "health and human services." And here it is likely to grow even further. Within the broad category of "health and human services," the Department of Social Services nearly doubled its spending. Most of this is for so-called SNAP benefits (Supplemental Nutrition Assistance Program), formerly called food stamps. Factors influencing this rise would include $6 billion per year of recently allocated "emergency allotment benefits," part of the state's response to the Covid pandemic. Another reason for the rise in spending is the decision of the state to award SNAP benefits to undocumented immigrants, but there is no publicly available data on how many of California's undocumented residents are recipients.

The eligibility of undocumented immigrants is also a factor in the biggest single line-item increase in the state budget over the past ten years, that of health care services. Most of this increase, $17.3 billion, is the result of the expansion of Medi-Cal (California's Medicaid Program) under the Affordable Care Act. By 2015, so-called Obamacare in California had grown to cover 12.7 million people, a nearly 60 percent growth in under two years. By 2018 there were an estimated 13.5 million Californians covered by Medi-Cal. By 2022, enrollment grew to nearly 14 million. Because most of the costs to cover Medi-Cal recipients qualifying under the Affordable Care Act are covered by the federal government, however, it remains unclear just how much of the overall cost increase is due to higher enrollment, and how much is attributable to higher costs per insured, the extension of benefits to the undocumented, and more bureaucracy. But the future could render California's current level of state control over health care trivial by comparison.

In 2023, Senate Bill 770 was passed by the state legislature and signed by the governor.[13] It is another attempt to enact single-payer health care, something so costly it has the potential to double the size of the state's general fund. SB 770 is a major step forward in the movement to bring single-payer health care to California. The bill directs the governor to prepare a plan to set up a "unified financing" program to pay for all health care services in the state. According to proponents, once fully implemented, all California residents will be entitled to receive a standard package of health care services; entitlement will not vary by age, employment status, disability status, income, or immigration status; and distinctions among Medicare, Medi-Cal, employer-sponsored insurance, and individual market coverage will be eliminated. Did you work continuously, full-time, for forty years and always made sure to pay your health care premiums? Tough. Get in line for government health care. You can call it equity, if that helps. Is your lifesaving medical treatment delayed? Waiting lists are a sacrifice we all must make. Ask the Brits how it works with their National Health Service (which nearly killed me, by the way—but that's another story).

Nobody could reasonably claim that California's health care system works perfectly today. But navigating a decentralized, mostly private system at least preserves competition among providers and choices to consumers. Turning this entire economic sector over to the state government of California is a perilous leap. The bureaucrats and public sector unions who have so catastrophically failed to deliver quality education, infrastructure, housing, or even law enforcement now that California's police have had their hands tied and radical prosecutors no longer do their jobs . . . these are the people who are now going to take over California's health care system. What could possibly go wrong?

You could ask the same question in relation to the "special session" of the legislature that Gavin Newsom imperiously convened in the late summer of 2024 in order to "take action" on high gas prices. Never mind that the most effective action he could have taken would be to reverse the Democrat policies that gave California the highest gas prices in America by far, namely the state's extortionate gas tax and the absurdly onerous regulations that require energy companies to treat California as a completely separate market. But no. Instead, in a drearily predictable pantomime of blame-shifting, the oil companies were accused of "price gouging," the proposed solution for which, preposterously enough, was for the state government to set and manage precise operating procedures for oil refineries.

This is Socialism. But direct government control over the economy isn't the only way Socialism can be realized in a society. Businesses can be forced to comply with unlimited rules that ostensibly advance the needs of the many, regardless of what happens to the business.

To see just how intrusive government regulations have become in California, let's start with a sector of the economy I know well: the restaurant industry. Years ago in London, my business partner and I (somewhat foolishly) started a restaurant called the Good Cook—an offshoot of our company, Good Business. Let's just say that it did not turn into a good business. We learned a lot—not least that the restaurant business is incredibly tough. So many factors, so much that can go wrong, such tight margins. A thoughtful government would treat this industry with care and sensitivity. Restaurants are often the beating heart of a community, provide great job opportunities, and should be cherished. The socialists in charge of California have taken the exact opposite approach.

Employing an estimated 1.2 million workers, this once-thriving, vital economic sector has taken two beatings over the past few years.[14] One, of course, is the devastating impact of the Covid pandemic, which scared away diners and drove costs through the roof. Much of that could have been avoided if those in charge had followed the actual science instead of superstition and groupthink. People often describe the terrible impact of the pandemic with the phrase "when Covid hit." We should remember that for a large part of the suffering and destruction wrought by the pandemic in California, a more apt phrase would be "when the lockdowns hit." Not the same thing at all. But even before Covid—and certainly during and after—for the restaurant industry, an endless onslaught of regulations has brought the entire sector to the brink. Here's one restaurateur's story.

"You have to pick which laws to break; it is impossible to comply with all of them." So says the owner of an independent restaurant in Los Angeles, coping with what is the most punishing regulatory environment for restaurateurs in the country. He claims he now has to spend 60 percent of his time not training cooks and servers, sourcing great food, and designing incredible recipes, but instead doing paperwork. For example, instead of being in the kitchen or dining room, he routinely spends several hours every week auditing payroll records for minor infractions of labor laws; violations could land his business in a million-dollar lawsuit.

A core belief of socialists is the naïve and complacent assumption that the economic growth and big profits they need (to provide tax revenue for their expansive schemes) will happen no matter what. You don't need financial incentives, smart financiers, visionary leaders, or less red tape. Nowhere in these United States does a state government demonstrate this part of the socialist dream more than California. The regulations are endless.

In most states, if you want to work in a restaurant, you apply for the job, get an interview, and if all goes well, you're hired and you go to work. If you need training, it's done on the job. But in California, a new law requires restaurant workers to obtain a "food handlers card," which means passing a state-approved exam in order to be certified.[15] And if you own a restaurant, you'd better understand the details.

Employers must pay the costs incurred by the employee to obtain their food handlers card, they must consider the time the employee spends getting the card as hours worked, and they are prohibited from restricting employment to applicants who already have these cards. Why? Don't ask. This may seem like a petty nuisance, but it affects the whole business. Employers not only have to be sure their employees all obtain these cards, but they also have to alter their timekeeping, their job advertisements, and their employee training and orientation procedures. This is just one example of the burden on restaurateurs in California. There's much more.

"My employees always want to work through their shift," our restaurant owner explains. "They like to be able to trade break times, and they like to skip breaks and end their shift earlier." But watch out. In California, employees get an unpaid thirty-minute meal break if they work more than 5 hours, at least one paid ten-minute rest break if they work 3.5 hours in a day, and a second paid ten-minute break if they work at least 6 hours.[16] And the employer must force their employees to take these unpaid breaks whether they want them or not.

"How am I supposed to force every person I've got working to be sure to take these breaks? I don't know exactly when they clocked in and we are all caught up in serving our diners. We have ten to fifteen people working during lunch and evening rushes, and most of the time they don't want to take an unpaid break. But if I'm audited by the state, I face fines for every violation they find, even if someone's shift was only a minute too long."

The regulations are endless. Another new law requires single-user restrooms to have signs that say "All gender toilet facilities." Not having this precise language outside a unisex restroom is a violation of the law. Another law that took effect in the summer of 2024 requires bars to make test kits available to any customer who wishes to determine if their drink has been spiked.[17] Bar owners will have to purchase these kits, with the collateral burden of now becoming part of the chain of liability for any related mishap that may befall a patron.

To ensure compliance, California's larger restaurant chains are now subject to oversight by a nine-member Fast Food Council, authorized to set the hourly minimum wage for most fast-food and "fast-casual" restaurant employees, and also "to recommend regulations related to health and safety working conditions, security, taking protected leave, and protection from harassment and discrimination."[18]

This council, with seven members picked by the governor, one by the assembly speaker, and one by the state senate's rules committee, is actually the result of a compromise reached after extensive negotiations between California's powerful unions and representatives of the restaurant industry. But with all council members owing their selection to politicians like Gavin Newsom and other leaders of the one-party state of California, the headwinds buffeting anyone trying to run a restaurant are just going to get stronger. Socialist utopia, here we come.

It's not just regulations, of course, that make owning a restaurant in California so tough. It's the new minimum wage. Rather than address the rising cost of living, which is blowing up household budgets for everyone, California's socialist legislators prefer to chase their own tails by mandating a higher minimum wage. Much higher. Starting in the spring of 2024, the minimum wage for a restaurant worker in California is $20 per hour.[19] The federal minimum wage? $7.25 per hour.[20]

Earlier we spoke about the Democrat Doom Loop in California. Here it is in action: introduce stupid policies that raise people's costs; panic that higher costs will cost them votes; hand out money to compensate for higher costs; raise taxes to pay for the handouts; which in turn raises people's costs . . . and so on, back to the beginning. Restaurants are at the sharp end of this idiocy.

The challenges afflicting restaurant owners are further magnified by California's Private Attorneys General Act (PAGA). This law empowers any employee to file a lawsuit on behalf of themselves and all other allegedly aggrieved employees for any violation of California Labor Codes that they experience or observe. Thousands of these lawsuits are filed every year. PAGA affects all businesses in California. It is so lucrative for trial attorneys that they will advertise on Instagram to recruit employees to file these lawsuits. Regarding PAGA, the California Chamber of Commerce writes:

> The default penalty for a violation of the Labor Code is $100 per
> employee per pay period for an initial violation and $200 per em-

ployee per pay period for each subsequent violation. For example [in 2018], a group of drivers sued Uber claiming they were misclassified as independent contractors and were owed expense reimbursements and converted tips. If the drivers were successful on their PAGA claim, PAGA penalties would exceed $1 billion.[21]

Even Uber might be staggered by a fine that big. But for small businesses, PAGA can be a killer.

Victor Gomez, who is now the executive director of the California chapter of Citizens Against Lawsuit Abuse, owned a small franchise business on California's Central Coast and lived in constant fear of lawsuit abuse.[22] Speaking for the small-business community, he said, "We are often the targets of shakedown lawsuits. I feared the threat of a lawsuit. There was nothing to protect me." Gomez describes how the process plays out as unscrupulous attorneys would file lawsuits based on technical violations and then not even allow business owners to correct the problem, even when the violation caused no harm.

"Aggrieved employees saw pennies, while these lawyers walked away with thousands of dollars," said Gomez. "Can you imagine being an employer and having to pay out thousands of dollars in penalties because you failed to have the beginning date and ending date, sick time or vacation time listed on the check stub even though every employee was paid, paid on time, and the checks always cleared the bank?"

Gomez said that along with labor law compliance, another avenue of assault for these attorneys was violations of the Americans with Disabilities Act. He claimed that opportunistic attorneys will scour the internet, utilizing Google Maps, to look for any "parking lot where the blue striping is starting to fade." They would then pounce, assuming the business is out of compliance with other trivial issues "such as a mirror that could be a quarter of an inch too high, or a sidewalk angled one degree off." Then, with no warning, business owners find themselves in court.

This could all be chalked up to bureaucratic zeal and not Socialism, except that they want to eliminate anyone from making it as a free-lancer. You have to work from a big business with close government ties or you don't work at all.

Assembly Bill 5 (AB 5), which went into effect in January 2020, required companies to reclassify independent contractors as employees.[23] Its impact was mitigated by a November 2020 state ballot referendum that exempted companies that hired app-based drivers, as well as some job categories such as freelance writers and musicians. But AB 5 wreaked havoc on many industries, including some that provided essential services such as trucking and nursing.

With respect to health care, the timing of AB 5 could not have been worse. Taking effect only a few months before Covid cases surged across California and the rest of the nation, thousands of Advanced Practice Registered Nurses (APRNs) were barred from working as independent contractors, and consequently, thousands of them—at a time when they were most needed—opted out of providing their caregiving services.[24]

One nurse, Sophia Khawly, enjoyed working in California as an independent traveling nurse practitioner. Then AB 5 came along and nurses weren't included on the list of exceptions. "This has created a lot of problems for us," wrote Khawly on her blog.[25] "We prefer working as a contractor because we can deduct a lot of expenses on our taxes. I had been looking to work in California for the beginning of 2021, and wanted to work through an agency that pays us as 1099 contractors. But this won't be the case. And since the agency will have to pay me as an employee, that means less pay since they are required to offer benefits. It also means that they can no longer provide me with a housing stipend, but only a reimbursement. This is a big disappointment and will deter myself and other nurse practitioners from practicing there in the future." Traveling nurse practitioners are in high demand around the country. Khawly has plenty of options. California's loss will be some other state's gain.

When AB 5 took effect, independent truckers were also excluded from providing shipping services.[26] Owner-operator drivers were forced either to accept jobs as employees with major shipping companies or leave California to work in states where they were still permitted to work as independent contractors. That tough decision confronted independent trucker Dee Sova, who had to choose between staying close to her home and losing her business, or taking her business elsewhere.[27] "The unfortunate part is, I'm away from all of my family because my kids are now in California," said Sova. "That's where they wanted to stay, that's where they were born and raised. And just not being able to get in the car and go over to a family member's house. That's the painful part of the decision."

Sova, along with seventy thousand other independent truck drivers, had their independent businesses either eliminated or driven out of state.[28] Even in California, that's a huge hit to our shipping capacity. And the human cost is incalculable. But the socialist dream must be pursued at all costs. Not only did AB 5 deny nurses, truckers, and other independent businesspeople the ability to practice their professions, but it raised the cost and lowered the quality of California's health care and shipping industries, since they could no longer expand and contract their capacity to meet the needs of the market, nor did they have access any longer to thousands of trained people who had previously given them that ability.

AB 5, however, is only one example of the barriers that California's legislature has thrown up against California's truckers and by extension the entire transportation and shipping industry in the state. The California Air Resources Board, acting under the authority of the Global Warming Solutions Act and subsequent legislation, has imposed continuously escalating emissions standards on truckers. While it is important to move the shipping industry steadily toward more stringent air quality standards, these standards are requiring truckers to replace their equipment before the end of its useful life. The added costs are particularly burdensome on small trucking companies and independent owner-operators, but even some large shipping companies are leaving the state.

There is a ripple effect on the entire economy when shipping capacity is constrained and shipping costs go up. These increased costs roll through every supply chain, putting additional financial strain on all businesses, undermining the ability of California-based companies to compete and creating another incentive for them to move to a less costly state. As we have seen, thousands of companies have done so.

The onward march of Socialism has recently hit electricity consumers too. In a healthy capitalist system, people pay for what they use. If your household consumes more electricity, you have a higher bill to pay each month. But that only works when utility prices are reasonable. California's gas and electric utilities already charge the highest prices in the nation, and they're raising prices even more. They have no choice. They are staring at a looming charge of billions in additional investments needed to generate "carbon-neutral" electricity, along with billions needed to address deferred maintenance on all the transmission lines and pipelines that have been neglected as billions were already being poured into solar farms, wind farms, battery farms, and new transmission lines to connect them all to an aging grid. With all those billions that have to be found somewhere, prices go up. Way up. And thanks to a state legislature that hasn't come to terms with the financial consequences of completely upending California's energy economy in a few short years, these renewable mandates have just been increased, not decreased in the face of completely unaffordable power. Because there is a socialist remedy: means testing. If you make more money, you'll pay more for your electricity and natural gas. Voilà. Problem solved.

This is part of a pattern. It always is with socialists. Now they are calling it "equity." The problems that low-income households are having paying their electricity bills could never be a result of socialist mandates causing shortages and high prices, or socialist taxes that the producers have to pass on to customers. According to the socialist narrative, high prices are the result of capitalist exploitation, and low-income households are the victims of systemic oppression. By this reasoning, the solution is clear: the more that you make, the more you will pay for your natural gas and electricity.

The scheme, long in the making, reached its first major milestone with the passage of Assembly Bill 205 in 2022. This bill "removed the statutory language requiring default residential rates to be almost exclusively charged on a volumetric basis and provided a framework to make the residential electricity rate structure more equitable." In plain English? The amount you pay will no longer be based on how much you use. How will your bill be determined? Within the bureaucratic gobbledygook, one key word offers a clue: *equitable*. Translation? If you make more money, you pay a higher "fixed charge."

In response to SB 205, and to adhere to the socialist mantra of "equity," California's three major utilities—Southern California Edison, Pacific Gas & Electric, and San Diego Gas & Electric—put together a plan they dubbed the Joint Investor Owned Utilities Income-Graduated Fixed Charge Proposals and presented it to the legislature in April 2023. Wading through the lengthy transcript, a new "rate design" can be discerned wherein a fixed charge per month will become the primary revenue source for utilities, and additional charges based on the rates that are tied to the amount of usage will be lower.[29] How the fixed charge differs according to how much you make is not subtle.

In PG&E's depiction of "theoretical fixed charges," a household making up to $30,000 per year would have no fixed charge at all. Between $30,000 and $60,000 in household income, the fixed charge would be just over $25 per month. Between $60,000 and $100,000 it would rise to $50 per month, and between $100,000 and $150,000 it would be around $80 per month. For households earning over $150,000 per year, the fixed charge would be a hefty $180 per month.

There are several takeaways here. To begin with, these charges, at least at the levels PG&E is depicting hypothetically, are not going to make a significant dent in the revenue requirements of the utilities. They are either going to have to sneak these fixed charges in at these relatively low levels, then ramp them up steadily each year until they do generate the hundreds of billions of additional revenue being sought, or the per use rates will not drop one bit, and these fixed charges will be entirely additive. But what about the utility finding out how much everyone makes?

Here again we have Socialism displaying its finest, collectivist essence. This income-based utility pricing scheme will empower California's public utilities to have access to the state's Franchise Tax Board, the agency that imposes and collects taxes from all state residents. This is private information that is now going to be in the hands of a public utility. But even more significant is the principle involved, and violating this principle is a core feature of Socialism.

Why should someone pay more for the same service because they make more money? Maybe they worked harder for that money. Maybe they spent years saving and investing, studying and training, and after decades of sacrifice have a higher-than-average income because there is high demand for their skills and hefty returns from the investments they only made because for years they denied themselves more immediate consumer temptations. Should they be penalized for that? And isn't that already part of California's progressive tax code?

Even more to the point, where does this end? Why, if we're now going to extend the socialist ideology that informs our tax brackets—the more you make, the higher a *percentage* of your income you pay in taxes—to how much we pay for electricity and natural gas, would we stop there? Why not require all public utilities, including cell phone and internet services, garbage collection and water and sewage services, to also collect more from households with higher-than-average incomes? Where's the difference? Aren't these agencies also starving for funds to address deferred maintenance and to comply with higher environmental standards?

The ideology of Socialism rests on the assumption that if you have more of anything—more income, more wealth, more privilege—you are morally obligated to share what you have with those who have less income, less wealth, and less privilege. But what if a person's high income and luxurious wealth were not acquired because of unearned privilege and capricious luck, but were the products of determined sacrifice and hard work? And what if someone else's low income and destitute poverty were the inescapable consequence of a lifetime spent *choosing* to do nothing productive, never striving, never sacrificing, never bothering to work?

Why can't California's Democrats picture two Black teachers working second jobs for a household income of $250,000 paying to subsidize a white guy with rich parents but no job of his own, sitting in the basement posting memes all day?

Take from the productive and give it to the nonproductive. Is this a sound moral premise on which to build a society? Or shall we cancel the redistribution if someone actually earned their wealth, and withhold the benefits if the prospective recipient never put in a hard day's work? And if that distinction is made—we only take from the "undeserving" rich and we only give to the "deserving" poor—who will make that distinction?

California's socialists have an answer to that difficult question: race. Which brings us back to reparations, the proposal moving through the California Legislature whereby Black Californians will receive payments as compensation for the evil cruelty and abuse their enslaved ancestors endured, and decades of subsequent discrimination. As I have argued elsewhere, there can be no dispute that there is a serious racial wealth gap, the product of deliberate government discrimination in matters like education and housing, and that we have a moral obligation to narrow that gap. But the right and effective way to do that is through what I have called "asset reparations"—policies that enable Black Americans to own homes and start businesses on a par with their white peers. Policies to increase opportunity must be a part of it too: school choice, strengthening families, and more. That is what an effective "asset reparations" agenda would look like. But that is not at all what the socialists of California were thinking of when they initiated the nation's first official reparations policy program.

We have questions.

First, how does this work in a state as diverse as California? Among K–12 students in California's public schools, the generation that represents California's future, white students are a small minority.[30] The cohort of so-called white non-Hispanic students musters only 20.1 percent of the total enrollment. Those students designated Black non-Hispanic account for only 4.7 percent of all students. The remaining 75.2 percent are all identified as other ethnicities—Hispanic 56.1 percent, Asian 11.7 percent, and a range of other ethnicities including "two or more races" constituting the remaining 7.4 percent.

Although advocates point to California's Fugitive Slave Act of 1852 as justification, there are plenty of reasons why a state like California, which was not a slave state, should not be leading the national movement to extend reparations to its Black residents. The simple demographic facts are powerful in their own right. Because according to the logic of race-based Socialism, wherein "non-Hispanic whites" are the oppressors who must have their wealth and privilege brought into parity with everyone else in the interests of "equity," it becomes necessary for 20.1 percent of the population to pay reparations to the other 79.9 percent of the population. But in practice, reparations will put a burden on all Californians regardless of whether or not they are "non-Hispanic whites": 95.3 percent of the population—*everyone* who is not Black, but most of whom are not white either—will pay through their taxes the reparations to 4.7 percent of the population.

It isn't clear that the proponents of reparations have, anywhere in their proposals, addressed this flaw. That is understandable, because even if they were to acknowledge the problem and fix it by only assessing higher taxes on white households in order to fund reparations to Black households, they would open up a new can of worms. Why, every other Californian who isn't a member of the dwindling "non-Hispanic white" community would ask, aren't *we* getting reparations? What about the First Peoples, California's Native American tribes? The grotesque savagery visited upon them surely merits reparation if slavery does? But the brutality was inflicted by Spain and then Mexico. Should we demand reparations from them? Perhaps a new tariff? What about Latinos themselves, who suffered decades of cruel exploitation at the hands of the invading white settlers? And what about Californians of Asian descent, whose ancestors labored under white overseers to build railroads and work in gold mines back in the 1800s, enduring abuse that rivals anything experienced by slaves?

To take this exploration another step further, imagine if the principles of race-based Socialism impelled proponents of reparations to extend them to 79.9 percent of the population—that is, to everyone who isn't non-Hispanic white. Wouldn't it be fair to ask which families actually had ancestors who were present in California in past centuries? Apart from California's 0.4 percent Native American population, how many can make that claim? Haven't most Hispanics in California, along with most Asians, arrived in the state much more recently? Millions of Californians of Mexican descent have family ties in the state that go back only one or two generations. What about recent arrivals from Vietnam, or the Philippines, or India? Shall they be eligible for reparations? Why? And, for that matter, how many of the non-Hispanic whites in California have relatives who were living here a century ago or longer?

Which brings us full circle, because even California's Black population cannot be universally assumed to be descended from slaves, even if you accept that California owes them reparations. California's relatively small percentage of Black residents includes a significant percentage who arrived in recent years, from the Caribbean or Africa, and have no family history of slavery in the United States, much less in California.

Exploring this complexity is exhausting, but if there is one thing that socialists love, it's complexity. Dense, byzantine, bizarre, convoluted, impenetrable, interminable rhetoric, designed to exhaust skeptics into submission.

Of course, the slippery slope is the point. Once you start giving away government money to one group, it makes it easier to give it to others.

However, here is a second method in their madness. Because the longer they persist, and the more outrageous their claims become, the greater the likelihood that they will end up with something. And in the meantime, true as well to the socialist playbook, the major advocates will have budgets with which to pay the members of their "task force" and commission sympathetic experts to produce studies and analysis.

Would the task force make the case that a "housing wealth gap" needs to be remedied? Yes. People are still alive from the days of discriminatory housing policies that were repealed in the 1960s and '70s. But of course this isn't the argument they made, because they are not trying to address anything so specific or logical.

The reparations process began in California in 2020 in San Francisco, with the creation of that city's African American Reparations Advisory Committee. After three years they came up with the San Francisco Reparations Plan 2023, which included the following:

- A lump sum payment of $5 million to each eligible person.
- An annual income supplement to guarantee any African American household at least the amount of the median income ($97,000 in 2022) for at least 250 years.
- Forgive all debt, including educational, personal, credit card, payday loans, etc.
- Provide participants "Black Cards" that offer discounts, free services, and preferences within the city and county of San Francisco.
- Tax abatement on sales taxes for 250 years.
- Guaranteed home, renters, and commercial insurance at no cost.

- All reparation payments are tax-free.
- Free down payments for home purchases.
- Exempt eligible homeowners from property tax.
- Zero percent housing loans for fifty years.
- Zero percent small business loans.

And much, much more.

A year after the work in San Francisco began, in 2021, Governor Gavin Newsom, heedless of the fiasco he was inviting, formed a statewide Reparations Task Force, perhaps with his future presidential aspirations in mind. The task force issued an interim report that June, detailing California's "history of slavery and racism and recommending ways the Legislature might begin a process of redress for Black Californians, including proposals to offer housing grants, free tuition, and to raise the minimum wage."[31]

To understand how slavery is applicable to California, one must sift through the report's five hundred pages of pretzel logic common to the victim industry in America. According to the report:

In 1883, the Supreme Court interpreted the 13th Amendment as empowering Congress "to pass all laws necessary and proper for abolishing all badges and incidents of slavery in the United States." However, throughout the rest of American history, instead of abolishing the "badges and incidents of slavery," the United States federal, state and local governments, including California, perpetuated and created new iterations of these "badges and incidents." The resulting harms have been innumerable and have snowballed over generations. Today, 160 years after the abolition of slavery, its badges and incidents remain embedded in the political, legal, health, financial, educational, cultural, environmental, social, and economic systems of the United States of America. Racist, false, and harmful stereotypes created to support slavery continue to physically and mentally harm African Americans today.

In other words, the task force is not actually recommending reparations for slavery, but rather for discrimination. And how do task force members recommend California pay for its mistakes?

The task force's preliminary findings identified a "housing wealth gap" and recommended granting $223,239 to every Black Californian who is descended from slaves, at a cost to California taxpayers of $501 billion.[32]

But this doesn't take into account possible additional reparations for "unpaid prison labor and years of lost income [while in prison]," or "disproportionate health outcomes," including shorter life expectancies that the group's economic consultants estimated to be worth $127,226 per year. And this is still not a complete list of the "injustices" and "harms" the task force is considering.

Practical suggestions from the task force as to how reparations might be implemented were issued in June 2023 after more "racial and financial data" was gathered from the state's Department of Justice to "make more accurate calculations."[33] Just the "Executive Summary" weighs in at seventy-four pages of small-font text.[34]

In predictably uncritical coverage by the *Los Angeles Times*, the vice chairman of the state task force charged with coming up with reparation ideas said "the process came down to three 'A's'—admitting the problems of the past; atoning for them by identifying appropriate reparations; and acting on that information in a unified way to make sure state legislators, who would finalize a program, follow through and get the work done."[35]

Certainly, one of those three A's—admitting the problems of the past—is healthy enough. There has been racism and discrimination in America's past, just as there has been racism and discrimination in the past of every nation. Any decent person with a sense of history should acknowledge the past and abhor racist or discriminatory behavior. It's the "atone" and the "act" parts of the three A's, however, where problems surface. It's not just, as already noted, determining *who* atones, and *who* acts, or, of course, who benefits. Those are big questions.

Imagine a group of programs created to assist those in need, disproportionately helping Black families to escape poverty. Sounds good? Fantastic. That's what CalWORKS has been doing for over twenty-five years, at a cost of about $5 billion per year.

The poverty rate in California is a little higher now than in 1990.

Whenever socialist reparations have been tried—not just welfare, but race-based discrimination—they have proven counterproductive. The sprawling welfare state fostered by the Great Society programs of the 1960s contributed massively to government dependency and Black student underachievement. Race-based discrimination obviously undermines the consistent standards necessary for a society to thrive as a cohesive and competitive meritocracy.

The consequences of race-based discrimination are as damaging to Black communities as welfare has been. The evolution of this type of discrimination into "equity," where proportional representation by race and ethnicity is demanded in everything—hiring, promotions, admissions, contracts, and even household wealth—clearly runs counter to the sense of justice and fairness that is vital for a healthy and pluralistic society to thrive. Most insidiously of all, both race-based discrimination and "equity" provide cover for the one place left in California where systemic racism still exists: the failing government schools run by the teachers unions.

If California's reparations task force really wanted to do something to help the Black community, it would start with improving California's K–12 public schools and addressing the failure of politicians beholden to the teachers unions to enact any real education reform. The task force recommendations include adopting a "K–12 Black Studies curriculum that introduces students to concepts of race and racial identity." But nowhere to be found is any call to action for California's schools to be held accountable for the fact that 83 percent of Black students did not meet grade-level math standards on the state's student assessment tests in 2023.[36]

Unfortunately, you will never hear anyone participating in the

Reparations Task Force, or anyone else whose career depends on the public sector, denounce the evident and catastrophic failure of California's government schools to provide equal opportunity to all students regardless of race or background. There is no chance that California's Reparations Task Force will address the true driver of current racial disadvantage: government failure. That's because in their socialist ideology, the government can do no wrong. It is always the solution, never the problem.

The specter of Socialism haunts California. It is expressed in an explosion in the size of the state government over the past ten years, with no end in sight. It is equally expressed in the avalanche of regulations, which effectively put entire industries under the control of government bureaucrats. The idealistic legislators who are engineering this decline haven't learned the lessons of history. Whenever power has been centralized, and equality of opportunity has been subordinated to equality of outcome, nations, and their economies, have tumbled into decline.

If Californians want to avoid the fate of every other socialist experiment in history, we must recognize the danger.

CHAPTER 7

BUREAUCRATISM

The town of Truckee sits near the summit of Donner Pass, connecting California to the rest of the United States. It is also one of the busiest freight rail corridors in the western United States. Several times a day, heavily laden trains rumble through, either eastbound or westbound on the double-track main line, shaking the buildings of the small town to their foundations. Just a few miles from the border with Nevada, and at a 5,800-foot elevation, Truckee is a vital staging area for Union Pacific, deploying snow removal and maintenance equipment up and down the line.

Things are about to change in Truckee.

In April 2023, the California Air Resources Board decreed that California's five thousand miles of railroads—that total doesn't include switching yards or the main lines, which are double track—would have to become zero-emission. In practical terms, that means replacing every one of California's over twelve thousand line-haul locomotives, and more than six hundred switch engines, with all-electric versions.

In a press release, CARB chairman Liane Randolph explained the reason for the ruling: "Locomotives are a key part of California's transportation network, and it's time that they are part of the solution to tackle pollution and clean our air. With the new regulation, we are moving toward a future where all transportation operations in the state will be zero emissions."[1]

This decision from CARB, with the full support of Governor Newsom and the state legislature, is part of its urgent mission to eliminate pollution from locomotives, which CARB has determined are sub-stantial contributors to air pollution. CARB estimates the regulation will deliver over $32 billion in health benefits, reducing respiratory illnesses, heart disease, and premature deaths.

This is a genuine concern. Diesel locomotives emit nitrogen ox-ides and particulate matter, which contribute to smog formation and pose severe health risks. Prolonged exposure to these pollut-ants has been linked to various respiratory and cardiovascular dis-eases, particularly in vulnerable populations such as children and the elderly. Transitioning to zero-emission locomotives will lead to healthier communities and fewer health care costs associated with pollution-related illnesses.

The cost of a new line-haul locomotive is around $3 million. Modern diesel-electric locomotives are much cleaner than their predecessors but will not be permitted to operate in California under these new regulations. It is uncertain how much zero-emission locomotives will cost. They would have to run either on batteries or hydrogen fuel cells, and given the long-range requirements of so-called Class I locomotives that often travel over fifteen hundred miles without refueling, it isn't clear that they are going to be techni-cally and commercially feasible soon enough to comply. Even at only $3 million each, it would cost the railroads $36 billion to replace every operating locomotive in the state.

But according to CARB, the cost of transitioning to zero-emission railroads is substantial but necessary. For switching yards and some routes, electric wires could be installed over the tracks to take away the requirement for onboard electricity storage. No matter how it is accomplished, this transition is going to involve developing signifi-cant new infrastructure.

Of course, concern about climate change is perhaps CARB's over-riding motive for the new regulation. The transportation sector is one of the largest sources of greenhouse gas emissions in California, and railroads are a significant part of this sector. Electrifying the rail system aligns with California's broader climate goals, including achieving carbon neutrality by 2045. To adhere to this aggressive timetable, which CARB and California's leaders believe to be inviolable, it is necessary to eliminate emissions from locomotives.

...

That's the case for replacing every locomotive in California. But as usual, the bureaucrats don't think about what might be practical. How will these sweeping new mandates affect short-line railroads in California that can't possibly afford to replace their locomotives and lack the lobbying firepower to attract the billions in subsidies that the big operators will receive? How will this affect everyone who has to pay for the much higher shipping costs, either directly or indirectly, as the industry grapples with this expensive transition? And what, for that matter, is going to happen to Truckee when every single train that arrives from east of the California line will have to stop so the four or five locomotives that pulled it up the mountain can be replaced with a new set that is emissions-free?

The core of Bureaucratism is the mantra, "That's someone else's responsibility."

It's reasonable to assume that most of California's bureaucrats believe themselves to be doing their best, sensitive to the real-world impact their rulings have on the rest of us. But collectively, the sheer size of California's bureaucracy, combined with its utopian and narcissistic aspirations, has turned our state into a place where only the wealthiest individuals and mightiest corporations can productively navigate the labyrinth they've built.

What ordinary Californians face, those of us who aren't billionaires and who aren't presiding over corporate boardrooms wielding billions in financial might, is the forced endurance of a stupefying array of regulations that often prove beyond a normal person's strength to deal with. Rules, regulations, procedures, permitting processes pour endlessly out of bureaucracies like CARB and so many other powerful state agencies, leaving us uncertain how we may ever build anything, restore anything, operate anything, do anything. The money required just for the permits, and the complexity of the permit applications and required reports, have left us all at a place where half the cost and twice the time is spent on government applications and fees and reporting, with nothing afterward to actually do the real work and live the dream.

All my life I've hated bureaucracy. In my personal life, the maddening, inhuman nonsense from government bodies, corporations, schools, vacation activities, and visitor attractions . . . you name it. Forms and requirements and protocols that make no sense and no one can explain but everyone just goes along with. As my family and friends can attest, often with mortified embarrassment, I always try to fight back. In my professional life, particularly while working in 10 Downing Street in London as senior advisor to British prime minister David Cameron, I spent long hours battling pointless and destructive officialdom. When starting and running businesses, the ridiculous compliance regimes seem to be the enemies of entrepreneurship. But never have I seen anything like this—like what we have in California. Bureaucracies have turned the California Dream into a nightmare.

Exploring the roadways of California yields scenery evoking two distinct worlds. On the big freeways, surrounding every major interchange, the twenty-first century asserts itself in an agglomeration of concrete and glass boxes surrounded by lakes of asphalt, each festooned with a recognizable corporate logo. Food. Fuel. Lodging. The corporate power they represent is reflected in their generic interchangeability: "We have taken over the world. We are everywhere." And they are. From California to the Carolinas, it's the same fast food, the same gasoline brands, the same motel chains. You can't tell them apart.

If you get off the main highways, a different world still exists, but it's fading fast. Along Highway 50, which connects Sacramento to the south shore of Lake Tahoe, there are several examples that take us back to the middle of the twentieth century, before the only sources of roadside food, fuel, and lodging were franchised cutouts backed by multinational corporations. On the eastbound ascent, just above the snow line, one of these relics sits, surrounded by a chain-link fence. Struggling for years against an economic deck stacked against it, Covid restrictions administered the coup de grâce. But there it stands, a spacious log cabin–style lodge, with steep Swiss roofs and windowed gables. Moldering in the rain, freezing in the snow, it is worth more dead than alive.

Across the highway, a few miles downhill but still in the High Sierra, a roadhouse stands abandoned. Thick wood framing, a peaked roof, a stone chimney, and a decrepit neon sign define this relic from the last century. Imagine this place in its heyday, with a fire roaring in the hearth, drinks being poured, glasses clinking, the hubbub of exhilarated travelers filling the bar. Imagine the lodge across the street, the same scene, with someone playing the piano in the lobby, while families lounge or play board games with their children beneath the vaulted timber ceiling. It's all gone now. The only thing these beautiful ruins offer are the real estate they're sitting on and the liquor licenses that will pass to the new owners.

To build a new restaurant in California today, much less build a motel, or in fact anything at all . . . don't buy materials and hire workers. First you must swim marathons in the bureaucratic ocean, and you'd better have a lot of money, a lot of time, and the patience of a saint.

How else does one tolerate the nearly infinite ecosystem of federal, state, regional, and local agencies, all with the power to stop your project in its tracks? How else to navigate the endless litigation, the overlapping regulations that often conflict with each other depending on which agency they're coming from, and change all the time? How else to cope when yet another lawsuit, or rule change, requires an entire new set of designs, and the need to resubmit them to every agency and start all over again?

Instead of a restaurant that's been in one family for a century, with a fire in the hearth and drinks poured by hand, we have corporate franchises with the menu and the interior atmosphere curated by behavioral scientists, and drinks measured out by a machine.

Against California's prohibitive backdrop, how can anyone expect small businesses to succeed, particularly if they're doing anything that requires construction or serving food, when there are dozens of agency bureaucracies that must be coddled and thousands of their regulations that must be complied with, because every one of them, often just on a whim, can fatally derail your business?

This punitive regulatory environment has precisely the opposite effect on big businesses. Multinational corporations can thrive in the presence of high-input costs and excessive regulations, because they have the balance sheet to withstand anything the government throws at them. They thrive even more if all their smaller, more innovative competitors have been put out of business by those regulations.

California's ruling class tolerates a parasitic government because parasitic government empowers oligopolies. If the government goes too far, big corporations have the power to sue it. How many smaller players, mavericks with a paltry million or two to burn, have lost everything when they tried to take on the Army Corps of Engineers, or the California Fish and Wildlife Service, or the Coastal Commission, or any others among a host of agencies fueled by an inexhaustible cascade of taxpayer dollars? Enough to provide cautionary tales aplenty.

A practical government in California that was committed to serving its citizens would not only deregulate and consolidate oversight agencies. They would also fast-track permitting for nuclear and natural gas development, fund water-supply infrastructure, and upgrade the roads. Doing this lowers the cost of housing and empowers small businesses to compete. This understanding is usually lost even among those who properly criticize government investment in wasteful, impractical, politically contrived, and unnecessary infra-structure.

We can't bring back the last century, nor should that be anyone's goal. But we can make it easier for small entrepreneurs to resurrect and restore the resorts and roadhouses that would otherwise face demolition. We can make it easier for small entrepreneurs to construct new refuges for the traveler and the tourist. We can create a policy environment that isn't punitive to the millions of honest dealers who want to create something that consumers want and to achieve financial independence by providing it. This decentralized wealth, the product of unshackled creativity and entrepreneurship, is the engine of culture and identity—and diversity—and an expression of freedom. We should not turn that over to multinational corporations alone. Nor should we continue to incentivize a synergy between oligopolistic corporations and government bureaucracies. But that is exactly what California's left-wing elites do best.

Bureaucracy is when most of the important decisions are made by state officials rather than by elected representatives, but Bureaucratism is when no one is making the big decisions or looking at what all the little decisions add up to. The bureaucrats don't write the laws; that's the domain of the legislature. But California's legislature delegates authority to over two hundred agencies, giving them the power to interpret state statutes, define the details of their implementation, then write and enforce the actual regulations.

To restate a theme that must define any analysis of how California's government has turned its back on the people it is supposed to serve, the employees of these two hundred or more state agencies are themselves represented by powerful unions that largely control which politicians are elected to write these laws and oversee these agencies. This is a circle of public policy decision-making completely internal to the government. The agencies are represented by the unions that control the politicians who control the agencies.

The sheer complexity of California's bureaucracy is mind-blowing.[2] If you have a business, your activities will be subject to oversight by dozens of state agencies. Do you want to work as a barber or hairstylist? Better check with the Board of Barbering and Cosmetology. That's the obvious one. But if you have employees, don't be surprised if you hear from the Occupational Safety and Health Division, the Labor Standards Division, the Division of Workers' Compensation, and the Employment Development Department. If you have premises, the Office of the State Fire Marshal. If you use chemical hair products, the Department of Toxic Substances Control. If you have trash, the Department of Resources Recycling and Recovery. If you sell hair products, you'll have to collect sales tax and file reports with the State Board of Equalization. Planning on doing something that involves betting? Talk to the Gambling Control Commission. Oh, and also the Bureau of Gambling Control . . . after all, it would be so boring to have just the one bureaucratic agency focused on your industry. And of course you have to register your corporation with the California secretary of state and pay taxes to the state's Franchise Tax Board. Then there are the county and city governments.

But that's easy compared to anyone running a business that actually disrupts the earth or produces tangible products. Are you laying a foundation? Building homes or, God forbid, building a factory, cutting timber, running cattle, farming, mining, or quarrying? Good luck with that. In addition to most of those listed above, here are some of the additional agencies that may come calling: the California Biodiversity Council, the Department of Fish and Game, the Board of Forestry, the Office of Tribal Advisor, the Department of Food and Agriculture, the California Natural Resources Agency, the California Air Resources Board, the Agricultural Labor Relations Board, the Contractors State License Board, Cal Fire, CalRecycle, the Industrial Welfare Commission, the Department of Insurance, the State Lands Commission, the State Mining and Geology Board, the Department of Pesticide Regulation, the Department of Water Resources, the Water Commission, the

Water Resources Control Board, and any number of state-run conservancies. Is your operation located near the ocean? Expect to tangle with the Coastal Commission. But you don't have to be close to the ocean, or a river, or a lake, to run afoul of California's water watchdogs. The California Water Resources Control Board is everywhere.

For example, businesses in California are required to regulate all of the outdoor runoff and discharges from their property. The original intent of this law was to deal with gross polluters who were dumping toxic pollutants on their property. But then SB 205 was signed by Governor Newsom in 2019, and this law made all businesses with certain Standard Industrial Classification (SIC) codes have to prove they held an Industrial General Permit in good standing before they could have their annual business license renewal approved by the cities where they were located.[3]

The SIC code is a way of classifying businesses that was developed in the 1930s.[4] The state Water Resources Control Board has prepared a list of "potentially regulated Standard Industrial Classification Codes" that lists over one thousand business categories that fall under their jurisdiction, ranging from "adhesives and sealants" to "yarn texturizing, throwing, twisting, and winding mills."[5] There isn't much you can do that involves a product or a tangible service that isn't on this list. The consequences of SB 205 have been devastating.

People who have been in business for decades, often for generations in the same family, were blindsided when renewing their licenses in 2020. Instead of a routine renewal process, they found out they had to acquire an Industrial General Permit. Most of them had no idea what that was and assumed they would just have to pay a reasonable additional fee and just acquire a permit. Not so fast.

The fee for an Industrial General Permit is $2,000 per year, and the implementation of it is twofold. If the business has any outdoor processes or outdoor storage, they can expect to have to pay between $30,000 and $100,000 in retrofits to their outdoor work area, then they will have to do annual reporting that includes providing from their worksite four storm samples per year. Typically, none of these folks know how to do laboratory work. That means they will have to hire an expert consultant to go into their yard, take samples, take them to a lab, get results, interpret the results, then upload the results and the report online into a massively confusing system.

To make matters worse, even if a business owner successfully takes all that lab data and uploads it for approval four times per year, over and over again, whenever they aren't meeting the threshold they are subject to enforcement actions. And these thresholds often seem like they've been pulled out of thin air by California's Department of Toxins and Substances Control.

A consultant with twenty-five years' experience helping businesses navigate California's regulatory morass claimed that this agency is using thresholds that are below the naturally occurring amounts. "Nobody is in compliance," she said. "They are nailing people all over the cities with fines between $3,000 and $1 to $2 million. If somebody is a gross polluter that's one thing, but for most of these people they simply didn't do their uploads correctly into their system or they aren't 100 percent in compliance and they don't have the money and skills to figure this out. I've closed more businesses since this law took effect than in the last twenty-five years. These guys are all getting killed."

Trying to save these companies would be easier, even in the face of tough regulatory oversight, except for the fact that not only are the thresholds for violations set at unreasonable if not impossibly low levels, but the mentality of agency staff is one of indifference if not overt hostility. Describing agency staff at the California Department of Water Resources, she said that "about one-third of them are deliberately hostile, another one-third are either sheep that go along with the culture or they are true believers and fanatics who set the culture, and there are about one-third left who are trying to help. But most of the ones who truly want to help are leaving or retiring."

Her conclusion is echoed by experts and entrepreneurs who try to work with state agency bureaucrats across any industry that has an impact on the environment, however small or benign. The people being hired have degrees in environmental planning, they are the product of activist professors, they have minimal field experience, and they seem to think all businesses, big or small, have the financial resources and time to comply with regulations that are poorly written and often impossible to fulfill.

The complexity and regulatory overreach of California's bureaucracy isn't just killing private businesses. It turns on itself as well, as countless state agencies all have the ability to paralyze any major public infrastructure project. By the time any project makes it out of the planning and approval process, the rules at some agency with veto power have changed yet again, and the process starts over. Typically the projects that finally get approval, perhaps thanks to an executive order that streamlines the process, are projects that make the least sense. And even these politically correct projects proceed at a glacial pace. An area where bureaucratic paralysis has been particularly harmful to all Californians is the state's badly needed new water supply projects. Every worthy project, from new reservoirs to desalination plants to aqueduct repair and levee upgrades, is tied up in bureaucratic knots. But it wasn't always this dysfunctional. There was a time when these projects were planned and executed in years instead of decades.

The California State Water Project was conceived in the 1950s for the "control, protection, conservation, distribution, and utilization of the waters of California, to meet present and future needs." In May 1957, Harvey Banks, then director of the California Department of Water Resources, submitted *The California Water Plan* to the governor and state legislature. Ten years later, a vast network of dams, reservoirs, aqueducts and pumping stations were already designed and completed. This is an accomplishment that would not merely be astonishing by today's standards; it would be impossible.

For example, the San Luis Reservoir, an off-stream behemoth that gets its water from the California Aqueduct and has a storage capacity of just over two million acre-feet, was built in just four years and operational by 1967. The project included the pumps to lift water over the 380-foot dam and the forebays below the dam where water is diverted from the California Aqueduct. The pumping plant has eight reversible turbines that can either consume or generate 424 megawatts of electricity, depending on whether they are using surplus solar power during the day to pump water from the forebay up into the dam or releasing water from the dam back down into the forebay during peak electricity demand in the early evening.[6]

This engineering marvel went from concept to design to reality in under ten years. Construction took less than five years. That was then. The San Luis Reservoir was intended to have a twin project already built and operating, the proposed Sites Reservoir, in an arid valley north of the Sacramento–San Joaquin Delta. It was planned to be filled by the Sacramento River during storms when the water is high, then gradually released throughout California's hot summers to serve farms and cities. But the Sites Project, stuck in the concept phase for nearly seventy years, remains stalled by bureaucracy.

Back in 2020, the executive director of the Sites Project, Jerry Brown (no, not the ex-governor) posted a video on YouTube to answer this question: What's taking so long to build the Sites Reservoir Project? Here's his answer:

> My experience is that for every one year of construction you have about three years for permitting, so for us we have about a seven year construction period, that would mean we'd have about a twenty year time frame for the total project. Our JPA [Joint Power Authority] started in 2010, we're estimated to be completed in 2030, so actually, we're pretty much on schedule.[7]

Pretty much on schedule. A project that once took less than ten years from initial planning to commencing normal operations is now expected to take at least thirty years, and that's "pretty much on schedule."

At the same time as the bureaucrats in Sacramento are holding everything up, they are churning out vapid verbiage and calling it "plans." While we were developing our own policy report, *Water Abundance,* at my California policy organization, Golden Together, I came across Newsom touting his own state water plan. Better read that, I thought, as I wouldn't want us to recommend things that may already have been underway. At least we should be aware of the projects the state government was proposing. I started reading the document. A nice generic introduction, full of the usual flim-flam and corporate/government-speak you see everywhere these days. But once we get into the specific chapters—that's where the detail will be. That's where all the specific projects will be laid out. To my astonishment, as I scrolled through page after mind-numbing page . . . there was nothing. Literally nothing specific. Just an endless string of platitudinous jargon and gobbledygook, "strategies" and "stakeholders" "working in partnership" for "equity" and "sustainability." Finally, toward the end of the document, I found a table with a few footling pilot projects. And I realized: This is the answer. This is why the government budget has doubled but everything is worse. This is why nothing gets done. *This is the bloat.* This is just the water document. Imagine all the other bureaucrats, in all the other agencies, sitting around churning out reports about equity and stakeholders with literally nothing actually happening in the real world.

This paralysis is business as usual in California and is one of the many facets of the bloated bureaucracy that has become self-serving and focused on *process* instead of results. California's voters approved funding for the Sites Reservoir in 2014, and to date there is not so much as a scratch in the ground. California voters approved high-speed rail in 2008, and to date not a single mile of actual track has been laid. To bring it back to the individual business level: The owner of a winery told me an astonishing story. She wanted to expand her operation to welcome fifty visitors a day, up from the total of thirty that was permitted. The process to get approval for an increase from thirty to fifty visitors took six years and cost over $1 million in fees.

Imagine if those who built the Golden Gate Bridge had faced the bureaucracy that confronts builders today. That marvelous, spectacular megaproject took four years and four months from start to finish. Imagine if the builders of the Oroville Dam had to navigate California's impenetrable array of state, regional, and local oversight agencies. Lake Oroville, part of the 1957 *State Water Plan*, holds over 3.5 million acre-feet. Construction started in 1961 and was completed by 1968.

The embattled Diablo Canyon nuclear power plant, which stabilizes California's precarious on-again, off-again renewables-heavy grid with 2.1 gigawatts of continuous carbon-free power, was approved for construction in 1968 and was operating by 1973. Reservoirs. Bridges. Power plants. We used to build them in a few years; now, if they get built at all, it takes decades.

A dairy farmer in California who is watching his industry get squeezed to death by regulators, with the smaller family operations falling first, has a theory about bureaucracy in California. "The people running these agencies are all making $300,000 per year or more," he said. "They're doing very well for themselves, and typically find that denying permits is a safer route than approving anything. It's harder for something to go wrong with a project that might reflect back on whoever approved the project if the project never gets approved to begin with."

This dairyman, who didn't want his name to be used, has a good point. Brian Kelly, the executive director of the California High-Speed Rail Authority, collected a pay and benefits package worth $576,000 in 2022. Other bureaucrats aren't far behind. The president of the California Public Utilities Commission, Alice Busching Reynolds, collected pay and benefits in 2022 of $323,073.[8] In that same year, Karla Nemeth, who directs the California Department of Water Resources, earned $284,559, and Liane Randolph, the chairperson of the California Air Resources Board, earned $269,361.[9]

For most Californians, these are pay and benefits packages that they can only dream of. To be fair, if you're running an operation that employs tens of thousands of people, and spends tens of billions of dollars, as is the case with the California High-Speed Rail Authority, a hefty pay and benefits package is easily justifiable. Except for the small matter of performance.

Bureaucrats preside over projects that barely get started, let alone finished, or if they are eventually finished, they are over budget and dramatically worse than what was originally promised. Or, in the case of the California Air Resources Board, the role of the agency has swollen far beyond its original mission, turning it into a sprawling monster that does more harm than good.

The Sites Reservoir, to return to that example, was intended to hold two million acre-feet and have pump storage, just like the San Luis Reservoir. But once compromises were reached with all the bureaucrats and litigants, the design for Sites was reduced to 1.5 million acre-feet of capacity, without reversible turbines to store and release surplus electricity, and a new condition that half of its annual discharge back into the river had to be withdrawn for the benefit of ecosystems instead of for use by farms and cities. Half of the water! That means half of the revenue that reservoir might have earned from farmers and municipal water agencies is forfeit. Will Sites ever get built? But the man in charge, Jerry Brown, will still have a job. According to his assessment of how long these projects should take, it will be a job for life.

Another bureaucrat who has a job for life is Brian Kelly, presiding over the sluglike progress of high-speed rail. And at least these highly paid bureaucrats are trying to build something. In most cases, California's byzantine bureaucracy exists primarily not to push actual public projects forward at a snail's pace, but to oversee, delay, and often deny the projects of private companies, and to harass private businesses. The impact is felt across California's embattled private sector.

For anyone operating a business in California—small, medium, or large—the experiences of the last twenty years have been a nightmare that gets worse every year. California's regulatory environment, its high taxes and exorbitant fees, and the overall cost of doing business are the toughest in the nation. Many businesses have voted with their feet, moving their operations to more welcoming business environments.

According to a list of Cali-Formers, companies compiled by the Sacramento-based Center for Jobs and the Economy, since 2020 over five hundred companies have either left California completely or opted to expand their operations in a different state while shrinking their operations here.[10] The list includes scores of household-name companies: Aerojet, Airbnb, Aligent, Alphabet (Google), Amazon, Amgen, and Apple, and that's just the A's. It spans the gamut from high tech and aerospace to energy (Chevron) and civil engineering (Bechtel) to arts and entertainment (Academy of Country Music, Disney). When including companies that have simply downsized their presence in California, opting to expand in other states instead, it's a challenge merely to find a large company that wouldn't be on this list.

Even companies that are intrinsically bound to remain in California because they are tied to the land—agriculture, logging, housing—are getting out. Soper-Wheeler, once a major logging company in Northern California, in 2001 began to move their operations to New Zealand, a process they completed by 2020.[11] Publicly traded housing developers, accountable to shareholders, lack a strong incentive to invest in California, because the returns are so much greater in states with less regulation and less litigation.[12] And as California's beleaguered farmers struggle to stay competitive, markets in the state are increasingly stocked with avocados from Mexico and beef from Brazil.[13] In 2020 California imported $14.3 billion worth of food products.[14]

The decline is everywhere. The total private sector labor force in California was 15.0 million in February 2020, immediately prior to the Covid pandemic.[15] It fell to 13.7 million in February 2021, then rose to 14.9 million in February 2022, 15.1 million in February 2023, and slightly higher to 15.2 million in March 2024. Over the past four years, the total employed private sector workforce has increased by only 1.6 percent. Even these dismal growth statistics obscure the scale of the problem. Unemployment in California in March 2024 was 5.3 percent, the worst in the nation.[16]

While California's private sector employment has been stagnant over the past four years, the bureaucracy has thrived. State government spending in California has dramatically increased. As previously noted, in just the last ten years, and adjusting for inflation, the California State General Fund, the budget that allocates taxpayer dollars to countless state government programs and departments, has nearly doubled. This spending spree at the taxpayer's expense corresponds directly to more government bloat: bureaucratic control of the economy in the form of more programs and more employees.

It should come as no surprise that the largest employers in the state in 2023 were government agencies, along with the University of California, with 227,000 faculty and staff. Altogether in 2023 an estimated 2.5 million Californians worked for state and local governments and agencies.

All of this raises the ultimate question: Who really runs these bureaucracies? It's not the voters. Why would voters agree to twice as much government in exchange for more crime, more homeless, failing schools, and higher prices for everything? The answer is in plain sight. It's the bureaucrats themselves, working through the public sector unions that represent them.

Taxpayers think they are voting on where the money goes. They fight over who gets the tax rebates, infrastructure spending, or government assistance. But in a bureaucratic state, the only thing money goes toward is more bureaucrats.

In 1968 California passed the Meyers-Milias-Brown Act, which made California the second state in the country to allow public sector collective bargaining.[17] This legislation has been amended repeatedly since 1968, most notably when Governor Jerry Brown (in his first term as governor) signed the Rodda Act in 1974, which expanded collective bargaining to public school employees and established the powerful Public Employee Relations Board.

Over the ensuing decades, California's public sector unions steadily increased their political influence. Today they are typically the biggest contributor to almost every member of the state legislature; virtually all of the Democrats and many of the few Republicans who are left owe most of their campaign financing to public sector unions. Government union control over the state legislature has been described by capitol insiders as "absolute."

The swaggering political arrogance of the unions in California was recently illustrated by a strange development. In a tight race for an Orange County state senate seat in 2024, the unions threw their considerable financial weight behind . . . the Republican candidate, Steven Choi. Why? Because the incumbent Democrat, Josh Newman, had dared to challenge the unions on one of their pet pieces of legislation, on union recognition within the University of California. They wanted to send a message to every other legislator: Step out of line and we'll come after you. Given the Democrat super-majority in the legislature, they didn't even care if they helped elect a Republican. Which they did. Such is the arrogance of the true masters in a one-party state.

It isn't hard to see what the consequences of this influence have created. The inevitable agenda of unions representing government employees is to grow government, and if government programs falter in their effectiveness, their solution is always to fix the problem with even more government. This increases their membership, their dues revenue, and hence their influence. Government unions, unlike private sector unions, can afford to be relatively indifferent to the consequences of their periodic demands for higher pay and expanded government employment, since government agencies are not required to compete in the market to earn profits, but instead are merely required to demand that the politicians—whom they helped elect—raise taxes.

California's public sector unions also tend, like most unions, to embrace a left-leaning, "Big Government" bias. This means that their preference for more bureaucracy, more regulation, and higher taxes has an ideological as well as an economic basis. In California today, public sector unions representing state and local employees collect and spend nearly $1 billion per year.[18] No other special interest in the state is so inherently focused on expanding the government, nor has access to such a large and perennial flow of discretionary funds.

In the most recent budget cycle, as Governor Newsom worked with the state legislature to roll out planned spending for the 2024–25 fiscal year, the consequences of a bloated bureaucracy were checked by a reduction in anticipated tax revenue. This should have been expected, given the fact that California's economy is notoriously cyclical due to the periodic surges in tech industry wealth whenever a new innovation comes out of Silicon Valley and captivates the world, then subsides until the next wave comes along. But in California, where public sector unions exercise almost absolute control over the state bureaucracy, growth in government can't be slowed down every time the economy hiccups.

Newsom had an opportunity to recognize the limitations of state spending. He had an opportunity to recognize economic reality and question the promises made and the priorities set by Democrats over the past several years. He could acknowledge that nearly doubling California's budget in only ten years, even after adjusting for inflation and population growth, cannot be justified. He could admit that even though per capita state spending had nearly doubled in only a decade, the citizens of California were worse off, not better, and that maybe it was time for a major shift in policies. But that would have run afoul of California's public sector unions, whose bureaucracies benefit from all these spending increases.

Taking the politically expedient path instead, Newsom made marginal cuts to the budget while sneaking in several indirect tax increases on businesses.[19] The biggest of these was a new tax policy whereby businesses that have lost money in prior years can't use those losses to offset gains in future years when they are profitable. The purpose of the original law is to allow those very businesses that in good years contribute so much to California's tax base and economy in general—high-tech companies that often incur huge losses when they are getting started—to lower their declared income by the amount they had previously lost once their products are shipping and they're making healthy profits. This is not only a fair-minded tax provision that makes businesses with volatile earnings able to compete with mature companies that earn more predictable profits; it is also an important incentive that keeps high-tech companies operating in California. But the bureaucracy must be fed. Newsom's budget advisors saw an estimated $18 billion on the table by making this change, and Newsom approved it.

To those of us in California who must deal with the state's innumerable laws and regulations and its heavy burden of taxes, fees, and fines, bureaucracy is a faceless, implacable, dehumanizing machine with infinite manifestations and layers of complexity that are impossible to navigate. It is the reason we are losing some of the finest aspects of our culture. We are losing family-owned businesses with unique venues and unique products: family farms, small manufacturers, and independent retailers. One by one, and by the thousands, California's bureaucracy is grinding them out of existence. California is increasingly becoming a state where only powerful corporations can afford to comply and prosper, and even those can only do so if they adhere to politically favored products and services and don't run afoul of a capricious and potentially malevolent bureaucracy.

Bureaucratism is a sickness, a parasitic infection that kills what would otherwise be the healthiest tissue in our state. It kills the ambitions, aspirations, and accomplishments of people who just want to invest, build, employ, and provide but lack the obsessive patience and duplicity, much less the time and money, to fight off a bureaucratic virus that demands more from them than the actual project they're willing to bet their lives and fortunes to complete. At the same time, the pathology of Bureaucratism empowers and corrupts the bureaucrats, as they multiply with abandon, serving only themselves. Bureaucratism is a parasite that eventually kills the host. Unfortunately, that is California today.

CHAPTER 8

COMPASSIONISM

When George Gascón was sworn in as the district attorney of Los Angeles County in December 2020, business as usual was over for the prosecutors he would now be supervising at the downtown Hall of Justice.[1] Imagine the scene as Gascón had his first meeting with the team of deputy district attorneys who would be responsible for implementing his directives, telling his team: I've taken on this role not to maintain the status quo but to transform it. We can no longer afford to ignore the evidence: that our criminal justice system too often fails to serve the best interests of society or the individuals who come into contact with it.

Gascón then would have described his reforms:

Effective starting today, we will no longer pursue the death penalty in Los Angeles County. We will not charge children as adults. Sentencing enhancements that do not demonstrably contribute to public safety and instead feed the cycle of mass incarceration will be eliminated. And cash bail will be removed for misdemeanor or nonviolent felony offenses. These are not just changes; they are a moral imperative.

The measures Gascón introduced were not minor administrative adjustments; they were a profound shift in how the criminal justice system would approach offenders. For decades the approach had been one of punishment. Incarceration was the default response to crime. But Gascón and his supporters believed, with some research to back them up, that incarceration does not always serve the best interests of either the offender or society.

One of the biggest criticisms of the traditional approach to criminal justice is that it doesn't address the underlying causes of crime. Many offenders come from backgrounds of poverty, trauma, and lack of opportunity. Locking them up does nothing to address root causes. Instead it can make everything worse, creating a cycle where individuals are released from prison only to reoffend, having received no support to change the circumstances that led them to commit crimes in the first place.

Gascón's reforms were a reflection of these criticisms. They began with the premise that our criminal justice system has to move beyond the idea that strict criminal penalties equate to greater public safety. What Gascón was attempting to do in Los Angeles County represents a shift toward greater compassion in both governance and justice. He believed that the criminal justice system should not merely be a means of punishment, but a way to rehabilitate offenders. According to this approach, offering opportunities for redemption and rehabilitation leads to better outcomes for everyone.

The policies that Gascón and his supporters promoted represent, for them, a commitment to empathy and understanding. By focusing on rehabilitation over retribution, and by recognizing the systemic factors that contribute to criminal behavior, they believed they were helping to reshape the criminal justice system into one that seeks to heal rather than harm. These reforms are not just about changing laws; they are about changing hearts and striving toward a society that values every individual's potential for growth and change.

Through these reforms, Gascón believed he was setting an example of how governance can be more compassionate, prioritizing human dignity and the possibility of redemption over retribution and harsh punishment. In doing so, he contributed to a broader movement that views these policy shifts as the compassionate, necessary next steps toward building a more just and equitable society.

...

Gascón's policies have been an extraordinary gamble. Imagine if they had worked. Fewer prisons and less crime. Nobody can argue with the goal. But it has been a terrible, tragic failure, in a city that is reeling under an epidemic of crime and homelessness that is worse than it's ever been.

Los Angeles is one of the great cities of the world. Flying in at night reveals this vast metropolis in all its spectacular glory. Sandwiched between the Pacific Ocean and inland mountain peaks nearly two miles high, Los Angeles is a panorama of glistening boulevards striped with oncoming white headlights and receding red taillights that carve into gigantic squares the quiet, endless grid of homes, sprinkled with glittering neon main streets that define countless diverse communities and neighborhoods with unknown pleasures in food, drink, fun, fashion, everything anyone could want, waiting to be discovered in strip malls and hidden alleyways and courtyards of palms and jacarandas, all capped by kaleidoscopic eruptions of high-rises where the city's multiple downtown districts push skyward. Some look out on the city and see "sprawl." I see something magnificent, an endless vista of human creativity and hustle. Los Angeles is a magical place, where dreamers and doers from around the world have made their stand and thrived.

Now a madness threatens this paradise, a madness called Compassionism.

Its poster child was George Gascón, a skilled politician who, buttressed by millions of dollars in campaign contributions from George Soros and a menagerie of Silicon Valley titans and Hollywood moguls, managed to get himself elected district attorney three times, twice in the city and county of San Francisco, then, in 2020, in Los Angeles County.

Everything about Gascón exemplifies California's dysfunction. A political insider, he was initially appointed San Francisco district attorney by then-mayor Gavin Newsom, replacing in that position none other than Kamala Harris. His campaigns, both in San Francisco and in Los Angeles, have been endorsed not only by Newsom and Harris, but by such notables as U.S. senators Bernie Sanders and Elizabeth Warren. Gascón is a creature of the far left, and while the millions showered on his campaigns by California's elite made his career in politics possible, it is his rhetoric that got him across the finish line with voters, time after time.

To understand how Gascón could pull off this success for so long lends insight into the entire fraudulent essence of Compassionism, not to be confused with compassion. The difference boils down to a simple truth that can't be repeated enough in our upended state with its inverted rules: genuine compassion brings with it tough obligations. To deter crime, criminals must know that if they are caught, they will be held accountable.[2] Individuals who are mentally ill need to be taken off the streets, as do drug addicts and alcoholics, and doing so is their best chance to finally recover their lives and their dignity, even if it takes away their freedom for a time.

But Gascón takes the opposite approach: Compassionism. This is the belief that there is no such thing as a criminal, that everyone, even including the perpetrators of violent crimes, is a victim. Not only is everyone a victim of circumstances beyond their control, in cases where the perpetrators are nonwhite, or LGBTQ, or immigrants, or simply coping with poverty, then their victim status is enhanced, and whatever crimes they may be accused of are excused as a desperate response to experiencing a lifetime of discrimination and hatred.

As bestselling author and Compassionism leader Ibram X. Kendi put it, "One either believes problems are rooted in groups of people, as a racist, or locates the roots of problems in power and policies, as an antiracist." It's not criminals versus victims. It's criminals and victims versus the system, and the system is the villain. Looking at it any other way is racist.

To atone for discrimination, systemic racism, police brutality, capitalist oppression, white privilege, and, oh why not, let's try to list them all:[3] institutional racism, structural racism, colorism, token-

ism, colonialism, sexism, ableism, ageism, classism, heterosexism/
homophobia, transphobia, xenophobia, Islamophobia, atheophobia,
and fatphobia—Gascón has vowed to "fundamentally transform our
criminal justice system." And wherever he has gone, that's exactly
what he has done.

For eight long years in San Francisco, from January 2011 through
most of 2019, and then once he assumed office as the forty-third
district attorney of Los Angeles County in December 2020, George
Gascón turned law enforcement and criminal prosecution upside
down, earning the enmity of police professionals as well as the prosecutors who have to work under him. Within minutes of taking
office in Los Angeles, he issued "special directives" that epitomize
what we might call "applied Compassionism."

Two of the highlights of Gascón's reign were the implementation
of "pretrial release" and the elimination of cash bail. According to
Gascón, cash bail creates a "two-tiered system of justice" that causes
"unnecessary incarceration" that will, as he puts it, "harm individuals, families and communities."[4] Unfortunately, this compassionist
approach puts criminals back on the street to commit more crimes,
whereas a genuinely compassionate approach might hold those criminals accountable, which would also better attend to the safety of those
individuals, families, and communities whom they preyed on.

Earlier we cited the definition of narcissistic compassion as a disorder where people reserve their empathy for the underdog while
exhibiting no empathy for hardworking people who muster the self-
discipline to be accountable and responsible. George Gascón is an
embodiment of narcissistic compassion. Criminals are "underdogs,"
misunderstood, disadvantaged, oppressed. Hardworking people with
stable, responsible lives, with jobs, homes, businesses, and families
they support, are privileged and entitled. Gascón turned these theo-
ries into practice on the streets of LA, with deadly consequences. The
laundry list of directives he issued was a recipe for dystopia.[5]

Along with pretrial release and the elimination of cash bail, Gascón decreed that more than a dozen misdemeanor crimes, including drug possession, prostitution, and resisting arrest, "shall be declined or dismissed before arraignment and without conditions," unless certain exceptions or other factors exist. Moreover, Gascón's office was directed to dismiss misdemeanor cases for crimes not included on his list if the charges fell "within the spirit" of his directive. Instead of trying and convicting these criminals, they were put on "diversion" programs. Effectively this means they are released on probation. Where they frequently reoffend.

In April 2020, to cite a particularly egregious example, according to the *Los Angeles Times*, Eric Medina was arrested four times for grand theft auto in the span of less than a month.[6] His escapades began early in the month, when he stole a van and was arrested and released. Within days, he was arrested for stealing a light truck. Released again, and again within days, he stole another truck, and for that, too, he was released without bail. Finally, only a few weeks after his first arrest, he stole another car. This is Gascón's version of compassionate California. Even repeat offenders walk.

For the people victimized by criminals who know that even if they are arrested, they will be swiftly released, it can be an extremely frustrating experience. Robert Powell, a plumber who lives and works in Los Angeles County, knows how this feels.[7] On March 28, 2024, his van was broken into and $30,000 worth of tools were stolen. Home surveillance cameras he had installed showed the criminals breaking into the van, hot-wiring it, and driving it away.

By April 5 a suspect had been arrested, booked, and immediately released. The police explained to Powell that "the state of California considers it a victimless crime."

George Gascón, who survived a recall attempt by Los Angeles voters fed up with his performance, lost his seat in the regularly scheduled election in November 2024. But even without Gascón, Compassionism toward criminals and indifference toward the victims of crimes remain the norm in California. And Compassionism, counterproductive and pathological, manifests itself in other ways in the Golden State. Gascón may have been an egregious practitioner of Compassionism, but he was just one instrument of what has become a dark and ubiquitous ideology. He was a symptom of something much bigger than himself.

In California, compassion has devolved into demented levels of performative "do-gooding" where no one can ever be held accountable for their behavior. This is realized in the failure of authorities to get homeless people into shelters, compel treatment for homeless addicts, and safely institutionalize the mentally ill. It is demonstrated in the epidemic of retail theft, where security guards are not even permitted to intervene. This is pathological altruism. It dominates public policy in California and the result is complete dysfunction. California's cities are overrun with criminals and homeless encampments because normal moral codes have been turned upside down: responsible behavior is penalized, while doing the wrong thing is incentivized.

Activist, compassionist district attorneys in California are exemplified by Chesa Boudin and George Gascón, whose consecutive tenures in San Francisco presided over that city, giving up entire neighborhoods to ungovernable chaos. As we have just seen, Gascón moved on to wreak the same havoc in Los Angeles County. But these men were joined by other radicals. Across the bay from San Francisco, Alameda County descended deeper into chaos under the compassionist District Attorney Pamela Price.[8] As reported by Capital Research, "In her first month in office, Price re-opened eight murder cases against Alameda county police officers, while offering a man charged with murdering three people in a shopping mall (by definition a mass shooting) an unusually soft plea deal, reducing the charges to one count of voluntary homicide and personal use of a gun. Price reportedly defended the decision by saying the killer 'was just 18 then and is very sorry for his behavior.'"[9]

Pamela Price's jurisdiction included Oakland, a great port city of 440,000 that is reeling under an onslaught of crime and homelessness.

It got so bad that in February 2024 CNN reported, "Rising crime risks turning Oakland into a ghost town."[10] The network claimed violent crime and felonies had fallen in 2023 in most major American cities, but that in Oakland, robberies were up 38 percent, and car theft was up 44 percent. These statistics, while indicating obvious trends, don't fully capture just how bad life has gotten on the streets of the city. In September 2023, business owners in Oakland went on strike for a day.[11]

The participating merchants said they were losing customers because of constant carjackings, car theft, robberies, and assaults. They said their insurance companies were refusing to renew their policies because the risk had become unacceptable. As Jennifer Tran, the president of the Oakland Vietnamese Chamber of Commerce, said, "Without basic safety, there is no business. Without basic safety, there is no community. Without safety, there is no city." And to this, what did Price have to say? "We have to defund police, defund prosecutors, and divest from prisons."[12]

Price lost a recall election in November 2024, but California's crime wave isn't merely the product of prosecutors who won't prosecute and law enforcement officers who are prohibited from engaging in law enforcement. Responsibility for criminality is shared by California's K–12 public education system, which remains in the grip of compassionists who have systematically stripped away accountability for teachers and firm expectations for students.

The inability to terminate bad teachers has been festering in California for a long time. The title of an article in the *Los Angeles Times* from 2014 says it all: "Firing Tenured Teachers Can Be a Costly and Tortuous Task."[13]

The *Times* investigated teachers who successfully contested their terminations and described the cases of some of the teachers whom Los Angeles Unified School District (LAUSD) had to keep in the classroom: The *Times* investigation cited several examples, including a high school teacher who kept pornography, marijuana, and cocaine stashed at school. A middle school teacher who allegedly had sex with another teacher on school property. A special education teacher who didn't report evidence of child abuse, yelled at and insulted her students, and didn't supervise her class. For each of these contested cases, and to no avail, the district had to pay hundreds of thousands of dollars in legal fees.

This is typical Compassionism. Misplaced, pathological compassion for the offending teacher, with almost cavalier indifference to the student victims. Everywhere you look, stories multiply. A broken public education system run by compassionists.

The LAUSD, with nearly 25,000 teachers and 563,000 students, is the largest K–12 school district in California.[14] Teachers in California are granted tenure after just sixteen months, effectively. The process to fire a bad teacher is time-consuming and confusing, and can take years. It requires extensive investigation, negotiations with the union, administrative appeals, court challenges, and endless rehearings. Most of the time, principals and administrators simply don't bother. The *Times* investigation found that in 80 percent of the dismissals that were upheld, classroom performance was not a factor. This is incredible. If you completely fail your students, if you don't teach them anything, you will keep your job. In order to get fired, you have to commit egregious crimes, and the evidence of your misbehavior has to be beyond any reasonable doubt. And even then, you may keep your job.

Larry Sand, a retired Los Angeles teacher who now advocates for students, has collected numerous examples of teacher misconduct.[15] He describes a physical education teacher he knew of at an inner-city school who would run out to his car, parked on campus, and replenish his alcoholic buzz between classes. That teacher was never terminated by the administration for this behavior, which went on for years.

There are two ways LAUSD, and other California school districts hamstrung by the labyrinthine firing process, manage to remove bad teachers from the classroom. The first, a method that has been increasingly employed as the obstacles to simple termination become increasingly difficult, is to just send them to a "reassignment center." These various administrative offices have been dubbed "rubber rooms."[16] These are the places where teachers accused of everything from drug abuse to sexual harassment while away their days, safely distant from students, still collecting pay and benefits. Some of them sit in these rooms for five years or more. As long as they show up, they get paid. They don't have to do anything.

If rubber rooms are where the most problematic teachers are warehoused, there's another path for the majority of troublesome teachers. Send them to another school. In a scheme reminiscent of how for years some Catholic dioceses would transfer priests accused of pedophilia into another parish instead of getting them completely away from children, what has happened in LAUSD and other public school districts is that teachers whom parents or administrators have deemed cannot stay in one school any longer are simply transferred to another school.

From student advocate Larry Sand, here is a stunning example of how merely transferring problem teachers would multiply the injuries to students:

> One day, a middle-school teacher allegedly touched a female student inappropriately. There were witnesses, but the student involved would not press charges so they put him into the district office for a while—the so-called "rubber room" or "teacher jail." Since firing him was not a viable option, the powers-that-be decided to transfer him to another school, where he was accused of fondling another student. So he was sent back to the district office, where he whittled away his paid vacation ogling porn. Busted, he was transferred to yet another school, where he got caught sharing his smut with some of his female students. He was then returned to the district office, where the last I heard, he was waiting for his next assignment, courtesy of his union lawyer.[17]

The closest anyone has come in compassionist California to holding bad teachers accountable for bad performance and bad behavior came and went over a decade ago in the *Vergara* case.[18] Initially filed in California state courts in 2012, the plaintiffs were nine public school students. The lawsuit alleged that California laws, run through the state legislature by teachers union lobbyists, violated the state constitution. In particular, the plaintiffs challenged the rules governing tenure, layoffs, and dismissal. The crux of their case was that these laws had a disparate impact on low-income and minority students because they were more likely to be assigned a bad teacher.

Initially, the results in court were encouraging. Attorneys for the plaintiffs argued that, under current law, teachers were granted tenure after only one full year of classroom observation, not nearly enough time to identify and remove from the profession those teachers who didn't have the necessary skills to teach effectively. They argued that "first in, first out" layoff rules meant that when school districts had to reduce teacher head counts, extremely talented younger teachers would be let go in order to preserve the jobs of older teachers, even those who were clearly underperformers. The plaintiffs also argued, accurately, that it was nearly impossible to fire negligent teachers.

The plaintiffs' closing arguments were articulated by lead attorney Marcellus McRae in a fifty-six-minute, mesmerizing performance in March 2014.[19] Often citing testimony and data that were presented by the *defendant*'s expert witnesses, McRae argued that because districts could not weed out bad teachers, and instead had consistently resorted to transferring them to lower-performing schools, the statutes governing tenure, layoff, and dismissal policies were unconstitutional.

The trial court agreed. In June 2014, the court ruled that the challenged statutes violated the equal protection clause of the California Constitution. In the statement from the bench, the court even said these laws "produced disparities that shock the conscience." If only that were the end of this story. But Compassionism is a deep, dirty river. Before the ink was dry, California governor Jerry Brown appealed the ruling, sending the case to an appellate court.[20] In April 2016, the trial court's ruling was overturned. The three-judge panel found that the plaintiffs had "failed to show that the statutes themselves make any certain group of students more likely to be taught by ineffective teachers than any other group of students."

One might argue this is circular reasoning. It is true that the statutes themselves do not explicitly state that school districts are required to transfer their bad teachers to bad schools in low-income neighborhoods. But as was proven beyond a doubt in the case, that is exactly what has been happening, and continues to happen. And if these laws had been overturned, that would not happen, and school districts would have been given new tools with which to retain good teachers and terminate bad ones. Nonetheless, in a split decision, the California Supreme Court refused to review the appellate court's decision.[21] *Vergara* died.

What the compassionists running California's public schools will not acknowledge, along with the union leaders who control them, is that nothing matters more in a student's development than the quality of the teacher. Not money. Not new buildings. Not creative new curricula. If the teacher is good at their job, the students learn. If the teacher is not good at their job, no amount of accoutrements will make a bit of difference. But we must protect the teacher at all costs, say the compassionists, and that is exactly what they're doing to this day.[22]

If Compassionism for teachers is destroying public education in California, that's only half the problem. Compassionism is also destroying the students. True compassion comes with obligations and requires tough decisions. This means that when students disrupt a classroom, they have to be removed from it. If these consequences don't exist, there is no deterrent to disruptive behavior, and it can snowball into a situation where classrooms, and even entire schools, become ungovernable. A small minority of disruptive students start problems and get away with it, which encourages a sizable additional minority of students who would otherwise behave to join in the fun. Before you know it, even the students who want to learn are deprived of that opportunity. And this, thanks to Compassionism, is where we are today in countless California schools.

A recent example of how bad it's getting in California's unmanageable schools—or, more precisely, to what extremes Compassionism is taking them—is Senate Bill 274, signed by Governor Newsom in October 2023. As reported in the *California Globe*, and quoting Nancy Skinner, the Berkeley Democrat who authored the bill, SB 274 "extends the ban on suspending a student on the basis of having disrupted school activities or otherwise willfully defied the valid authority of supervisors, teachers, administrators, school officials, or other school personnel."[23]

Instead of suspension, much less expulsion, Skinner prefers "restorative justice" measures, and cites the Oakland Unified School District (OUSD) as an example of this policy. Oakland Unified School District? That Oakland? The one collapsing into crime and chaos? Where roughly one of every thirty Oakland residents had a car stolen last year?[24] Brilliant! Let's do what they do.

Oakland Unified School District is a pioneer in restorative justice, and the concept sounds good. Compassionist rhetoric and compassionist concepts typically do sound pretty good. It's reality that tends to intrude, however, even when the conceptual framework survives first impressions. On the website of the Oakland Public Education Fund, dedicated to raising money for Oakland public schools, restorative justice's "school wide model" is defined in three tiers.[25] One, Relate, where the restorative justice facilitator "trains and coaches teachers and students on restorative practices for community building." Two, Repair, where the facilitator "provides restorative conversations." And three, Restore, where the "facilitator conducts re-entry circles and individualized circles of support."

This all sounds great. "Re-entry circles." "Individualized circles of support." On a website filled with photographs of earnest elementary school students posing companionably together in pristine classrooms, paragraphs like this inspire visitors:

> The OUSD Restorative Justice (RJ) initiative is dedicated to transforming OUSD into a healthier community that is rooted in racial and gender equity. By working in partnership with all members of the community we intentionally build meaningful relationships, repair harm, and welcome new and returning members. In OUSD, Restorative Justice is a set of principles and practices inspired by indigenous values used to build community, respond to harm/conflict and provide individual circles of support for students.[26]

"Racial and gender equity." "Partnership." "Members of the community." "Meaningful relationships." "Repair harm." "Indigenous values." "Circles of support." The jargon and platitudes represent a philosophy of restorative justice that isn't inherently flawed. The problem is the compassionist extreme to which it's being taken. At some point, some students have to be held accountable for their behavior. Some may need to be removed from the campus. In a previous era, a student who was expelled would end up in a reform school, where they would be subjected to strict discipline. In some cases that was exactly what those students needed. They didn't need to sit in a "circle of support" with a "facilitator" who they knew wasn't going to do a thing to stop them from misbehaving again. And here is where Compassionism has just leapt to a statewide new extreme: if a student displays willful defiance, you cannot suspend them.

When bad behavior gets a slap on the wrist, it encourages more bad behavior from everyone. Even the good kids lose faith in the institutions that serve them.

According to the *Economic Mobility Catalog*, published by Results America, a nonprofit dedicated to, among other things, "evidence based strategies" to advance economic mobility, willful defiance is "a notoriously vague category of disciplinary incident."[27] Fair enough. So what shall we call it when a student is willfully defiant? And what shall we do when a student is utterly indifferent to anything that anyone says to them, and won't change their disruptive behavior? Restorative justice in California's public schools, without necessary balance in the form of the ability to suspend or expel defiant students, is a recipe for anarchy. Sometimes the only way to instill respect for authority is to exercise authority. Restorative justice that isn't ultimately backed up with tough consequences for the tough cases is the carrot without the stick. Perhaps for the majority of students, restorative justice is a useful new approach. For those on whom it leaves no impression, however, it is a green light to unleash chaos in the classroom as a student, graduating to crime and violence as an adult. The streets of Oakland are proof of this consequence. Compassionism run amok, California-style.

The disease of Compassionism has overwhelmed California's elites to the point where they have, as previously noted, volunteered the state's beleaguered taxpayers into footing the bill for undocumented immigrants to receive state-funded food supplements, state-funded health care, and access to free public education. That's not all. In the 2024 session a bill was approved by the state legislature that would help undocumented immigrants to get access to state assistance to buy homes.[28] In a state where the vast majority of working people cannot afford to buy a home, their tax money would be handed to illegal immigrants so they can. Imagine how offensive that is to a hardworking family of legally documented Mexican immigrants doing everything in their power, year after year after year, to save for their own California Dream: a nice house, with a yard to enjoy the sunshine, in a safe neighborhood. That California Dream had already been snatched away by Democrat policies that have inflated the typical house price to over $900,000, out of reach for all but 15 percent of California households. And now to add insult to injury, the government wants to give free down payment assistance to illegal immigrants who just wandered across the Democrats' open border? This is pure Compassionism in action: The far-left extremists who pushed this grotesque policy probably think they're being compassionate. In reality they are cruel and heartless, throwing working-class Californians' struggles back in their faces as they sneer: "Sorry, you're not our priority."

Further evidence of this mentality is found in Senate Bill 960, signed by Governor Newsom in September 2020, authored by (who else?) good old Nancy Skinner from Berkeley.[29] Taking effect in January 2024, SB 960 permits law enforcement to hire noncitizens as police and correctional officers. Compliant media immediately took pains to debunk claims that "illegal immigrants" could become police officers, stressing that the law only opened the doors to noncitizens with valid work permits.[30] So what could possibly go wrong?

As it turns out, a lot. A law like SB 960 leaves police and correctional organizations more vulnerable to infiltration by members of foreign criminal networks, or worse. It is far more difficult to perform background checks on people who have spent most of their lives living outside the United States, or on people who still have most of their family and friends living outside the United States. For example, while an applicant may not even be a member of a criminal gang, they may be under pressure from a gang threatening them or one of their family members here or abroad.

This isn't hypothetical. California's law enforcement, correctional institutions, and customs officials are already infiltrated by foreign criminal gangs. In 2022 the *Los Angeles Times* reported on "the Mexican mafia's money-making operation inside L.A. County jails." According to the article, gang members were able to successfully corrupt a sheriff's deputy to assist with smuggling heroin and methamphetamine into the jail.[31] In another case, a U.S. customs official was paid by drug smugglers to wave through truckloads of marijuana and illegal immigrants.[32] In April 2024, a correctional deputy in Southern California was arrested for transporting an enormous cargo of fentanyl pills, and prosecutors allege he was working for "the cartel once led by the drug lord known as 'El Chapo.'"[33]

Nobody knows the extent to which cartels and other malevolent foreign actors have infiltrated California's law enforcement agencies, but their growing wealth and reputation for ruthlessness suggests they have probably managed to bribe or intimidate far more members of law enforcement than we've caught so far. As their power grows, these attempts will escalate. The three huge counties that occupy most of the northwest corner of California—Humboldt, Trinity, and Mendocino—are places of spectacular beauty, hosting vast redwood forests and rugged mountain ranges. Today these pristine regions are largely off-limits to the casual visitor, much less an aspiring property owner. They've been dubbed California's "Emerald Triangle," an allusion not only to the endless evergreen forests that carpet their mountains and canyons, but to the Golden Triangle in Southeast Asia, a remote region that is the heroin production capital of the world.[34]

In this increasingly lawless region, outgunned sheriffs refer to "blood cannabis," which in another allusion calls to mind the "blood diamonds" coming out of lawless regions of Africa. Here in California, as the illegal marijuana trade spills into neighboring Shasta and Siskiyou Counties, sheriffs contend with gangs from Mexico, China, and Laos. From a 2023 report published in *USA Today*, "Workers are lured to the Emerald Triangle by an image of the past—one of peaceful hippies who established a cannabis community decades ago, but who are now known as the few remaining legacy farmers. Instead, workers are far more likely to be greeted by aggressive guard dogs, an elaborate security system, potent pesticides, a towering perimeter fence and an arsenal of weapons."[35]

People tricked into working for these operations are often held against their will and threatened, beaten, or even killed if they try to leave. The women are sexually abused. In an ironic twist, many who do manage to escape from these gangs have to flee to Mexico to elude recapture.

In a state that was run by serious leaders, sheriffs would team up with the feds to go up there and root out every one of these gangs in massive shows of force until the problem was permanently solved. But that would not be compassionist. A court case resolved in 2021 in Siskiyou County, immediately west of coastal Humboldt County, is an example of what is happening instead. Starting around 2015, the county became host to thousands of Hmong farmers, immigrants from Laos. They were attracted by cheap land and the legalization of marijuana, and began planting the lucrative weed on thousands of small parcels. Unsurprisingly, the *Los Angeles Times* ran a sympathetic feature on the migration, "Hmong Pot Growers in Siskiyou County Seeking Identity."[36]

But in the meantime, what by 2021 was estimated to be six thousand illegal greenhouses were creating a demand for water that was causing local wells to dry up, depriving long-established farmers and ranchers of water for their crops and livestock.[37] These illegal greenhouses were so numerous and so portable that it was virtually impossible to regulate them. So the county passed ordinances that prohibited selling well water without a permit and banned water trucks on roads servicing the areas with marijuana greenhouses.[38] Then, in came the compassionists.

With the help of the American Civil Liberties Union, the Hmong pot farmers filed a lawsuit alleging "law enforcement racism." In September 2021, a federal judge ruled that "Northern California county officials can't stop trucks from delivering water to Hmong farmers who are illegally growing marijuana, saying the practice raises serious questions about racial discrimination."[39] The ruling was upheld, and to this day, as these illegal grows multiply, farmers and ranchers confront a dwindling supply of groundwater with no recourse. In October 2023 Siskiyou County sheriff Jeremiah LaRue, in a California Insider interview, described how cartels have taken over Northern California's rural counties.[40] There is no end in sight.

In California's Central Valley, when I recently asked a sheriff what his top priority was, he replied, "Theft of farm equipment." I thought he meant small items like shovels. "No, it's tractors and backhoes." He went on to explain the new dynamic. The Mexican drug cartels, entrepreneurial multinational businesses that they are, have expanded into the avocado market in Mexico. So they need farm equipment. Lots of it. According to this sheriff, the cartels send large trucks up the Central Valley, pack them with stolen farm equipment, and take it all back to Mexico. "Why aren't they stopped at the border?" I asked. "It's not exactly like taking a baggie of fentanyl across." "Because they control the border," the sheriff replied.

On tribal lands and other rural expanses throughout California's far north, to the streets of San Francisco, to gangs in every corner of the state, foreign criminal organizations are extending their control.[41] California's law enforcement agencies don't need to start hiring foreigners to wear badges and carry guns; they need a state government that will give them the laws and the resources to take back our territory from the armies of foreign criminals who are terrorizing our citizens, stealing our property, and taking over our territory.

Compassion for criminals instead of victims. Compassion for negligent—or worse—teachers instead of students. Compassion for incorrigible and violent students instead of diligent and self-disciplined ones. Compassion for undocumented foreign migrants instead of hardworking citizens, and compassion for drug traffickers instead of the ranchers and farmers they are terrorizing and displacing. These are the faces of Compassionism, not compassion, and they define policy in California today. The state legislature has the ability to correct these failed policies, except for the sad fact that this perverse and out-of-touch pathology of Compassionism now afflicts a supermajority of the legislators. Even the most egregious extremes of Compassionism manage to command a majority, as the example of Senate Bill 1414 demonstrates.

One of California's ten Republican state senators (out of forty members in the state senate) is Shannon Grove, representing rural

Kern County.[42] This is one of the last Republican strongholds in California. It is a gigantic expanse of irrigated farmland dotted with oil wells, taking up over eight thousand square miles. But things haven't been going well. Its agricultural industry depends on the whims of the California State Water Board, and its oil industry depends on the whims of the California Department of Conservation's Geologic Energy Management Division. In both cases, Kern County has been under relentless assault for years. To, ostensibly, save fish, farmers are having their water allocations cut and their fields go fallow. To ostensibly save the climate, oil producers are having drilling permits denied and existing wells are being capped. Because both of the primary drivers of its economy are slowly getting squeezed to death by Democrats in Sacramento, voters in Kern County elect Republicans.

Thank goodness. Thanks to the Kamala Harris crime downgrades, astonishingly, for years it was not considered a felony in California to solicit, agree to engage in, or actually engage in any form of commercial sex with a minor. In 2024 Senator Grove introduced SB 1414, which would have made it a felony. That seems reasonable enough. The only real question ought to be why this conduct was only a misdemeanor. Grove's bill was so unimpeachably justified that she convinced two Democrats to cosponsor the bipartisan bill. That's when the compassionist shenanigans started.

If Senator Grove represents the dwindling Republican minority in the legislature, Senator Nancy Skinner (yes, her again!) is a typical member of the Democrat supermajority.[43] Skinner's Senate district spans the eastern shore of the San Francisco Bay, with Marin County across the water from its northern half, and the city of San Francisco across the water from its southern half.[44] The district includes almost all of Oakland, with ultraliberal Berkeley in the center. Skinner is a political veteran, having served eight years as a member of the Berkeley City Council. She is also an avid environmentalist, having founded the organization Cities for Climate Protection and other like-minded groups. To round out her progressive credentials, Skinner's compassionist proclivities extend to sex offenders.

On a Democrat-controlled committee, Skinner engineered what amounted to a hostile takeover of SB 1414, so by the time the bill made it out of committee for a floor vote, it included amendments that watered it down to the point of irrelevancy. Here is Compassionism in action:

Instead of making it a felony to pay a teen for sex, the revised bill left it up to the discretion of the prosecutor to charge the offender with a felony or a misdemeanor. The only conditions under which a felony charge could still be mandated was if the child being purchased is fifteen years old or younger, *and* it's the buyer's second offense purchasing a child under sixteen, *and* the buyer is more than ten years older than the child. That's a lot of hoops. Under the revised SB 1414, if you're a twenty-four-year-old who pays a fourteen-year-old for sex, and it's the first time you've been caught, depending on the prosecutor, you could receive what amounts to a slap on the wrist. Where compassionist district attorneys run the county's prosecutors, count on misdemeanors to come down on these sex criminals, not felonies. That's the way to hold sex offenders accountable, according to California's compassionist legislators.

Grove should be grateful that at least her bill passed this time. A previous and related bill that she introduced, which would have made sex trafficking a "serious and violent crime," with jail time attached, was initially blocked by Democrats. She had to bring it back a second year, when it was blocked again—and only finally approved after the intervention of Gavin Newsom, who could sense a looming PR disaster. When you've become a party that explicitly opposes making sex trafficking a crime for which perpetrators can be incarcerated; when you've become a party that actively amends a bill on selling a child for sex to make sure it's okay if they are sixteen, or if there is "only" a ten-year age gap—you've officially lost the plot.

Skinner justified her maneuvering with the following statement for the record: "Selling sex has been within human cultures for millennia. It is a very difficult area of law to get into." One might say that all aspects of law enforcement are "very difficult areas to get into." Murder, rape, aggravated assault, and home invasion are crimes that continue to occur, despite all attempts to curb them. And they've been "within human cultures for millennia." But when we design our laws, the only compassion worth incorporating is the one that recognizes that criminals are deterred if they believe there is a high probability they will be caught and held accountable, and that victims deserve justice. Otherwise it is not compassion but Compassionism: posturing, narcissistic, counterproductive, out of touch with reality.

Compassionism defines how California's legislature passes laws, how its agencies write the rules to implement the laws, and how the courts interpret the laws. It touches everything, including how we prosecute criminals and deal with the homeless, how we hold teachers accountable and teach our children and youth, how we cope with the relentless growth in the power of organized crime. In every case, it is causing more harm than good. Compassionism, which may sound good but never does any good, is the opposite of genuine compassion, which can often sound tough and cruel but is grounded in reality and hence far more likely to be effective. Someday we may hope that California's leaders are cured of Compassionism. Results are what matters, not rhetoric.

CHAPTER 9

CRONYISM

In August 2024, city and state leaders gathered in Los Angeles to celebrate the grand opening of Weingart Tower 1, the largest supportive housing project in the city's history.[1] Distinguished leaders present included Los Angeles mayor Karen Bass; Congresswoman Maxine Waters; the governor's senior advisor on homelessness, Hafsa Kaka; California Department of Housing and Community Development (HCD) director Gustavo Velasquez; and many others.

Constructed at a cost of $165 million, this twelve-story building has 228 studio apartments and 47 one-bedroom apartments that will be made available to the homeless people who live in the neighborhood.[2] As announced on the California HCD website, "Each unit is completely furnished and includes a television, central heating and air, and a fully equipped kitchen. The tower also provides on-site supportive services, a gym, an art room, a soundproof music room, a library, four dog runs, a ground floor cafeteria, and more."[3]

As reported in the *Los Angeles Daily News*, Kevin Murray, CEO of the Weingart Center Association, the nonprofit organization that is managing the project, said, "This is not just a building. This is about people, about giving people dignity and respect." He went on to say that "people who have been living on the streets deserve a place they're proud to call home, and that having a gym where people can work on their physical therapy, or a music or art room for art therapy, are important to helping residents heal physically, mentally, or emotionally."[4]

The same report quoted Mayor Karen Bass, who agreed with

Murray, citing the need to provide outlets like art and music to help residents heal from traumas they have experienced while living on the streets. At the opening ceremony, Jim Andersen, chief development officer of the project's development company, Chelsea Investment Corporation, said, "The whole concept of this building is to serve the whole individual, not just give them a bed and a sink and a shower, but a place to grow and live and heal and express themselves and really rejoin and reenter active life. It's a place to grow, live, and heal."[5]

One of the tower's first residents, Amya Backa, told KABC-TV of her experience moving from the streets into a new apartment. "When I was homeless it was like a little dark hole. I went from being in that hole to just coming out, like, it's a lot of love and support out here. . . . I'm so speechless right now."[6]

Weingart Tower 1 is phase one of a two-phase project that, as the developers explain, "is providing hope, options, and wrap-around services to help the city's unhoused break the cycle of homelessness." Construction started in September 2021, and at that time, Los Angeles mayor Eric Garcetti said, "This development is a clear marker of how far we've come in our mission to deliver the high-quality, permanent supportive units that unhoused Ange-lenos urgently need and deserve, and is an extraordinary example of the type of project that will make real progress in this crisis."[7]

These ambitious apartment construction projects, products of public-private partnerships, are intended to help California's "un-housed" get off the streets and reclaim their lives. If they are given a safe, clean environment, they can experience the stability that will eliminate the need for them to steal and eliminate the anxiety that compelled them to turn to substance abuse. This is the essence of the "Housing First" policy to address homelessness in California. It is designed to save the unhoused and revitalize neighborhoods.

According to the Housing First approach, the most important thing is to get an unhoused person into a home. If we just build enough "permanent supportive housing" for the unhoused, our streets will be safe again. And if these housing units are built in upscale neighborhoods on expensive real estate, the quality of these affluent neighborhoods will have a positive influence on the behavior of the newly housed. And in any case it is "exclusionary" to not include in affluent neighborhoods a few buildings devoted to free housing for the unhoused.

Projects such as the Weingart Towers and other supportive housing projects are examples of public-private partnerships, fulfilled through legislative mandates, executive orders, taxes, bonds, and incentives, that accomplish important shared objectives, but they aren't the only ones.

Proponents believe we will also benefit economically and ecologically if we use a similar mix of government and private sector coordinated efforts to install "renewables" to replace our existing sources of electricity, which are expensive and unsustainable. Transforming our energy supply to renewables will save the planet; if we don't make this transition to clean energy, we are not doing our part to combat climate change. But government can't do this alone. It has to be in partnership with the private sector. While electricity rates may rise in the short run, if we just keep building more wind and solar farms, then costs will eventually drop.

That's the dream. If we all do our part, a healthy planet with housing for everyone can become a reality.

•••

But these dreams become nightmares. The partnerships may be delivering for the private companies, but certainly not for the public. Electricity is expensive and unreliable. And there are more homeless people than ever before. Constructing Weingart Tower 1A, paid for largely through government subsidies and government tax incentives for private investors, cost $600,000 per unit. At that cost, it would take $45 billion to make supportive housing available to every one of the 75,000 unhoused individuals in Los Angeles County.[8]

The impact of these policies has been devastating to the hard-working residents of Los Angeles, who must endure higher prices at the same time as they have to cope with the degradation of their neighborhoods.

After working several years in New York City, Soledad Ursua moved back to her native state of California and invested her life savings in a triplex in the Venice Beach section of Los Angeles. With two units available for renters, she lived in the ground-floor unit and began building a life in LA. But not so fast.

Venice, a picturesque coastal enclave located just north of Los Angeles International Airport, has long been a haven for artists and hippies, and for decades its famed boardwalk along the beach has been a magnet for skaters, surfers, and tourists from all over the world. The canals for which Venice is named, lined with quaint homes and built over a century ago, have been mostly filled in today, but six of them still survive in a beautiful neighborhood a few blocks from the beach.

This idyllic community, a bohemian island in the middle of a giant city, is what attracted Ursua to the neighborhood. But the dream quickly devolved into a nightmare. Thanks to government policies that have had the precise opposite of their intended effect, Venice Beach has been overrun with homeless encampments. Thousands of vagrants, most of them drug and alcohol abusers, and many of them predators and thieves, have descended on the place. And why not? There are no enforceable laws to remove them, and government agencies and non-profit organizations provide them with free food and other services. Venice Beach, a victim of its own allure, is now an occupied city, and there is no end in sight.

There's a reason towns like Venice Beach have become unsafe and unpleasant places to live. The presence of homeless people in Venice

Beach and elsewhere is profitable. The collection of special interests that has been dubbed the "homeless industrial complex" is exploiting and benefiting from tens of thousands of homeless people—and if the problem is ever solved, the profits will go away.

How California's policies affect the homeless, how government spends billions, and how the more billions they spend, the worse the problem gets, is an example of Cronyism at its worst. Cronyism can be defined as a political system where an exclusive and incestuous elite controls government policy and budgets on the basis of their private interests, with the impact on everyone else of secondary concern. This antidemocratic model epitomizes California, and the homeless industrial complex is a prime example. It has corrupted governance and harmed the people.

What is happening in Venice Beach, elsewhere in Los Angeles, and in most other large cities in California (including the disastrous situation in San Francisco) is that a collection of government bureaucracies, "nonprofit" corporations, unions, and for-profit real estate developers have all embraced a homeless policy that will make homelessness worse while enriching each of these coalition partners with almost unbelievable sums of taxpayers' money.

Based on the self-serving premise that homeless people cannot be treated for substance abuse and/or mental illness or trained for a job until they have a home of their own, billions are spent on "bridge housing" and "permanent supportive housing." Bridge housing, which used to be called homeless shelters, is now located on prime real estate and extremely expensive. The bridge housing project recently completed in Venice Beach cost $8.6 million to house 154 adults and youth. By their own admission, that's $56,000 per bed.[9]

This is a ridiculous cost. Why is a shelter being constructed three blocks from the California coast on some of the most expensive real estate on earth? Why is the shelter being built from the ground up, instead of being located in an existing building in a less costly part of town and away from residential neighborhoods? The clincher? This

$8.6 million structure isn't even a permanent building. It's a huge, temporary tent, set to be dismantled within a few years.

"They call this a 'low barrier shelter,'" said Ursua, who lives less than a quarter mile away. "This means that no sobriety is required for admittance, there is no curfew, and there are no background checks. If you are a convicted criminal, you are only asked to 'self identify' when you check in. There is also a 'weapons amnesty box' for visitors to give up their weapons, but it's the responsibility of the person carrying a weapon to decide if they want to relinquish it. People are afraid to go out at night."

If shelters at $56,000 per bed are ludicrously costly and wasting billions of dollars, far worse is the "permanent supportive housing," which is wasting tens of billions of dollars. Back in 2016, Los Angeles voters approved the issuance of $1.2 billion in bonds to create "thousands" of units of permanent supportive housing. Six years later, only twelve hundred apartment units had been built, and costs were skyrocketing. A 2016 city audit uncovered one project where the costs had risen to $837,000 per unit.[10] These are studio and one-bedroom apartments.

This cost, staggering though it may be, is far from an isolated case. In Venice, the city has been trying for several years to build permanent supportive housing on a three-acre site that currently serves as public parking and occasionally hosts craft fairs and farmers markets. Located just one block from the beach, surrounded by one- and two-story residences, this massive structure is planned to be up to five stories in height, all to create 140 apartment units. Half of them will be offered to "artists" on low incomes and the other half will be "permanent supportive housing" for homeless people.

And the cost?

Despite numerous California Public Records Act requests to the city of Los Angeles, the official estimate remains undisclosed. But the "Monster on the Median" will almost certainly be in the $750,000-per-unit range, for several reasons. There is a high water table close to the beach. That, plus concerns about sea level rise affecting a structure so close to the shore, will compel extra work on the foundation. Also, the structure will be built to wrap 360 degrees around a parking garage in the center. This parking garage, unlikely to offer enough spaces to accommodate residents and visitors to the beach, will use an elevator— they call it "automated lift parking"—to deliver vehicles from the street level to the garage. Imagine the automobile queues on North and South Venice Boulevard as people patiently wait to be hoisted up the car elevator. But why be practical?

If that weren't enough, the structure actually will have to pass over the north end of one of Venice's scenic canals, completely covering a block of this historic amenity that is central to the identity of Venice Beach. This government-sponsored project, like so many in California, and like virtually all publicly funded projects to help the homeless in California, fails to pass a cost-benefit analysis based on any reasonable criteria. Vacant, developable land in Venice Beach lists for as much as $50 million per acre.[11] The city of Los Angeles could divest this three-acre property and realize a profit that would probably be well in excess of $100 million, and they could invest that money in cost-effective shelter space somewhere that isn't prime real estate. But if that were their strategy, they might actually solve the problem.

That wouldn't achieve the aims of Cronyism; not at all. Developers, already heavily subsidized, who build "permanent supportive housing" are exempt from normal zoning laws including height limitations, density maximums, setback requirements, parking space minimums, and even compliance with the California Environmental Quality Act. Is there even a sincere intention here to help the homeless? Or any regard for the beleaguered taxpayers who are conned into supporting these scams, much less the residents whose neighborhoods are being ruined? It's all about payoffs to the cronies.

We see it everywhere. The term *Cronyism* might normally conjure images of shady deals between individual people—the real estate developer paying off a local politician, the kind of run-of-the-mill corruption that, frankly, can be found everywhere. But in California it is not just individualistic (although there is plenty of that). It's systemic. The homeless problem only worsens because the homeless industrial complex siphons all the bond money, tens of billions to date, to build "supportive housing" at prices averaging over $500,000 per unit. The governor issues no-bid contracts to donors and cronies to supply medical equipment during Covid. The state legislature puts initiatives on the ballot to block measures that make it harder to raise taxes, while through additional initiatives and legislation demonstrating their insatiable appetite for higher taxes and more debt. Public sector unions openly boast about owning politicians, as they are the biggest campaign donors in the California Senate and Assembly, and crush any politician who doesn't approve their wage and benefit increases.

To understand the corrupt drive to squander what is now well over $30 billion of taxpayers' money in just the last twenty years to supposedly address the homeless crisis, we have to recognize what a lucrative transfer of wealth this is for the participating parties.[12] Government agencies are flush with this cash, "nonprofit" corporations collect additional billions, labor unions mandate "project labor agreements" that further inflate costs, and the lion's share goes into the pockets of politically connected real estate developers who build palaces in paradise, when simple bunks in converted vacant buildings on public land located well inland could be set up practically overnight. Accommodations for hundreds of people could be built for the cost of just one of these subsidized units of "permanent supportive housing." But this problem is not meant to be solved. That would stop the money.

One of the barriers to California's voters demanding reform, regardless of their political ideology, is the popular and carefully nurtured misconception that "nonprofits" are by their very nature not self-interested parties. Of course there are many wonderful nonprofits doing vital work in many fields. But when it comes to homelessness, the scale of the disaster they've presided over belies a charitable judgment of good intentions. At the very least, as the programs they oversee continue to make the problems worse, why aren't they willing to change the model?

Someone who runs a nonprofit that is actually trying to help homeless people in Venice told me, "There's a guy around here who is CEO of two separate homelessness nonprofits. He does that to get around the salary caps. In total he's paid over a million a year."

The model still in effect in California is housing for free, with no conditions, at a construction cost and operating cost that guarantees the supply of "permanent supportive housing" will never meet more than a fraction of the demand. Indeed, the model as it is currently derived guarantees that demand for free housing will increase even if the price of building and the pace of construction were to increase by an order of magnitude. There is a growing awareness of the problem, but no change so far in policy. With "Housing First" state law since 2016, preventing any homelessness project that receives state funding from requiring sobriety from its clients, California has effectively made it illegal to actually solve the homelessness crisis that it created.

San Jose, in the heart of the fabled Silicon Valley, is another example of a large California city that has thrown money at the homeless epidemic only to see it get worse every year. Located in what was once known as the Valley of the Heart's Delight, the verdant Santa Clara Valley at the southern end of San Francisco Bay, this region was once the largest fruit producer in the United States. Starting after World War II, the valley transformed within a few decades to become the world's technology capital. Now blessed not only with near-perfect weather, surrounded by mountains carpeted with redwood groves, and freshened with breezes off the nearby Pacific Ocean, Silicon Valley has become host to one of the greatest concentrations of wealth the world has ever seen. It is also home to perhaps the world's greatest concentration of incredibly intelligent and creative people. (Plus me.) But when it comes to helping the homeless, apparently none of this matters.

Irene Smith, a San Jose–based attorney who has been investigating the dismal performance of nonprofits dedicated to helping the homeless, released a series of reports in the first half of 2024 that provide abundant evidence as to how deep the dysfunction goes and how essentially corrupt the system has become. Smith is calling for a Nonprofit Registry to do what, at least to the blissfully uninitiated, seems like basic accountability.[13] She alleges that "no one can tell you how much is being spent or has been spent on homelessness services in San Jose." Continuing, she lists specific examples of unaccountability:

> The list of entities committing financial mismanagement is sadly long: The Feds certainly can't tell you, although they give plenty of funds. Neither the State nor the County can tell you, although there have been plenty of bonds. The Housing Department of San Jose can't tell you, even though they are the public entity directly charged with managing the funds. And non-profits who accept money from government agencies as well as individual donors and corporations can't tell you, even though they're the direct recipients of taxpayer funds.

Smith states explicitly what a growing number of critics across the state have been saying for years. Cities like San Jose are relying on outside nonprofits to deliver city services including housing and mental health, but these nonprofits are not required to respond to public record requests or subject themselves to the same audit rules that would apply to city-run services. But, as Smith puts it, "the word 'non-profit' conveys an undeserved benign glow," and "we must recognize non-profits for what they truly are: unaccountable and well-funded advocacy groups."

The *San Jose Mercury News* is a legacy newspaper with a generally left-wing editorial position, hanging on by its fingernails to solvency in the digital heartland whose inventions sealed its fate. But even this outlet has begun to publish one account after another on just how bad conditions have gotten in the housing projects built for the homeless and managed by these nonprofits. The stories are shocking.

One downtown permanent supportive housing complex, Second Street Studios, is an early example of failure. But all of the initial reports touted it as a glowing success. Opened in 2019 thanks to an $18.4 million grant from the city of San Jose, plus an annual budget of $1.5 million "to fund the critical supportive services for residents," this 135-unit building was portrayed as a triumphant step forward to address the homelessness crisis.[14] Ongoing public expense was also baked into this project in the form of a two-thirds rent subsidy to be paid by the Santa Clara County Housing Authority. Since rent for basic studio apartments in downtown San Jose starts at around $1,600 per month (good luck finding one of those), this two-thirds subsidy amounts to an additional expense of around $2 million per year.[15] That's a lot of public money, contributed either directly in the form of government grants and subsidies or indirectly in the form of tax-deductible contributions from the local tech giants. But how much good did all of this largesse deliver?

Five years later, the Second Street Studios are a disastrous and very typical example of what remains California's official strategy to combat homelessness. While still managed by a nonprofit, the building had "more than 500 police and medical calls, four preventable deaths, and more than ten fires" in one year.[16] Because one of the few accountability metrics the nonprofit operators are measured on is retention—based on the assumption that if tenants stay for a long time, that constitutes a long-term successful "rehousing"—building managers have an incentive to overlook behavior that would ordinarily be grounds for eviction. Even with this perverse incentive, in this building they issued 433 lease violations in ten months, but "tenants quickly fought back against the rules with free attorneys."[17]

When this property was finally investigated by the Santa Clara County Board of Supervisors, they uncovered "substance use and sale, human trafficking and sexually inappropriate behavior, fighting, yelling, leering at youth and staff, and weapons." The county's response? They awarded the nonprofit managing the property a $26 million "bailout."[18]

These horror stories have proliferated at a time when California's largest cities continue to fund homeless programs that are proven failures. Helping the homeless cannot possibly succeed at the necessary scale unless the model shifts to inexpensive shelters in inexpensive parts of California's counties. In all cases, behavioral violations should be criteria for immediate transfer. For example, if permanent supportive housing is to remain part of California's homeless strategy, if a tenant commits a crime or in any manner violates the terms of their residency through violence, vandalism, or disorderly conduct, including failing to remain sober, they should be moved back to a shelter. And if shelter residents violate the terms of their residency, they should be moved to a high-security one.

Operators of private shelters put conditions on entry, unlike government-funded shelters. To get admitted, the homeless person has to commit to sobriety, counseling, and job training. These programs are successful. Every professional homeless advocate operating privately funded shelters has shared the same conclusion—the majority of chronically homeless people are substance abusers, mentally ill, or both. Whether that's the cause or the effect of their homeless status is irrelevant. They need to be compelled into shelters where they can get treatment and recover their dignity. But that would stop the money train.

A few miles up Highway 101 from San Jose is San Francisco, now an international poster child for lawless chaos. But the crony network in San Francisco, as in San Jose, resists change. In 2023, facing a two-year estimated deficit of $744 million, Mayor London Breed nonetheless proposed spending an additional $692 million on the city's homeless over the next twelve months.[19] This proposal came on top of billions the city has already spent, yet the number of homeless in San Francisco is not going down. The average cost of a shelter bed in San Francisco—not an apartment in "permanent supportive housing," but a shelter bed—is reported to be $70,000 each. None of this is financially sustainable.[20] None of this is working. But are they changing the model? Are they trying anything new?

The answer to that question is yes, but not by doing what any sane observer might expect. San Francisco decided to allocate $5 million per year for a program that gives out free beer and vodka to anyone identified as suffering from an "alcohol use disorder."[21] This is modeled after the so-called safe supply strategy, the same one that informs the decision in San Francisco and other California cities to provide free needles to people addicted to drugs requiring an injection. A critic of the program, quoted by the *New York Post*, said, "Inside the lobby, they had kegs set up to taps where they were basically giving out free beer to the homeless who've been identified with [alcohol use disorder]. It's set up so people in the program just walk in and grab a beer, and then another one. All day." Continuing, he posed the obvious question: "Providing free drugs to drug addicts doesn't solve their problems. It just stretches them out. Where's the recovery in all of this?"

The fact still ignored by California's elites and their crony beneficiaries is simple: There is no recovery in any of this. Homeless people in California are not being helped. But the money keeps flowing into the pockets of politically connected developers, nonprofits, and government bureaucracies, and that's the point. Successfully treating the homeless would constitute failure for the cronies.

Confronting and reversing this long history of Cronyism, corruption, and failure was the central message of the 2024 San Francisco mayoral campaign of Daniel Lurie, a friend of mine who had previously run a nonprofit, Tipping Point, focused on tackling poverty in the Bay Area. To the surprise of many seasoned political observers, Lurie, the outsider, won a clear and decisive victory, showing that even in this city dominated for so long by the far left, people are demanding change. Let's hope Lurie can succeed in turning around one of the most iconic and beautiful cities in the world.

To be fair, the reasons Californians confront a multifaceted onslaught of lawlessness and chaos can't be traced to any single cause. Background conditions play a major role. The state has become one of the most difficult places to earn a living wage, thanks to a legislatively engineered epidemic of scarcity and high prices for every essential, including food, fuel, and housing. At the same time, the state has become one of the easiest places to be homeless—which is not to say being homeless is easy—thanks to the mildest weather in the U.S. and a lack of laws to control vagrancy, drug use, and petty theft. But it certainly doesn't help that these so-called background conditions are not mitigated, indeed are actually catalyzed thanks to a massive homeless industrial complex that won't collect billions of dollars per year anymore if the problem is ever solved.[22]

To return to San Jose, Irene Smith has suggested some concrete steps to restore accountability to the nonprofits in California that are collecting billions of dollars every year merely to make the problem worse.[23] They include the following:

> Annually report size, efficacy, and growth of nonprofit contracts with a city or county. Prevent city staff simultaneously serving on nonprofit boards that contract with the city thereby eliminating conflicts of interest. Treat nonprofits as lobbyists and make all meetings transparent so that nonprofit organizations cannot use taxpayer money to lobby city council. Require financial and governance transparency from all nonprofits that contract with a city or county. Audit the city or county's housing department annually for a cost to benefit analysis.

The destructive policies that enrich the homeless industrial complex and loot taxpayers, while actually incentivizing more people to migrate here and take to the streets, are just one example of Cronyism becoming the dominant economic framework in California. Other examples are just as egregious and wreak, if anything, even more havoc on the lives of ordinary Californians.

Another particularly virulent variant of Cronyism, California-style, involves a coalition of elite special interests who manipulate laws to create scarcity. To this end, they lobby for and secure the passage of antigrowth laws and regulations that create high prices in every significant sector of the economy. The most obvious example of this is the price of gasoline.

The average retail price of regular gas in California as of April 3, 2024, was $5.15 per gallon.[24] Californians now pay more for their gasoline than Hawaiians, which is quite an accomplishment. The state of Hawaii is a remote archipelago in the middle of the Pacific Ocean, with no in-state petroleum resources to speak of, whereas California is sitting on some of the most abundant reserves of oil and gas in the world.

Despite proven reserves of 2.3 billion barrels of oil and potentially another 10 billion barrels locked in California's so-called Monterey shale formation, California imports over 70 percent of its crude oil. Some petroleum geologists claim that if oil exploration were permitted in the Golden State, the quantity of proven reserves would be likely to triple. But through a relentless barrage of legislation, regulation, and permitting abuse, California's legislature and the activist agencies that oversee the industry are doing everything in their power to shut it down.[25] The same regulatory assault is underway with the state's natural gas industry, where despite plentiful in-state reserves, over 90 percent is imported.[26]

It's not just energy that is expensive and in short supply in California. Every essential building block of a successful economy is subjected to politically engineered scarcity. The state's water infrastructure is neglected, and instead of investing in new ways to harvest and store the roughly 200 million acre-feet of rain that hits the state even in dry years, billions are being invested in systems designed to ration urban water use while farms throughout the state are taken out of production for lack of irrigation water.[27] Freeways are neglected as billions are wasted on a high-speed rail project that, even if it is ever completed, will do virtually nothing to alleviate freeway congestion.[28]

California even has a shortage of developable land, which is absurd, since the vast majority of California's nearly 40 million people live in urbanized areas that only consume 5 percent of the state's total land area.[29] You could build homes for 10 million people, at four per household on quarter-acre lots, with an equal amount of space set aside for roads, retail centers, parks, schools, and commercial/industrial facilities, and you would increase California's urban footprint only to 6 percent. Such new "sprawling" developments would consume only 2,000 square miles, in a state that occupies 156,000 square miles.[30] But there's "no room." There's also not enough water, energy, or good roads and freeways to accommodate newcomers.

All of these points, of course, were noted in previous chapters. But here let's focus on the fact that all of it is by design, the result of cynical collusion in a crony coalition of special interests that combined to wield almost unimaginable power.

Two examples:

California's public sector unions collect and spend nearly a billion dollars per year, using a sizable percentage of that money to make or break the campaigns of every elected politician, all the way from local water boards to the governorship.[31] They want endless environmental regulations so they can grow their regulatory and enforcement bureaucracies, and to pay for it, they don't want to see public money invested in practical physical infrastructure. They're not alone.

California's public utilities, quasi-private and owned by stockholders, are held to a fixed profit by regulators. This means that the only way they can increase their earnings per share is by raising their revenue. No wonder investing in "renewables" is so favored by these utilities. With no competition and captive ratepayers, their stock price will be a lot higher when they're charging $0.50 per kilowatt-hour and passing 9 percent down to the bottom line than when they're charging $0.05 per kilowatt-hour. How convenient that the state has decreed "net zero" by 2045.[32]

Antigrowth politics can also benefit some sectors within the state's home-building industry, or at least what's left of it. As noted previously, with exorbitant fees, artificially inflated land prices, ridiculously overwrought building codes, unnecessarily costly building materials, since almost nothing can be sourced in-state, and punishing delays in acquiring permits from a byzantine array of hostile agencies, it is impossible to profitably build most types of housing in California without subsidies. But why fix that? The small builders are forced to give up and find new professions. The big builders that have opportunities to profitably build affordable market housing in less-regulated states without crawling to the government for subsidies have done so. That leaves California with a handful of politically connected megabuilders collecting billions in subsidies to build "affordable housing."[33]

Here we also see the baleful influence of private sector unions cynically exploiting environmental laws to block new housing from being built. Calculations from Jennifer Hernandez, a respected land-use attorney with decades of experience fighting for housing, suggest that over a million housing units in California that have passed through every regulatory hoop and local zoning process are nevertheless blocked by "environmental" lawsuits, most of them filed by unions to use as leverage in negotiating "project labor agreements" that include euphemisms like "prevailing wage" (three or four times market rate), "skilled and trained" (union workers only), or both. It all reminds me of sclerotic 1970s Britain, before Margaret Thatcher's union reforms.

If that were a complete list, it would be enough, but almost every special interest in California wants scarcity. "Green tech" loves it, because elevated prices for energy allow them to develop and sell every manner of "green" product, from energy management systems and electric cars to chipsets for "connected" appliances in the "internet of things." The data-gathering sector stands to gain billions in revenue by collecting and parsing behavioral data from consumers using connected appliances. In a state where energy and water were abundant, these products and services wouldn't sell. As it is, not only does the backdrop of high prices make them rational consumer choices, but just in case, the state legislature is mandating their adoption.

None of this happened by accident. It is the result of Cronyism, the opposite of healthy capitalist competition. Whenever a socialist-leaning government overregulates and subsidizes an industry, the biggest, most politically connected corporations can afford to comply and prosper, while the smaller emerging potential competitors are eliminated. The failures of society—homelessness, high prices, and failing schools—constitute success for the special interests that have created the dysfunction in order to feed off it. Wherever politics and business are blended into an exclusive insiders' game, Cronyism flourishes.

Playing out in the November 2024 election was a battle between grassroots citizens groups and businesses desperate to stop the onslaught of new taxes versus a state legislature and municipal governments that are wholly owned by the public sector unions. Precipitating this battle was a citizens' initiative that qualified for the state ballot, the Taxpayer Protection and Government Accountability Act.[34] This initiative would have restored constitutional limits on the ability of California's state and local elected officials to raise taxes, which over the years have been undermined by union-sponsored ballot initiatives, legislation, and court rulings.

In response to this dire threat to Cronyism in California, Governor Newsom's attorneys filed a case with the California Supreme Court arguing that the Taxpayer Protection Act would "hamper state and local government's ability to pay for key services provided to taxpayers, from trash collection to public safety."[35] The court, with six out of seven members appointed by Democratic governors, agreed with Newsom and, outrageously, took the Taxpayer Protection and Government Accountability Act off the ballot before the voters could have a say.

Meanwhile, because the legislature can place initiatives onto the state ballot without having to undergo the messy and expensive process of gathering signatures on a ballot petition, the Democratic supermajority swiftly came up with a pro-tax initiative, the Housing and Public Infrastructure Amendment.[36] Designed to further undermine constitutional limits on how taxes can be authorized in California, the initiative asked voters to lower the approval threshold from two-thirds to 55 percent for "housing projects and public infrastructure"—an extremely broad definition. Such is the fight against taxes in a state that already has the highest overall taxes in America. One step forward, two steps back.

As with the election of Daniel Lurie in San Francisco, however (along with the eviction of George Gascón in LA and Pamela Price in Oakland's Alameda County), and indeed the overwhelming vote in favor of Proposition 36, common sense prevailed and the voters rejected the legislature's Proposition 5. So at least some limits on endless tax increases will remain. The same pathology has been at work with every attempt to take on probably the most costly aspect of Cronyism in California: the government unions' never-ending extraction of excessive pay, pensions, and luxury health care (known as "other post-employment benefits," or OPEB) through their political corruption. The nonprofit organization Govern for California estimates that the total amount received is around $100 billion a year. Not a bad return on the unions' $1 billion investment in political bribery.

Like all of the pathologies afflicting California's elites, Cronyism is masked by a facade of virtue. The goal is more taxes in order to fund more projects and programs operated by cronies. But that isn't the message. Instead voters are reminded, in what amounts to thinly veiled threats, that everything from "trash collection to public safety" is at risk without more taxes. Governor Newsom himself has made it a priority to warn Californians about another threat: the "right wing." On his Campaign for Democracy fundraising website, the governor warns that "extremist Republicans" are "undermining the most basic tenet of our democracy, the right to vote."[37] The hypocrisy is strong. Newsom sent his attorneys to the California Supreme Court to offer implausibly thin arguments to rule against the "right to vote" on an initiative that merely seeks to restore taxpayer protections enshrined in the California Constitution by voters nearly a half century ago. Such is Cronyism when its money train is threatened.

CHAPTER 10

INCOMPETISM

On a cool, sunny day in January 2015, Governor Jerry Brown and assorted dignitaries gathered in downtown Fresno to celebrate the "groundbreaking" of the California bullet train project.[1] Participants were in high spirits as the governor and his wife, Ann Gust Brown, along with EPA administrator Gina McCarthy, High-Speed Rail Authority board of directors chair Dan Richard, Fresno mayor Ashley Swearengin, and other notables wrote their signatures on an actual steel rail that had been brought in for the cameras.

Brown spoke about the event's historical significance: "What is important is the connection that we are rooted in our forebears and we are committed and linked to our descendants. And the high-speed rail links us from the past to the future, from the south to Fresno and north; this is truly a California project bringing us together today." Agreeing with the governor was Dan Richard, who said, "This is an investment that will forever improve the way Californians commute, travel, and live. And today is also a celebration of the renewed spirit that built California."[2]

It seemed like a great idea.

California's high-speed rail was going to connect every major metropolitan area in the state with trains going 220 miles per hour. From Sacramento to San Diego, and from San Francisco to Los Angeles, a network of ultramodern track and ultramodern trains was planned that would knit the state together as never before. For the first time, commuters living in California's vast Central Valley would be able to hop on a "bullet train" and in under one hour disembark in a coastal city hundreds of miles distant to go to work.

This was an inspiring prospect. At an initial, official total project cost estimate of only $30 billion, California's high-speed rail was going to be the envy of the nation and set an example for the world. Its sleek, aerodynamic trains were designed to run on clean electricity, emitting no greenhouse gas. Millions of Californians were expected to ride it, taking traffic off our congested freeways and helping us to fight climate change.

At the time of the groundbreaking ceremony in 2015, the expectation was that "heavy construction on a 29-mile stretch of track between Avenue 17 in Madera and East American Avenue in Fresno will ramp up soon after the groundbreaking. Next, the authority plans to lay 60 miles of track between Fresno and the Tulare–Kern County line and 40 miles between the county line and Standard Road north of Bakersfield. Those segments and stations in Merced, Fresno, Hanford, and Bakersfield are to be completed by 2018 at a cost of roughly $13.8 billion, according to an authority report."

Having high-speed rail serving as a transportation backbone running from north to south in California is seen by mass transit enthusiasts as a necessary part of a much broader strategy. Regional mass transit solutions throughout the state, intercity rail, light commuter rail, and buses would all link to each other and to the high-speed rail system to offer a fully integrated and "net-zero" transportation option for all Californians. The state would become more like Europe, where many consider it unnecessary to own a car. Without needing car ownership, households would save thousands every year: no longer needing to purchase gasoline, pay for auto insurance and registration, or maintain their vehicles.

High-speed rail was enthusiastically sold to California's voters as just one part of a great leap forward whereby our consumption of resources and our carbon emissions would be dramatically lowered

while we would be able to get around more conveniently and pleas-
antly than ever before.

...

Well, it has been a full decade since the "groundbreaking" and still not one train has rolled down a track. The estimated total construction cost has now increased to well over $130 billion. The Central Valley segments that were expected to be complete by 2018 are now esti-mated to be completed sometime between 2030 and 2033.[3] Nobody has any idea when the entire San Francisco–to–Los Angeles system will be done, if ever. But the possible—and, in California, frankly predictable—downside of delays and overruns wasn't part of how this project was presented to the public by its proponents, nor how it was portrayed by the media.

To skeptics back in 2015 who questioned the need for high-speed rail and found the cost estimates, ridership projections, and con-struction timetable all to be wildly optimistic, Brown had this to say: "Everything big runs into opposition." As for the handful of critics who showed up to protest during the groundbreaking, Brown called them "weak of spirit."[4]

Perhaps Governor Brown was right, and only those who are bold of spirit can imagine these beautiful trains zooming through a verdant California countryside, presided over by benevolent, gently spinning wind turbines. Riders will be able to get from San Francisco to Los Angeles in two hours. Who among us, apart from the weak of spirit, would not have supported this wonderful vision?

Visions are easy, of course. And they do their job. The alluring images they present take up residence in our hearts, moving us to support these ideas that look and feel so fine. So many visions have been presented to Californians in recent years.

Imagine, for example, California's formerly "unhoused," thoroughly rehabilitated, strolling through patios lined with trees, framing brand-new midrise apartments that provide these residents the support they always deserved but never had a chance to realize until now. For a few billion more, we can house them all. Or picture the devoted teacher, no longer underpaid, encouraging an eager group of diverse students who are absorbing the skills they need to succeed in an ever-more-complicated modern world. Our intrepid teachers. Our enthusiastic students. Of course the California Teachers Association knows what's best for our kids.

These are the visions we've been sold. Sadly, the reality is often the complete opposite.

Of all the ideologies this book has covered, "Incompetism" might seem the most far-fetched. After all, the acceptance of mediocrity, or even failure, as a desirable virtue cannot be reasoned and purposeful, can it? Remember, though, that California's ruling elites believe immovably in the moral clarity of their vision. What does it matter if the results aren't what everyone hoped, as long as the noble intention is evident? Incompetism says there is always more money if the cause is just, and eliminating projects or people for doing the wrong thing is the real injustice. There is no accountability for failure if it is in service of a "progressive" ideal.

In California over the past two decades of one-party rule, as the absence of real political challenge has produced stratospheric levels of arrogance and complacency, incompetence has risen from mere ineptitude to something more menacing. Incompetence in California's government is now so routine, so entrenched, so *unremarkable*, that it has congealed into an almost total contempt for the citizen and taxpayer and complete disregard for their interests or opinions. It is pathological.

Anyone searching for examples of incompetence among members of California's political elite will find a target-rich environment. A plethora of cases where our ruling class has displayed a stupefying inability to "get the job done." But the iconic bullet train stands out.

On the drive down Highway 99 in the San Joaquin Valley, as you pass through the southern outskirts of Fresno, a strange apparition looms in the distance. Visible from miles away, it grows larger as you approach, turning out to be much bigger than you might have thought. It is the Cedar Viaduct, a 3,700-foot elevated causeway with an elaborate dual span of concrete cast-in-place arches to facilitate its overcrossing of the highway.[5] Completion of this impressive bit of construction engineering was announced in May 2023. Eventually this viaduct will support the weight of bullet trains traveling on tracks atop the structure.

Eventually is the key word here. Welcome to California's high-speed rail project. Sixteen years into this massive endeavor, not one mile of actual track has been laid. It's grotesquely over budget, decades behind its original schedule, and not likely to cost-effectively accomplish a single environmental or economic objective.

As we examine the bullet train fiasco, it is important to recognize that this disaster is merely first among equals. As will be seen, incompetence finds its way into every corner of Californian governance, wasting tens of billions of dollars on projects and programs that only occasionally manage to inflict minimal harm, while usually making much worse whatever problem they are intended to solve. The bullet train checks all the boxes. It will go down in history as a financial, environmental, and social catastrophe.

In December 2023 the Biden administration awarded more than $6 billion to California for high-speed rail. You would think that might make a difference.[6] But in California, a billion dollars doesn't go very far anymore. And when it comes to the bullet train, $6 billion is chump change. High-speed rail was originally sold to voters in 2008 as a marvelous antidote to automobile transportation.[7] The train was supposed to travel at 220 miles per hour—and get built at a total cost of $33.6 billion. The original 2008 "business plan" wisely refrained from estimating a completion date, and that's about the only thing they got right.[8] Some of the claims they made reveal eye-watering levels of delusion. According to the initial plans, laying track from San Francisco to Los Angeles would "alleviate the need to build"—at a cost of nearly $100 billion—"about 3,000 miles of new freeway plus five airport runways and 90 departure gates over the next two decades." The entire project was envisioned to extend north to Sacramento and south all the way to San Diego.

A revealing way to look at the utterly fraudulent claim that high-speed rail will reduce freeway driving is to recall the motivation behind the entire rail project: to combat climate change by reducing vehicle miles traveled. People will stop driving their cars and board the train instead, and voilà, less greenhouse gas will spew into the atmosphere. To that end, the California High-Speed Rail Authority boasts that the initial segment of the train will reduce total vehicle miles traveled in California by 183 million.

That may sound like an awful lot of "vehicle miles traveled," but it's actually a drop in the bucket. In 2022 Californians logged 340 billion vehicle miles.[9] This first segment of high-speed rail, expected to be completed by 2030 at a cost of $35 billion, was actually planned to reduce California's vehicle miles traveled *by one-twentieth of 1 percent.* Put another way, based on those economics, high-speed rail would reduce California's total greenhouse gas emissions by one full percentage point at the price to taxpayers of $2 trillion—that's *trillion* with a *t*—dollars.

As it is, however, it is fair to wonder if this project will ever be completed.

Today, sixteen long years later, the bullet train remains nothing more than an expensive assortment of monumental viaducts and additional miles of cleared corridors where no construction is yet evident, and even this only along an initial stretch that will connect the San Joaquin Valley towns of Merced at the northern end to Bakersfield at the southern end. This "first phase" involves completing a mere 171 miles of what was planned to be 800 miles of high-speed rail. And to date, as noted, even here where efforts have been focused, not one mile of track has yet been laid.[10] The cost for this initial segment—being built on the flattest, most forgiving topography of the entire eventual route—is now projected to exceed $35 billion.[11]

Do California's math-challenged incompetents realize that even in corrupt, costly California, that means they're going to be paying a staggering $204 million *per mile* of track? Wait till they try to tunnel through Pacheco Pass to connect the Central Valley line to the San Francisco Bay Area, or try to punch through the San Gabriel Mountains to connect the system to Los Angeles. And imagine, if you will, how much it will cost to blast a corridor for high-speed rail through the actual metropolis of greater Los Angeles, or through the dense suburbs that run uninterrupted from south San Jose all the way up into the heart of San Francisco.

With these constraints in mind, even at $204 million per mile, the whole 800-mile system will cost $163 billion. And if anyone thinks a track that costs $204 million per mile on some of the flattest farmland in America will "only" cost that much to tunnel through mountains and displace fully built-out areas, well, run for the state legislature. You'll fit right in.

In deference to shreds of honesty while maintaining the required capacity for incompetence and delusional thinking, the current plan for California's high-speed rail is only to extend the system from San Francisco to Los Angeles. The latest official estimated cost to do this is a paltry $128 billion, but every year that number goes up. In 2008 it was $33 billion. By 2012, already scaling back the projected speed via "blending high-speed train-sets" with low-speed commuter rail (where all the passengers would be), the total cost was increased to $68.4 billion.[12] In 2018, the "middle range" cost estimate was increased to $77.3 billion.

What is in store for Californians at this point is a "high-speed" system that is now planned to rely on slow commuter trains in the Bay Area and Los Angeles, at a cost of $128 billion. It will be a system that will never pay its operating costs, much less pay back its construction cost, which is sure to increase even further.

The most perfect encapsulation of the scale of Incompetism in the bullet train project was the reaction of a high-speed rail team brought in at the start of the project from France, where the TGV has been operating successfully in a comprehensive national network for decades. After a few years in California, the French team quit in order to work on a high-speed rail project in a "less dysfunctional" setting. They went to Morocco, whose bullet train opened for business in 2018.[13]

High-speed rail is just one example of supreme incompetence emanating from Sacramento but afflicting the entire state. Sticking with transit, consider the incompetence of California's many regional transit districts. In these examples, as with the high-speed rail project, incompetence manifests itself in two ways, both of them inexcusable.

The first is simply to carry on with a crazy idea. In its most ebullient initial conception, California's high-speed rail was marketed as a way to "travel from San Francisco to Los Angeles in two hours and forty minutes."[14] *Why would anyone want to do that?* Apart from the occasional tourist or train buff, this is not an efficient means to get from point A to point B. Getting to the station, going through security and boarding, then getting from the destination station to a final destination is not going to be any faster if the mode of transportation is a bullet train instead of a jet. The actual flight time from San Francisco International Airport to Los Angeles International Airport is 55 minutes.[15] Compare that to the promised 160-minute travel time using high-speed rail, which is a best-case estimate that would require upgrading the entire route to top-speed corridors and nonstop service. Taking a plane is much faster, and always will be.

Equally to the point, and illustrating the other type of incompetence that grips California's transportation planners, why carry on with a project when the cost is *incredible*? High-speed rail, plagued by cost overruns that would make any rational planner cut their losses and pursue more sensible alternatives (like enhancing California's freeways and existing railroads), is the prime example.

But the high-speed rail delusion is contagious. Take for example the trains that are part of the Bay Area Rapid Transit system (BART). This system of mass transit, built in the 1970s, when infrastructure projects were not mired in incompetence and litigation, connects the East Bay cities to San Francisco. The trains roll along at 80 miles per hour, and for years the ridership was robust enough to make the system nearly able to pay its operating costs from fare revenue. Then came Covid, which caused ridership to plummet. At the same time, passengers were increasingly reluctant to use the system thanks to a compassionist pathology that required BART management to ignore drug addicts and violent criminals who took over stations and trains. Want to ride BART? Navigate syringes, pools of urine, psychopaths, and predators. What a way to start and end your day!

So what did BART management do to bring back riders? Did they expel the crazies and the crooks, clean up their trains, and create a safe environment for passengers? No, no, and no. Instead, begging all the while for bailout funds, they proposed to build more tracks to extend the system into downtown San Jose.[16] And the cost for this "Phase II extension"? A staggering $9.3 billion, for a six-mile project.[17] That's $1.5 billion *per mile*. It makes the high-speed rail boondoggle look like a bargain by comparison.

When it comes to incompetence in California's public institutions, telling all the stories would take lifetimes. The Covid pandemic exposed many of these glaring deficiencies in public administration, but they had been simmering all along. How California's Employment Development Department (EDD) handled unemployment claims during the pandemic is a choice reminder of how unsafe your tax dollars are when they're handed to incompetent, indifferent, unaccountable bureaucrats.

The first mistake was to shut California down. Other states and nations managed to endure the Covid pandemic without going to the extremes that Governor Newsom imposed on Californians. So when California's EDD was expanded to hand out unemployment compensation to people who lost their jobs thanks to the lockdowns, there were millions of applicants who might have managed to keep their jobs in a less authoritarian environment.

This mistake was magnified, however, by an almost total lack of control over who was getting unemployment benefits. Just how easy it suddenly became to fraudulently obtain unemployment insurance payments is illustrated in the story of Daryol Richmond, who was part of an EDD fraud ring operating inside and outside the prison where he was serving nineteen years for robbery.[18] Using the identities of fellow inmates, before he was caught, Richmond and his coconspirators managed to file fake pandemic claims with the EDD totaling $25 million. Of these claims, prosecutors said that over $5 million was actually paid by the EDD to these criminals. The money was used by members of the crime ring to purchase cars, jewelry, and other items. Richmond himself was convicted of being responsible for submitting $1.4 million in fraudulent claims that led to $382,000 in actual payments.[19] He did this from a cell in Kern Valley State Prison.

While the accomplishments of Richmond and his cohorts are impressive, they represented only one small fraction of a fraud stampede that the EDD wasn't remotely prepared to handle. In all, most estimates put the total amount of fraudulent claims actually paid at over $32 billion.[20] And why not? It was so easy.

Attempting to explain what happened when the magnitude of the fraud first came to light in mid-2021, then–California labor secretary Julie Su was forthright, if damning. "California has not had sufficient security measures in place to prevent this level of fraud, and criminals took advantage of the situation."

That's an understatement. Controls were so lax at the EDD that they failed to verify the authenticity of claimants, which meant that someone could file for benefits using someone else's name, and the benefits would typically be granted without verifying the identity of the claimant.[21] The state didn't check unemployment applications with prison rolls, something that ought to have been automated and routine. Hacking rings and organized crime took full advantage of the situation, relying on the EDD's even weaker oversight as it struggled to process the flood of applications and expanded eligibility during the pandemic. If the EDD had simply followed standard vetting procedures before approving claims, billions could have been saved.

When it comes to incompetence in California, Climatism tends to exacerbate the problem. After all, an appropriate and desirable solution, poorly executed, is still better than a poor solution that is poorly executed. So it is with California's energy policies. They are mismanaged through incompetence, but they are misguided to begin with. And it is fair to question the competence of the elites who have designed California's current energy policies, because they reflect an inability to grasp even the most basic aspects of feasible energy supply-and-demand scenarios.

California has decided to achieve "carbon neutrality" by 2045. The state legislature has set this goal despite the fact that, according to the latest available report from the U.S. Energy Information Administration, released in April 2023, the state still derives 45 percent of its energy from petroleum products and another 31 percent from natural gas.[22] And of the 9 percent of its energy imported from other states in the form of electricity, about 40 percent comes from "thermal" sources (that is, electricity-generating plants relying on combustion of either coal or natural gas). In all, California still relies on fossil fuel for 80 percent of its energy, which, despite decades of effort and billions of investment, is no better than the average in the rest of the world.

This clearly is an affront to California's climate extremists, but it raises the obvious question: How is it possible to displace fully 80 percent of the fuel the state relies on with "renewables" in barely two decades? The short answer should be obvious: it can't be done. But in the attempt, a more competent administration, partnering with a more competent state legislature and more competent state agencies, might at least make a credible effort. They might weigh the staggering economic cost and environmental impact of the solutions they have chosen, and change course. But to date, rationality eludes our ruling class.

These examples of incompetence have consequences. They extract hundreds of billions of dollars out of the pockets of working families in California, directing that money into projects that not only are incredibly costly to build, but also, once completed, will become permanent drains on the economy.

To recap what we've covered so far:

Mass transit that will *never* transit massive numbers of people, but consumes billions of dollars, if not tens of billions of dollars, every year. Up to $30 billion was lost in fraudulent claims by the EDD thanks to antiquated and inadequate internal controls. The most expensive energy in America and thousands of square miles of habitat were compromised by solar and wind farms based on a complete inability on the part of state legislators and regulators to conduct a competent cost-benefit analysis.

But there are still more examples of how California's elites have imposed epic incompetence on working families.

One of the most worrying failures of government to hit Californians in recent years is the state's insurance crisis. It is impossible for many now to even get homeowner's insurance in California. Why are so many insurance companies leaving? California's legislators and mainstream journalists claim it's because of climate change. This is a stretch. If California's forests were properly managed, fire risk would also be manageable, and premiums could drop back down. And if California's regulatory environment weren't so hostile toward any form of logging, milling, mining, quarrying, and manufacturing, and weren't so hostile toward issuing building permits, and weren't so completely captured by the unions, insurance claims would be far lower because the costs to repair and rebuild would be affordable.

The same is true for motor insurance, also now either impossible to get in some cities or ludicrously expensive. It's hard to blame this one on climate change, but they won't admit the real reason either: the explosion of crime.

Compounding all of these problems is the complete cluelessness of the state's elected insurance commissioner, whose only response to the increasing cost and diminishing availability of insurance has been to impose caps on rate increases. Price controls! Brilliant! Except that the controls are one of the main reasons insurers are leaving the state, thus throwing more and more Californians onto the last-resort state insurance provider, the California FAIR Plan. That plan is so catastrophically underfunded relative to its liabilities that any kind of major claims event would lead to a cascading financial crisis.

Why do Californians continue to put up with this? Year after year of politicians building their bureaucracies and enriching their cronies, all the while engaging in performative Compassionism.

There are many reasons. To begin with, Golden State voters often don't get to hear the truth unless they look for it in unlikely places. Google "California wildfires" and the top results you get are all oriented to instilling more climate alarm. Google "renewables" and you will find nothing but glowing reports on their efficacy. Search-engine bias delivers a far-left perspective on every issue of consequence, and while there are alternatives available, Google still controls over 90 percent of the search market.[23] This institutional bias extends to California's public television and radio, its major newspapers, and most social media. Alternative sources of information—for example, Fox News and X—are universally and incessantly demonized as not credible and even dangerous. Californians are conditioned to avoid them and dismiss their point of view. For that matter, Californians are conditioned to dismiss any point of view that isn't on the extreme left. A key player in abetting that process is the California Teachers Association.

We have already seen how the CTA has influenced public school curricula to indoctrinate California's next generation in far-left ideology at the expense of a decent education. We have seen how the CTA exercises nearly absolute control over state legislators, and we have seen how they have protected incompetent teachers from accountability. But the CTA in 2024 continues to push the envelope of incompetence.

Senate Bill 1263, sponsored by the CTA and working its way through the California Legislature, will do away with the California Teaching Performance Assessment, known as the CalTPA.[24] The assessment requires that as a condition of receiving their credential, teachers demonstrate their competence via video clips of their in-class instruction and through reports they must write describing their practice. This test is the last opportunity to screen new teachers before they get their teaching credential. And in many respects it is the only opportunity to assess these teachers' verbal and written aptitude, since the rest of the credential program involves only coursework. What audacity to expect accountability from those who aspire to become public school teachers! Why would we bother to assess the capabilities of those who are supposed to train the next generation? California lags behind most other states according to almost every metric by which public schools are judged.[25] But the CTA wants to take away one of the last barriers to letting even more incompetent teachers into our system of public education.

Every single day, often more than once a day, California Democrats do things to our state that are so obviously, gratuitously destructive and insane, you assume it can't be true. But it *always is*. The CTA's commitment to protecting incompetent teachers is perhaps the worst example of Incompetism in California, because it doesn't just harm the taxpayer, the businessperson, the working family, the economy, the environment, manufacturing . . . It destroys opportunity for the next generation of Californians, and that harms everything.

This commitment by the CTA to bad teachers—which causes bad schools, which causes bad life outcomes for the next generation of Californians—may also help to answer the question: Why don't California's voters see through the ideologically driven far-left pathologies that have done so much to destroy opportunities in this great state?

The answer is they are not only conditioned to believe far-left ideology by every institution they're exposed to: they are also denied the balanced education that would make it easier for them to see through the rhetoric to grasp the relevant reality.

Sadly, Incompetism has reached into our most elite universities and graduate schools. We have seen how DEI mania is an American twenty-first-century variant of Maoism. But it is important to recognize what happens to the products of schools that succumb to DEI. It doesn't just lower the quality and focus of the faculty, increase tuition costs thanks to a bloated DEI administrative bureaucracy, and charge the atmosphere and culture on campus with an intolerant, Maoist culture. DEI also means these schools are not producing as many graduates who are competent in their chosen fields. UCLA's medical school is a recent victim of DEI.

An in-depth report by the Washington Free Beacon in May 2024 exposed how DEI is rapidly destroying the reputation of UCLA's medical school and the quality of its graduates.[26] In 2020 the medical school hired a new dean of admissions, Jennifer Lucero, who immediately set out to ensure that the small, elite student body of future physicians was sufficiently diverse. Lucero reportedly claimed in one meeting that "candidates' scores shouldn't matter, because we need people like this in the medical school."

"People like this," according to Lucero, are any applicants who aren't white or Asian. Those applicants typically have to log perfect scores on the Medical College Admissions Test (MCAT) and have perfect grade point averages from elite undergraduate programs—and even then their admission is not guaranteed. But these highly qualified applicants are being rejected in order to make room for students who will help the medical school fulfill diversity objectives, even though these students end up struggling to succeed academically. As reported in the Beacon, "Racial preferences, outlawed in California since 1996, have nonetheless continued, upending academic standards at one of the top medical schools in the country. The school has consequently taken a hit in the rankings and seen a sharp rise in the number of students failing basic standardized tests, raising concerns about their clinical competence."

Since Lucero was hired in 2020, UCLA has lost its status as a top-ten medical school, dropping from sixth to eighteenth place in *U.S. News & World Report*'s research rankings of the best medical schools.[27] The inability of many UCLA medical students to perform academically is shocking. Again from the Beacon: "One professor said that a student in the operating room could not identify a major artery when asked, then berated the professor for putting her on the spot. Another said that students at the end of their clinical rotations don't know basic lab tests and, in some cases, are unable to present patients."

"Berated the professor for putting her on the spot." This is a perfect example of how the proper roles of teacher and student have been inverted. Was it ever so bad that a student, especially the conscientious student who is driven to succeed academically, might fear being challenged by their professor? Today the professors must fear the students. This reversal of the traditional power balance between teacher and student cannot possibly bode well if the objective is to turn out competent medical professionals.

Not only has UCLA's medical school lowered admission standards to achieve diversity, they have also watered down the coursework. They have reduced the preclinical curriculum from two years to one year and added to that one year of coursework extraneous classes such as "Structural Racism and Health Equity" and "Foundations of Practice," a seven-hour-per-week class on "interpersonal communications skills." Lucero has forced dissenting members of the faculty or admissions committee to submit to mandatory diversity training.

We've seen evidence of DEI impacting social sciences and the humanities, but at UCLA it's impacting the quality of the doctors the rest of us rely on to keep us healthy, to diagnose and cure our ailments; people whose competence may determine whether or not we live or die before our time. This is Incompetism bordering on criminality, and this, too, is a consequence of diversity, equity, and inclusion.

California's failed approach to homelessness also represents incompetence in every sense of the word. It is in this context that we must view what has to be one of the most tone-deaf, delusional proclamations in the history of California, which is Governor Newsom's claim in May 2024 that California's homeless policies may serve as a "model for the nation." It is difficult to imagine something more inaccurate coming out of the mouth of a politician in America today. It is a stunning inversion of reality.

Newsom's comments were made in reference to the recent approval by California voters of Proposition 1, an initiative that was on the March 2024 state ballot with the noble-sounding title "Behavioral Health Services Program."[28] In a low-turnout primary election, by a razor-thin margin of just 28,000 votes of the 7.2 million ballots cast on the measure, Californians were conned yet again into supporting failure. Nothing in this $6.4 billion bond represented a significant shift in homeless policies in California. All of it, however, committed to spending far more money than would ever be necessary if policies were revised to adopt a more commonsense approach.

To understand how California's voters could approve of wasting still more billions on failed programs allegedly to help the homeless, the campaign spending offers revealing insights. There was no organized opposition to the measure. In a state with over 22 million registered voters, where successful campaigns either for or against ballot initiatives typically spend $10 million or more, the opponents of Prop. 1 spent almost nothing.[29] This shouldn't surprise anyone. Many established special interests in California are part of the homeless industrial complex, and those moneyed influencers who aren't, such as retail store chains, probably saw this proposed spending as better than nothing. That might even be true, but the return on investment is inadequate. If the model isn't changed, it will guarantee that the problem just gets worse.

To support Prop. 1, Newsom put all his fundraising ability to work, evidently viewing this measure as something he could cite as one of his major accomplishments as governor. His own committee, named Newsom's Ballot Measure Committee, Yes on Prop. 1, raised over $13 million to launch a massive campaign in support of the initiative.[30] Unwilling to challenge the governor and the special interests backing the initiative, and lacking the time and the unity to propose commonsense alternatives, there was no organized opposition to Prop. 1. Opponents raised a reported $1,000; that is, they were outspent by over $13 million to nothing. And in spite of this overwhelming advantage in campaign financing, the outcome was too close to call and wasn't announced as having passed until March 21, two weeks after the election and only after mail-in ballots were finally counted.[31]

While Prop. 1 did allocate funds to increase the capacity of the state's mental health system, it ignored the elephant in the room. Every approach this bill would fund, either through state borrowing or through mandating increased spending by the counties, was more of the same failed approach. The fundamental, fatal flaw was simple: at the rate these existing approaches provide housing and treatment for homeless people, the problem will never be solved. The math doesn't add up.

The measure calls for the state to borrow $6.4 billion to build 4,350 housing units and add 6,800 mental health and addiction treatment beds. That equates to a construction cost of $573,000 per homeless person either granted a housing unit or assigned to a mental health facility.[32] The most recent federal report on the homeless population in California estimated 181,000, with 68 percent of them "unsheltered" homeless, that is, living on the streets.[33] That means the target population for Prop. 1 to help numbers 123,000 people, and at the rate Newsom has proposed via Prop. 1, just constructing the facilities would cost over $70 billion.

This is impossible, and is only compounded by the fact that, absent other changes in policy, most notably a requirement that anyone receiving shelter or housing assistance must commit to sobriety, job training, and counseling, these programs will only attract more people to move to California. That is exactly what has been happening for the past several years. California has become a magnet for homeless people from around the country, because there are no laws in effect to restrain their behavior, only benefits and services.

Newsom may tout the passage of Proposition 1 as the centerpiece in a strategy to help the homeless that is a "model for the nation," but for those who truly care about helping homeless individuals, he is tragically wrong.[34] The first principle governing homeless policy is to recognize that free housing cannot be of an obviously higher quality than the commercial rental units working families in California can occupy only if they spend an inordinate percentage of their household income. Moreover, any form of government-subsidized housing must come with strict conditions on behavior.

In the end, it seems that even Newsom knows that the jig is up when it comes to homelessness. Asked by an interviewer in August 2024 why California has so many homeless people, he replied: "Because of our policies. And our neglect."[35]

Incompetism is the price of progressive pathologies. All of them combine to produce leadership and organizations that are compromised, where ideology comes before meritocracy, where presentation comes before performance, and where equity is more important than equal opportunity. In every aspect of governance, we are the victims of Incompetism. It manifests itself in the politicians we elect, the legislation they enact, the agencies they manage, and the private institutions that are bound by their rules.

The pathologies that California's ruling elite have succumbed to are dragging California down, year by year, into the mire of mediocrity. The wondrous achievements that our private sector still produces are in spite of these pathologies. Imagine what we might be capable of if they were cured.

PART II: CALIFUTURE

CHAPTER 11

A REVOLUTION IS BREWING

These nine isms, these political pathologies and the mental states that drive them, explain California's many failures. But there is hope. Californians are waking up. There is a growing realization that for every issue affecting our ability to live well, we have been betrayed by our political leadership. For every policy—housing, crime, homelessness, education, energy, water, transportation, taxes, wildfires, and more—the politicians have gotten it badly wrong.

There are practical solutions. For example: Deregulate housing development permits. Hold criminals accountable for their behavior and ensure certainty of prosecution and punishment for crime. End the disastrous Housing First policies and instead give homeless people safe housing in inexpensive congregate shelters where sobriety is a condition of entry. Focus on educational standards, not ideology; enable school choice and diversity. Build nuclear power plants and develop California's abundant energy reserves. Build new reservoirs and desalination and wastewater recycling plants. Widen California's freeways and highways. Let the timber companies harvest more lumber in exchange for maintaining fire roads and power line corridors. Repeal the many laws and regulations that have given California the most hostile business environment in the nation.

Above all, take an ax to the absurd and destructive proliferation of bureaucracy in Sacramento, the alphabet soup of agencies, the endless supply of bureaucrats and busybodies bossing everyone around, spending more and more of our money telling us what to do and in the process making it impossible to get anything done. Sweep it away!

As if it were that easy. None of this can happen without replacing the isms, the ideological pathogens, the nine superbugs that have infected California's elites. The antidote to these pathologies is their opposite. The antidote to Elitism is populism, which would require California's leaders to recognize the harm that their ideological beliefs are inflicting on the working class in particular. California needs an optimistic, positive populism that helps working people climb the ladder of opportunity in practical ways: a good job that provides enough to raise your family in a home of your own in a safe neighborhood with a school that gives your children a great education so they can have a better life than you.

The pathology of Narcissism is cured by empathy. With empathy it is impossible to blithely indulge ideological fantasies that only cause harm in the real world. Infected by Narcissism, it is easy to resist exposure to real-world results, whether it's crime rates or recidivism, the cost of housing or gas. When a narcissist is presented with real-world evidence that conflicts with their self-image, it is easy for them to ignore or deny what they've seen. It is even easy for a charismatic narcissist to convince other people to ignore or deny what they're seeing. But when Narcissism is replaced by empathy, the consequences of bad policies are impossible to ignore.

If there is any pathology that urgently needs an antidote, it's Maoism. Of all the diseases that make up the ideological pandemic that's pushing California off a cliff, this is the most virulent. It is also, paradoxically, the most universally discredited. The evidence of history is unequivocal: Maoism isn't merely an intolerant, inherently divisive ideology that destroys societies and nations. It can mutate into murderous and even genocidal variants. But Maoism is also capable of extreme deception, taking different forms and appearances to fit the time and place. In California, Maoism masquerades behind the imperatives of social justice and "equity." Once it has infected its host, it is hard to cure. There is only one antidote that strikes at the root of Maoism in its current incarnation, and that is true humanity. To recognize that people cannot be stereotyped as either oppressor or oppressed, based on some group characteristic. Race, gender, income, age, and every other group identifier are secondary to every person's individual humanity.

As for Climatism, this is an illness of excess. To grab global warming as a metaphor and apply it to this ideology, if a normal healthy temperature is 98.6, Climatism is characterized by a fever of 104. Which is to say that if concern for our environment isn't overheated and unhealthy, but is brought down to a normal temperature, it becomes a necessary and vital part of any policy agenda. The antidote to Climatism is moderation and balance, a commitment to pursue *all* environmentalist goals, and to do so while assigning equal priority to the needs of people. In pursuit of climate mitigation, are we tearing up rain forests in Brazil to grow cane ethanol or fouling watersheds in West Africa to mine cobalt? Healthy environmentalism must always take into account the human cost, whether it is laborers abroad or working families right here in California. Lower the temperature. That is the cure for Climatism.

The antidote to Socialism is a dose of limited government. At the same time, the source of Socialism's virulence—the romantic idea that the government must engineer equal outcomes for all citizens—must be replaced with an equally attractive aspiration. In California that is surely freedom: be who you want to be, live how you want to live. Same goes for Bureaucratism: the warped, burgeoning, self-perpetuating, obstructionist child of Socialism. When the government grows out of control in order to pursue socialist dreams, the apparatus of regulation, redistribution, administration, and enforcement becomes truly monstrous. Shrinking the government is the first step. But then we must restore and honor the finest ideals of public service. The people who work in government departments and agencies must be inspired to remember the values that attracted them to the public sector to begin with; they must strengthen their understanding and embrace of the core mission of government, which is to serve the people in a responsive and cost-effective way.

The opposite of Compassionism is true compassion, and that is the antidote to this dread pathology. Compassion is not always easy and, on the surface, may not always appear soft or kind. Exercising compassion brings with it obligations. Compassion for lawbreakers without compassion for victims is a symptom of Compassionism. Failure to see that it is cruel and inhumane to leave a homeless drug addict or mentally ill person on the street to suffer: that's Compassionism. Pretending that property crimes are just "quality of life" inconveniences, so perpetrators who suffer challenges in their lives should be excused, is Compassionism. Accountability and responsibility are part of true compassion.

Cronyism is an ugly disease. It is endemic throughout history and can never be completely eradicated. But California's case is deadly. The incestuous collusion within an insular ruling elite whose agendas align constitutes the power behind California's betrayal of working families. If Cronyism can't be entirely cured, it can be significantly mitigated. In part that will be achieved just by cutting back government to a reasonable size. Less government, less opportunity for corruption. But we also need specific reforms to control special-interest self-dealing and pay-to-play.

Finally there is Incompetism. Part of the cure is better scrutiny and transparency, so government officials and agencies are faced with actual accountability. But beyond that we simply have to raise our expectations. California did not become a great state by nurturing mediocrity or by telling its citizens their disappointments in life are somebody else's fault. Incompetism is a pathology that can be treated with a healthy dose of meritocracy.

None of this will be possible without real political revolution. The good news is that a revolution is brewing in California. The conventional wisdom among Democrats still holds that as the percentage of white voters continues its demographic decline, the grip Democrats hold on power will only solidify. This is naïve. In California's 2020 election, while 57 percent of "likely voters" were white, only 48 percent of Democratic voters were white.[1] Based on K–12 enrollment today, within a generation, 60 percent of California's electorate will be Latino, with Asian and white voters holding about 15–20 percent each, and the remainder primarily African American.[2] But California's Democrats are making a huge assumption to think their dominance is going to be enhanced as white voting power diminishes.

An insightful and devastating takedown of Democratic policies in California was published in 2021 by Jennifer Hernandez, a San Francisco–based attorney who specializes in cases involving land development. In a lengthy and scrupulously documented essay titled "Green Jim Crow: How California's Climate Policies Undermine Civil Rights and Racial Equity," Hernandez explains how policies coming from, for example, Marin County liberals are making it impossible for low- and middle-income families to afford to live anywhere in California.[3] In painstaking detail, she itemizes what amounts to a comprehensive Democrat assault on lower-income households, through extreme environmentalist laws that have made everything cost too much. By now this is familiar territory, but to recap: housing, rent, gasoline, cars, electricity, and good jobs—all out of reach. Hernandez describes how manufacturing and energy industry jobs have been driven out of California at the same time as wealthy, mostly white liberals perform work that can be done remotely with a keyboard and screen, while living in low-density neighborhoods in homes they inherited or purchased before prices became prohibitive. She also exposes the hypocrisy of green policies that offer subsidies and tax credits to people wealthy enough to purchase rooftop solar or all-electric vehicles, subsidies that are funded through rate increases that disproportionately affect low-income communities.

The facts Hernandez presents, and the reasons for them, are becoming increasingly clear to all of California's struggling voters. It is reasonable to wonder just how long California's nonwhite voters are going to tolerate politicians and policies that just push them deeper and deeper into poverty. Any political leader who steps forward and is willing to challenge the existing structure, whereby "green" policies are breaking businesses and household budgets, and is willing to demand new policies, is now more likely than ever to be taken seriously by voters who have had enough. And for good measure, these reformers can accurately claim that if there is racism to be found, it is found in the laws that Hernandez has appropriately dubbed the new "Green Jim Crow."

California's system of public education is similarly ripe for a bipartisan rebellion. This popular uprising of parents transcends ethnicity and will, once again, indict as the true racists all those opportunists who have been blaming problems on racism all these years. Academic underachievement is not caused by racism, nor is it caused by lack of funding. It is caused because the teachers union protects bad teachers, allows unqualified teachers into the profession, and favors seniority over competence whenever a school district has to lay off some of its teachers. The quickest and most effective way to improve public education in California, and save billions of dollars at the same time, is to introduce competition and break the union-run government school monopoly. A political leader who will assert this unequivocally will get elected and will find the strongest support from low-income neighborhoods where parents are desperate for educational alternatives that might better secure their children's future.

The same hopeful possibilities for structural change lie in California's muddled system of criminal justice. We have already seen signs that change is coming. In 2022, far-left district attorney Chesa Boudin was recalled in San Francisco. In 2024, the sweep was comprehensive: Los Angeles County DA George Gascón was kicked out of office by a huge margin; Oakland's mayor and the county DA were both recalled; San Francisco mayor London Breed lost her reelection bid; and, perhaps most stunning of all, Proposition 36, a statewide ballot initiative repealing some of the worst features of the notorious, crime-inducing Proposition 47, was passed by an overwhelming margin, with over 70 percent of Californians (and every county) voting in favor. Another reason for hope is the U.S. Supreme Court's decision to overturn *Martin v. Boise*, a landmark case that held that cities cannot enforce anti-camping ordinances if they do not have enough homeless shelter beds.[4]

And once again, the trope is wearing thin that crime is the inevitable and excusable result of racial oppression, or that police conduct and sentencing are driven by racism. The overwhelming majority of California's people of color want real and reliable public safety, and at this point they have had plenty of time to recognize that the "progressive" approach has been a total failure. They want safety and security for their families and their possessions. A politician that will fight for that with humanity but also with firm resolve is going to win elections.

Another structural obstacle that can be overcome is simply the electoral math. Almost invariably the votes in recent years in statewide elections have broken 60 percent in favor of Democrat candidates, and 40 percent in favor of Republicans. That's a wide margin. Or is it? As we have seen, the policies that Californians have been subjected to have, for the vast majority of voters, destroyed their prosperity and upward mobility, destroyed their children's chances for a decent education in the public schools, and left them feeling unsafe in their homes and neighborhoods. The excuses have been repeated too many times. "We have to save the planet." "We have to fight racism." But they are not saving the planet. They are not fighting racism.

This brings us to the meta-structure that is going to be overturned, the core values that are both a cause and a consequence of California's pathological isms. That is the "era of limits" mentality that was injected into California's culture by Jerry Brown during that landmark speech he made in 1976. If you were to pick a turning point when this state turned from a mentality of abundance and affordability to one of rationing and high prices, it would be on that day nearly fifty years ago when Brown announced that things were going to be different from now on. Tougher. And while Brown was right about that, it was not inevitable. It was a political choice.

Evidence of how restructured California's politics have been ever since, and more so with each passing decade, is offered through every chapter of this book. Government control. Limits. Restrictions. Shortages. High prices. Scarcity.

California's legislature already passed Senate Bill 1157 in 2022, which will limit the indoor water consumption of Californians to 42 gallons per person per day.[5] As noted earlier, it will impose on every property owner with landscaping to submit for approval by the water utility an outdoor "water budget." The expectation is that this new bill will save another 400,000 acre-feet per year, which will reduce California's annual water withdrawals for cities and farms by about 1 percent. *One percent.* The estimated cost to monitor and enforce this bill, including the need to install *two* water meters at every property—one to measure indoor use and one to measure outdoor use—is about $7 billion.[6] Literally every alternative category of new water supply infrastructure could produce more water for less investment. Reservoirs. Desalination plants. Wastewater recycling. Anything. But that isn't the point. The point is to limit consumption. Enforced scarcity. Bureaucratic micromanagement. Surveillance. Use less.

Perhaps the epitome of this era of limits we're living in is a new state law proposed by San Francisco state senator Scott Weiner. His bill would require automobile manufacturers to install sensors and controllers on every new vehicle that will automatically slow the vehicle down if the driver attempts to go more than 10 miles per hour above the posted speed limit.[7] If California's political structure that imposes an era of limits on every resident doesn't change, how long before a law like this is not laughed at—or vetoed, as it was in 2024 by Governor Gavin Newsom—but becomes reality?

The extremism and absurdity of all this is why we can be confident that the revolution will come. It will extend to every aspect of our society. The commonsense principles and values of a work ethic and accountability can translate into a return to laws and policies that worked before and will work again. We see it in microcosm in

Huntington Beach, Orange County—"Surf City USA." In 2022, a team of energetic Republican candidates overturned a long-standing 6–1 Democratic majority on the city council to take control, 4–3. Two years of commonsense, pragmatic policy on crime, homelessness, and other local "quality of life" issues saw this band of Republican rebels storm to a 7–0 clean sweep in 2024.

At the same time, a more rational approach to land and infrastructure development, also well established in California history, can turn us back into a state where the essentials of a good life are abundant and affordable again. There is no reason why California's best days cannot be yet to come.

This is the vision for California that has extraordinary appeal. We can rightsize the environmental movement to balance the needs of nature with the needs of people. We can fight for social justice and inclusion by fixing the schools and making the streets safe. We can embrace abundance instead of scarcity, and we can embrace competition and meritocracy instead of resentment and victimhood. This optimism can be the contagious meta-antidote that only has to attract an additional 10 percent of the electorate to its message and its agenda, and a politically realigned California will have new governance.

Califailure does not have to be California's reality any longer. There are pathways to eradicating the pathologies that have corrupted our political leadership. There are issues and antidotes that can captivate a majority of our electorate and in so doing empower a new generation of political leaders to fundamentally restructure the state. California is ripe for rebellion. People are sick of the frustration and failure, and are demanding change.

California can be golden again. *We can—and must—restore the California Dream.*

CHAPTER 12

RESTORING POLITICAL BALANCE

Today, California is a one-party state. The good news, if you want to call it that, is that a) California's Democrats have no one else to blame, and b) California's Republicans have nowhere else to go but up.

That is exactly what is happening. In 2024, California voted Republican without realizing it. Apart from the high-profile defeats for DAs and mayors in Los Angeles and the Bay Area and the overwhelming success of "tough-on-crime" Proposition 36, the Republican position also prevailed in statewide ballot initiatives on taxes, the minimum wage, and rent control. In the presidential election, Donald Trump won a higher share of the vote than any Republican in decades. Ten counties flipped from blue to red. Senate candidate Steve Garvey scored well over 40 percent of the vote, despite being significantly outspent by his Democratic opponent. It's still true that Republican seats in the state legislature are the lowest they've been in the history of the state; they hold 20 out of 80 seats in the Assembly and 10 out of 40 seats in the Senate.[1] Every higher office in the state, from governor down to state superintendent of public instruction, is occupied by Democrat politicians. In statewide elections, Republican candidates typically get 40 percent of the vote. That sounds like an insurmountable margin. It's not.

When evaluating how many voters support Democrats, it is revealing to calculate how much their campaigns spent per vote.[2] For example, in November 2022, Governor Newsom was easily reelected with 59.2 percent of the vote to Republican challenger Brian Dahle's 40.8 percent. But Newsom, who collected 6,470,104 votes, spent

$38.5 million on his campaign, whereas Dahle spent a mere $4 million, barely one-tenth as much. Put another way, Newsom paid $5.96 per vote, whereas Dahle only spent $0.90 per vote.

In battleground districts, Republicans have won in California even against massive Democrat spending advantages. In 2022, in California's Assembly District 7, Republican Josh Hoover edged veteran Democrat incumbent Ken Cooley by eight-tenths of 1 percent, despite being outspent $4 million to barely $1 million.[3] Republican candidates with strong messages can win in California.

Further evidence of an awakening electorate was evidenced in the fate of Proposition 1 in March 2024.[4] As we saw earlier, this was Newsom's pet project to fund more of the same failing homeless policies. Skeptical voters nearly stopped the initiative, which only passed by three-tenths of 1 percent. For weeks the count was too close to call. Yet Prop. 1 had no organized opposition. Spending to convince voters to reject this proposition was nonexistent, while the special interests supporting the measure spent $13.7 million. If even a handful of donors had stepped up to fund a competent opposition campaign, Californians wouldn't be on the hook for another $6.4 billion to fund policies to allegedly help the state's burgeoning homeless population that are proven failures.

To underscore just how ripe for realignment California's electorate has become, consider how poorly Democrat-supported ballot propositions performed in November 2020. Californians voted on twelve state ballot propositions on November 3.[5] On nine of these propositions, California's government and private sector unions spent significant amounts of money: over $1 million in five cases and over $10 million in two cases. But of these nine, the unions got their way on only one of them, Prop. 19, which changed some of the rules on how property taxes are applied.[6] Meanwhile, California voters rejected a property tax increase, an attempt to reintroduce affirmative action, a measure to grant seventeen-year-olds the right to vote, rent control, unionizing dialysis clinics, and a measure to retain zero bail.

The defeat of Prop. 16, which attempted to bring back affirmative action, is perhaps one of the most encouraging signs in the 2020 election, because despite being outspent by more than 10 to 1, the opponents prevailed. Californians saw Prop. 16 for what it was, a transparently racist meal ticket for trial lawyers, "equity and inclusion" bureaucrats, and the victim industry masquerading as antiracism. With only 42 percent of Californians voting yes, it wasn't even close.

With just a few exceptions, on ballot initiatives they have been presented with over the past few elections, California's voters made the right, commonsense choices. This is an encouraging development. Consistent majorities—often as high as two-thirds majorities— believe the state is headed in the wrong direction, the polling precursor of political change. With committed political investors prepared to match the sustained (and corruptly gained) financial resources of the unions, California's political landscape could see a real shakeup. The votes are there. Republicans now need to go out and get them.

In order to persuade an additional 10 percent of voters to vote for them, California's Republican candidates have to make sure they talk about solutions as well as problems. They need energy, and optimism, and a clear and compelling commonsense plan. They must have solutions to problems that are of universal urgency. These solutions shouldn't be primarily ideological because they need to appeal across lines of income, age, ideology, and ethnicity. Everybody in the state is concerned about the cost of living, quality education, crime, insurance. These problems, and their solutions, reach into every aspect of our lives. Making California affordable, with great schools and safe streets, is a goal that everyone shares. These are issues that are nonpartisan. They must be the focus. All these things of course sound obvious. It's surprising, then, how often they are ignored.

Some of the problems that Republicans and conservatives have had in California are pretty obvious. A biased media. The alleged legacy of Prop. 187, a policy dating back to the 1990s that was branded anti-immigrant (it passed overwhelmingly at the time), aimed at denying some categories of public services to undocumented aliens.[7] Then in

2008 there was Prop. 8, the ballot initiative to ban same-sex marriage.[8] These measures were passed decades ago but the memory of both of them has been manipulated to stigmatize Republicans as bigots. The Republican "brand" in California, in the absence of a strong, positive, homegrown version, has also been shaped by national associations that may be an advantage in other states but less so here.

Of course, none of these are insuperable barriers. In fact, they are probably best described as excuses. The fundamental values of California at its best—the pioneer spirit, independence, freedom, the rebel and the creator, the visionary and the builder—these values are best captured by Republican ideals, not the grim, joyless, controlling dogmatism of the Democrats.

CALIFORNIA'S FUTURE VOTERS

The California Revolution will obviously mean adding voters to the stable 40 percent floor (and ceiling!) that Republicans already have today. Right now, 50 percent of California's white electorate is Republican. Meanwhile, California Democrats enjoy support from supermajorities of Latino, Asian, and Black Californians. California's white Democrats tend to live in higher-income neighborhoods with better schools; often they live in their parents' or grandparents' house, which means they have no mortgage and minimal property taxes. By virtue of these legacy advantages, the policies that are killing everyone else in California are merely theoretical to many white liberal Democrats. If they aren't already, they are probably never going to be Republican or conservative.

Unlike the state's overall population, based on the 2020 election, California's electorate is still majority white—57 percent. Latinos constitute 35 percent of eligible voters, even though, based on 2020's turnout, they're only 22 percent of the people who actually voted. In 2020, Asian, Black, and white Californians turned out in percentages roughly proportional to their percentage of eligible voters. It was Latinos who were underrepresented—big-time.

Political candidates who offer positive, practical solutions to the everyday issues of housing, the cost of living, education, and crime, in a commonsense and nonideological manner, could start to turn this around.

CALIFORNIA'S FUTURE IS LATINO

It isn't much of a stretch to assume that today's students are tomorrow's voters. In California, school enrollment today is about 60 percent Latino. The white population may decrease somewhat further, and the Asian population may gain a few percentage points.

Even today, less than half of California's registered Democrats are white. Even within the Democrat Party, they are already an absolute minority. And it has just begun.

To see where this is headed, consider California's current K–12 enrollment and extrapolate it to the future. In other words, if registration patterns by ethnicity stay constant between now and the very near future, this is where Democrats are going to have to get their voters. In California, within the foreseeable future, it is not going to matter if white voters are converted to become Republicans, because they're going to be an insignificant portion of the electorate.

But the future in California is primarily Latino, projected to be 60 percent of the electorate, with Asian and white percentages likely to hold at about 15–20 percent each. California's Black population has been consistent for decades at about 5 or 6 percent of Californians and may not change very much. This demographic profile is not likely to be America's destiny, insofar as the Black population is much higher in the rest of the nation and the populations of Asians and Latinos in most states are much lower. But California's demographic future predicts America's in one crucial respect: trying to convert American "progressives," whose relative affluence insulates them from the worst effects of the increasingly far-left policies they support, is not worth it. Not only because these rich white "progressives" are less likely to experience the hardships that Democrat policies inflict on everyone else, but because the percentage of the electorate that they represent is in steep decline.

The key to reviving the Republican Party in California lies in a phrase that I first started using in 2016, as we began to see the emergence of a political realignment, first in the UK with the Brexit vote to leave the European Union, and then here in America with the election of Donald Trump as president. I spoke then of the Republican Party's opportunity to become a "multiracial working-class coalition" focused on lifting up the people and families left behind by establishment policies. This was what I referred to as "Positive Populism," which was the theme of *The Next Revolution*, my Sunday night show on Fox News, and my 2018 book, *Positive Populism: Revolutionary Ideas to Rebuild Economic Security, Family, and Community in America*.

At the national level, it is clear that the promise of a Republican multiracial working-class coalition was decisively delivered by Donald Trump in his emphatic victory in the 2024 presidential election. In California, it remains more opportunity than reality. But the opportunity here is greater than anywhere else. There is no doubt that the increasingly far-left policies of the political establishment in California, the product of the pathologies outlined in part I, have absolutely hammered working-class Californians, with Latinos among the hardest hit. Consequently, building the multiracial working-class coalition in California, with energetic effort placed behind a commonsense, positive policy agenda that will restore the California Dream, is the key to reviving the Republican Party in California—and indeed reviving the state itself.

An encouraging sign of the potential for such a transformation: In the 2024 presidential election, while ten of California's fifty-eight counties flipped from Democrat to Republican, one of those was especially notable. Imperial County, in the south of the state, swung by over twenty points from Biden to Trump between 2020 and 2024. Imperial County is 86 percent Latino. My friend Jeff Gonzalez flipped a Democrat-held State Assembly seat in the same area. In the neighboring assembly seat, Leticia Castillo did the same.

In 2024, my California policy organization, Golden Together, sponsored a study led by Joel Kotkin at Chapman University, "El Futuro Es Latino." It compared outcomes for Latinos in California with their peers in Florida and Texas on key indicators like income, education, and home ownership. Of course it was all worse in California. The report laid out a road map to turning things around, a vision very much aligned with some of the specific policies we have been developing at Golden Together. The most important point, however, is captured in the title: El Futuro Es Latino—the future is Latino. Yes, it is.

CHAPTER 13

A FOUNDATION OF PROSPERITY AND ABUNDANCE

The foundation of prosperity and opportunity in California is a healthy business environment. We will never be able to restore the California Dream for everyone without a thriving private sector in which every business, of whatever size and in whatever sector, can flourish and grow. California should be the best place in the world to start and grow a business. We are so disastrously far from that today. Of course it's true that businesses should operate subject to reasonable regulations that prevent abuse and promote competition. As it is, however, businesses in California are under siege. Despite all our advantages—great universities, great weather and scenic beauty, the world's fifth-largest economy, and diverse industries, including leading-edge technology companies—California is consistently ranked as the worst state in America in which to run a business.

Businesses of all sizes are affected. Hundreds have either scaled back their operations in California or completely relocated to other states. Big businesses confront a fantastically more complex and onerous regulatory regime than in any other state. Corporations that choose to stay and take the punishment are forced to pass the costs of compliance on to customers, suppliers, and the wider community. Small businesses, increasingly started and owned by Latino and Asian Californians, lack the resources available to larger companies and struggle to adhere to literally thousands of rules coming from countless state and local government agencies.

California, the land of opportunity and promise, a worldwide symbol of entrepreneurialism, innovation, and start-up hustle, is slowly being degraded and demoralized into stagnation and sclerosis.

The problem has worsened in the last few years, and much of it can be attributed to the rapid growth of the state government. When Governor Jerry Brown took office in 2011, California's budget was $98 billion. Over eight years in office, Brown doubled it to $199 billion (despite there being no measurable increase in population served). Under Governor Gavin Newsom the budget has grown to just under $300 billion—and now must cope with a $73 billion projected deficit—at the same time as the state actually lost population. Bigger government, shrinking population. This can't go on.

There is an alarming complacency surrounding California's attitude to business right now, an assumption that the goose will continue to lay golden eggs regardless of the blows inflicted on it by misguided public policy.

While it is true that California's capacity for growth and reinvention is difficult for even this generation of ideologically driven politicians to extinguish—as evidenced by the Bay Area–led AI boom and California's dominance in green technology—it is completely ridiculous for our great entrepreneurs and business leaders to be forced to succeed *despite* the overall business climate, rather than being helped to succeed *because* of it.

As in so many other areas of policy, California today seems gripped by a negative and limiting ideology of scarcity, intent on stopping and blocking rather than starting and enabling. We need to move into a new mindset of abundance: positive, dynamic, ambitious. On every aspect of the business climate and economic incentive structure, on every issue affecting those things . . . energy, water, housing, infrastructure . . . our regulatory, tax, and policy framework should be saying "Yes We Can" rather than today's grim and crushing mantra of "No You Can't."

There is an inspiring opportunity here. By improving the business climate in California, more companies will compete to offer goods and services, lowering the cost of living and the cost of doing business at the same time as creating millions of new jobs and driving forward innovation that makes life better here and around the world. Making California the best place in America to start and run a business will make a major contribution to restoring the California Dream of entrepreneurship and upward mobility.

PATHWAYS TO RECOVERY: DEFENDING AGAINST DECLINE

California's regulatory environment, protracted and expensive permitting processes and other compliance costs, along with high income and corporate tax rates, all make it difficult for businesses to thrive. Solutions include streamlining regulations, reducing needless bureaucratic obstruction, reducing the complexity of the tax code, reducing uncertainties surrounding future tax policies, and lowering taxes. But moving beyond these generalities to specific policy suggestions can be an overwhelming task, magnified by the fact that most business advocacy organizations have to spend much of their resources simply defending against new legislative burdens.

For example, every year the California Chamber of Commerce publishes a list of so-called job-killer bills introduced in the state legislature.[1] While they have an impressive record of managing to prevent many of these bills from becoming law, the sheer volume and scope of these bills reveals the mentality of California's legislators and the political momentum of antibusiness forces in the legislature.

In 2023, two of the job-killer bills that were signed into law by Governor Newsom included SB 525, which increased the minimum wage for any health care worker to $25 per hour, and SB 616, which nearly doubled the existing sick-leave mandate. The chamber dropped their opposition to SB 525 after it was modified to restrict the $25 minimum wage to larger health care facilities, but the burden will still affect the cost of providing health care, and, more to the point, this avalanche of bills targeting business puts organizations like the California Chamber of Commerce on permanent defense. In 2023 alone, the chamber fought against no fewer than twenty-three bills in the state legislature they deemed to be job killers.

All of this legislation increases costs to businesses, and these costs are inevitably passed on to consumers. California not only has the highest energy prices in America; it has the highest cost of living in general. This systemic failure is policy-driven, creating an economy that is broken in so many respects. In particular, the high cost of living harms the working class and the state's most vulnerable, those members of low-income communities who must allocate 100 percent of their income to purchasing food, shelter, and health care, and have no discretionary income to buffer the impact of price increases for these essentials.

California's high cost of living is the direct and entirely predictable result of government bloat and regulatory overreach, but rather than address that the state legislature attempts to cope by passing even more regulations—increasing the minimum wage is a prime example—in an exercise reminiscent of a cat chasing its own tail. Reforms to improve California's business climate need to be both systemic and specific. They must aim to change the culture and break the cycle.

WAYS TO REVIVE CALIFORNIA'S BUSINESS CLIMATE AND ECONOMY

Many of the most damaging laws and regulations that need to be either repealed or revised are discussed at length in part I. Here they can be considered in four categories: labor law and regulations, environmental law and regulations, taxes and fees, and reforms designed to reduce the size and complexity of California's bloated bureaucracy. Below are some of the specific changes that would put the state on track to have the best business climate in America instead of the worst. And to be clear, this is a start—not a comprehensive list!

Reforms to Labor Laws and Regulations

1. Repeal the Meyers-Milias-Brown Act, which in 1968 established collective bargaining for many of California's government workers.[2] It is important to remember that even if they can no longer unionize, public employees will still enjoy civil service protections.

2. Enact right-to-work laws to prohibit union membership being a condition of employment.

3. Outlaw mandatory "project labor agreements" requiring unreasonable pay rates, forced union workforces, or both on any construction project receiving a portion of its funding from taxpayers.

4. Repeal AB 5. Businesses and individual workers are entitled to the freedom and flexibility that is provided by having the right to work as an independent contractor.

5. Remove from all regulation AB 5's so-called ABC test: "The worker performs work that is outside the usual course of the hiring entity's business." This provision, the worst of the three, denies businesses the ability to rapidly respond to rapid growth or decline in demand for their services.

6. Repeal the Private Attorneys General Act and instead bolster state labor law enforcement.[3]

7. Enact right-to-cure, whereby businesses facing civil enforcement either from government agencies or third parties have the ability to correct infractions in lieu of fines or lawsuits, particularly in cases where there are only technical violations, minimal impact, or no harm.

8. Enact a de minimis law that automatically dismisses third-party civil lawsuits whenever alleged infractions in payroll reporting are technical violations without evidence of negligence or abuse.

9. Permit employees to work through their shifts without a break if that is their preference.

10. Repeal the law that mandates overtime pay when an employee works more than forty hours in a week. The requirement to pay overtime on any day when an employee works more than eight hours is sufficient to protect their interests.

11. Repeal the law that requires employers to prove they were not retaliating if they terminate an employee within ninety days of that employee engaging in any "protected activity," such as making complaints or claims to the state labor commissioner.

12. Review the entire framework of minimum wage laws to protect workers while increasing job opportunities. Local, regional, sectoral, and age-related factors should all be taken into account.

Reforms to Environmental Laws and Regulations

1. Implement the recommended reforms noted in the Golden Together policy paper "Universal Housing Affordability" to revitalize California's building industry and increase the supply of affordable homes, thus lowering the cost of living for California's workforce.[4]

2. Review and reform unfunded environmental mandates.

3. Repeal the climate disclosure law that requires businesses with revenues over $1 billion to report their greenhouse gas emissions, including estimated GHG emissions from their entire supply chain.

4. Repeal the climate disclosure law that requires businesses with revenues over $500 million to report their "climate-related financial risks."

5. Repeal the climate disclosure law that requires any business selling, purchasing, or using carbon offsets, or making any claim to be reducing their carbon emissions, to publish detailed accounting to document the offset project or document their claims.

6. End the private right of action under the California Environmental Quality Act (CEQA). Restricting the right to file lawsuits to district attorneys in California's counties and the state attorney general will eliminate what are now countless lawsuits that delay and deter investment in housing, infrastructure, and all manner of new business operations, denying businesses opportunities for growth and job creation.

7. In order to balance environmental protection with the need for job growth and the interests of working families, review the greenhouse gas (GHG) limits pursuant to climate change legislation that have led to restrictions that are eliminating business competitiveness in California, costing jobs, and raising the cost of living.

8. Adopt more realistic goals for reducing GHG in order to allow businesses more time to adapt to new guidelines, more time for technology to mature, and to allow businesses to fully depreciate their existing equipment before having to replace it.

9. Review the functions and authority of the Coastal Commission to restore focus on its primary purpose of environmental protection, reverse its damaging "mission creep," and rebalance the overall regulatory framework by returning responsibilities to counties.

Reductions and Restructuring of Taxes and Fees

1. Restore the two-thirds vote requirement for any legislation or ballot initiative to pass that involves an increase of taxes or fees.

2. Repeal the "windfall profits tax" imposed on California refineries, which limits the percent profit they can earn. This tax will further diminish supply and discourage reinvestment in refinery upgrades, even those that might support California's long-term climate goals.

3. Establish and permit businesses to write off their equipment

purchases using accelerated depreciation schedules instead of having to carry so much of it over year after year.

4. Eliminate the $800 corporate minimum tax. If a business has negative taxable income in a year, it should not owe taxes.

5. Eliminate the fee to file the required yearly renewal of the Corporate Statement of Information with the California secretary of state.

6. Revoke the scheduled unemployment insurance payroll tax increases that are planned in order to pay debts incurred by the Employment Development Department, which businesses had no role in creating.

7. Eliminate the business personal property tax. Business owners are required each year to pay taxes equivalent to 1 percent of the value of their furniture and equipment (inventory is excluded). The reporting is complex and time-consuming, especially for small businesses. Alternatively, raise the exemption to $100,000 of business personal property.

8. Establish a commission, to report within six months, to make recommendations for a radical reduction and simplification of taxes in California, with a focus on promoting enterprise, job growth, and widely shared prosperity.

Reducing the Size and Complexity of the State's Bureaucracy

1. Until per capita general-fund spending by the state government is brought back to under $5,000 per resident (in 2023 dollars), impose a hiring freeze on state employees.

2. Drastically reduce the number of executive branch employees from the current number of over 250,000.

3. Revisit all contracts granted to twenty-one public sector union bargaining units and adjust salaries down to market levels.

4. Terminate OPEB (other post-employment benefits, primarily retiree health care) for state employees, which are being provided

despite the availability of Medicare, Obamacare, and successor-employer health care.

5. Provide new state employees with defined contribution plans only and adjust defined-benefit levels for existing employees for years not yet worked to the benefit levels in place before Senate Bill 400 elevated benefit levels in 1999.

6. Eliminate duplicative state bureaucracies and ensure that there is proper accountability in agency actions and enforcement.

7. Review the entire twenty-nine sections of the existing State Legislative Code, with the default assumption or priority that regulations will sunset unless reviewed and reaffirmed.[5]

8. Require all existing and new regulations to expire periodically.[6]

9. Revise the state's regulatory agencies' roles and enforcement approaches with a goal to streamline requirements to aid businesses in compliance strategies and reduce their compliance workload.

10. For any proposed new regulations, require agencies to 1) commission a comprehensive cost-benefit analysis *to be conducted by an independent, private sector outside firm* before imposing a rule, 2) require agencies to consider public feedback on the cost-benefit analysis, and 3) allow citizens to challenge burdensome regulations or a faulty agency cost-benefit analysis in court.[7]

11. Expand access to civic participation in regulatory processes by allowing courts in locations across the state to hear cases that involve challenges to bureaucratic regulations.[8]

12. Rewrite guidelines for regulatory department board member appointments in order to achieve balanced representation on oversight boards from all stakeholders.

13. Drastically reduce, if not completely eliminate, head counts in state agencies by requiring that any state function that can be done by the county should be done by the county with minimal state oversight.

14. Streamline the process for charter cities to form, or for general-law cities to convert to charter cities, and to this end, loosen up the Local Agency Formation Commission (LAFCO) process to make it easier for local and regional governments to form, merge, or split.

IMAGINING A CALIFORNIA WHERE BUSINESSES ARE WELCOMED

The reforms proposed above are by no means an exhaustive list. But they represent, and capture, the new mindset we need: pro-enterprise, pro-growth, anti-bureaucracy. Low-tax, high-ambition, unlimited opportunity. California should not be ranked as the worst state in America to do business. Our spectacular weather and scenic beauty, along with our rich natural resources, make California a naturally hospitable place to live and work. These advantages are augmented by the legacy of earlier generations of Californians who in the 1950s and 1960s built freeways, a power grid, the state water project, and the best universities in the world. What they built is now stretched to the limit, thanks to a generation of neglect, but it remains the backbone that keeps California running. To the extent California retains a huge and diverse economy, it is thanks to these innate gifts and inherited legacy, and in spite of current government policies.

Making California a magnet for businesses again, instead of driving them out, requires a comprehensive program. California's natural resources are being squandered in the name of preservation. Managing our vast reserves of timber, natural gas, oil, and farmland is an opportunity. We can harvest these resources sustainably, using best practices that have developed over the last few decades, and also drive down prices.

At the same time, California's neglected infrastructure needs upgrading and expansion. Rather than pouring hundreds of billions into projects of dubious long-term value, we should be investing that money in repairing and widening our existing roads and rail, dredging and seismically retrofitting our dams, reservoirs, flooding channels, and levees, and coming up with creative and cost-effective ways to harvest storm runoff from the Sacramento–San Joaquin Delta. We should be carefully evaluating what public investments will create a backdrop of affordable abundance in the foundational elements of economic growth, lower costs, and broadly distributed prosperity: transportation, energy, and water.

Every part of California's government needs to undergo a cultural transformation, to recognize that the choices made in all three areas—natural resources, infrastructure, and business regulations—must balance the needs of the environment with the needs of the human beings who actually live and work here—and especially the working class. Our government must recognize that when businesses can thrive and compete for customers, the relative cost to customers goes down, and when this happens, it not only benefits *everyone*, it imparts disproportionate benefit to the least fortunate, those members of California's low-income communities.

Each time a state legislator proposes new legislation or prepares to vote on it, they should ask themselves: Will this help businesses thrive? Will it foster competition between businesses to provide services and products that are—to borrow a mantra from Silicon Valley—better, faster, and cheaper? They should ask themselves: Will this benefit *everyone*, and not merely mitigate a problem for a few people? Will this remove burdens to prosperity or merely shift the burden elsewhere?

The perception among most businesspeople in California today is that their state and local government is not trying to help them, but in fact is out to get them. This must change. Government agencies should be partners with businesses, assisting them with permits and offering productive oversight. Even with meaningful regulatory reform and a streamlined bureaucracy, it is essential to also have a culture within government that views business as a vital partner, not an adversary, and strives to communicate that to the public.

We need our government to reflect the optimism and ambition that has always drawn people to California and defines it still today. It is in the air, from the Hollywood Hills to Silicon Valley, from the shores of Lake Tahoe to the surf hitting the Santa Cruz beach. Californians want to change the world. We want a brilliant future, and we want to be the ones to build it. To make the world a better place. With that motivation intact, there is great hope. California can bring back opportunities for businesses and families. California can be number one again, a magnet for business, an example to the world.

CHAPTER 14

RESCUING K–12 EDUCATION

We saw in part I that despite the vast and increasing resources that have been thrown at California's public schools, the results they produce amount to a betrayal of our children. It is common to see school districts where fewer than half the students meet basic standards in English and math. In some districts it is barely a quarter. And as always, the victims of Democrat government failure tend to be the exact people the party claims to speak for: the poorest and most vulnerable; Latino and Black children. We simply cannot tolerate this failure. Each year that passes with these dismal outcomes is another year lost for a student who will never get that chance again. California's public school system is destroying opportunity on an industrial scale, and it is quite simply intolerable. So we should not tolerate it.

There are at least three necessary steps we need to take. We must strengthen the rights of parents to exercise school choice options for their children, and we should set up education savings accounts (ESAs) that are offered first to low-income households and special education students, so they can get the education they so desperately need. But both of these structural reforms will take time. So the third step—and in some ways the most urgent—is to reform the operational framework immediately for all public schools, introducing real accountability and serious consequences for failure.

Each of these will be bitterly opposed by the people who run—and currently benefit from—California's government school system: the teachers unions. The reforms will be blocked at every turn by the Democrat politicians who pocket bribes (sorry, political donations) from those unions. But the school system is not supposed to be run for the benefit of unions or politicians. We pay our taxes to fund government-run schools in order to benefit students. If they are not benefiting, then the government has no business running those schools. It is a cliché, but in this case it is literally true: the only acceptable attitude here is zero tolerance for school failure. There is no reason why the next generation of Californians has to continue to attend one of the worst public education systems in America.

REWRITE THE OPERATIONAL FRAMEWORK FOR ALL PUBLIC SCHOOLS

Let's start with the most immediate changes that need to be made. Structural solutions like school choice and education savings accounts are an important part of any reform plan, but too often Republicans make the mistake of thinking that such reforms are the only way to improve public education. In practice, where they have been implemented elsewhere, structural changes take time to have an impact. Initially, uptake may be slow. That doesn't mean we shouldn't prioritize such reforms, but simply that they cannot be the be-all and end-all. Children in failing schools cannot wait. They need our help now. We need an emphasis on raising standards immediately.

There is a lot that can and should be done in the short term to bring much-needed accountability to government-run schools and to rescue the children from a pathway to failure and crushed opportunity.

The first set of changes were included in the *Vergara* case, brought by nine public school students who argued that the teacher work rules reflected in current statutes denied them their right to a quality education as guaranteed by California's constitution.[1] The *Vergara* plaintiffs lost their case in appellate court in 2016. But these along with other similar reforms have been proposed in Sacramento repeatedly over the years. Today there is growing, bipartisan recognition among legislators in Sacramento that these work rules need major revision if

California's K–12 students are to have a better chance at receiving a quality education. Nothing matters more in a student's development than the quality of the teacher. Not money. Not new buildings. Not creative new curricula. If the teacher is good at their job, the students learn. These five reforms will immediately improve the quality of teachers in California's public schools:

1. Introduce merit pay for teachers. Those who do a great job of closing attainment gaps and helping their students improve their performance should be paid more. Those that don't should be paid less. It's just common sense.

2. The entire concept of tenure should be revisited. It is fair to question whether tenure, which was initially established to preserve academic freedom for university professors conducting scientific research, is even appropriate for K–12 public school teachers. But while that larger question is being resolved, at the very least the evaluation period necessary before tenure can be granted to a new teacher should be extended from under two years to five years.

3. Criteria for layoffs shall prioritize retaining the best-performing teachers, without regard to seniority.

4. The process to terminate ineffective teachers will be streamlined. If a teacher is not performing effectively, according to established metrics, they should be removed from the classroom as soon as possible.

5. We also need to make sure taxpayer money is being spent wisely and goes to the uses that will deliver results for students. There are far too many administrators, many of them paid obscene salaries and benefits, certainly in comparison to teachers. And there is far too much emphasis on construction and facilities, instead of the quality of teaching. Tens of billions of dollars are wasted—an unconscionable diversion of resources away from student needs.

When it comes to metrics, we need to bring accountability to schools as well as teachers. Right now, parents struggle to understand how their child's school is performing. While there is data out there about aggregate school performance, it is confusing and hard to find. That's why we need to bring back standardized aptitude tests. They are the best way to tell if our schools are working or not.[2] The importance of standardized aptitude tests was demonstrated in California when, for a brief time, they were used to identify low-performing schools and compel administrators to implement reforms. So all accredited schools in California should be graded annually based on established metrics, including performance on standardized academic achievement tests. Every year, these results should be published within months, not years, and made publicly accessible using reports that are easy to access online and formatted in ways that are transparent and easy to understand— for example a simple A, B, C, or D grade for every school.

This inevitably raises the question of what to do with the information. Simply publishing a grade is useless unless it leads to real change. The most obvious change from the current tolerance of calamitous school failure would be to introduce serious consequences for a school that ends up with the lowest grade. It must not be allowed to continue failing. So, for example, a school that gets a D grade two years in a row would be put into "special measures"—taken out of school district control, the principal replaced, and the school taken over for emergency improvement action.

We could think of this as an updated version of the 2010 Parent Empowerment Act—also known as the Parent Trigger Law. Written by my friend and Golden Together colleague Gloria Romero (then state senate majority leader for the Democrats) and passed by a bipartisan majority, the act created a process allowing parents by a majority vote to force low-performing schools to adopt specific "intervention models."[3] These included replacing teachers, converting the traditional public school into a charter school, closing the school, and transferring the students to other schools.

The fate of the Parent Empowerment Act exemplifies just how powerful the teachers union monopoly is in California.[4] By 2015, the California Department of Education revised the annual proficiency tests in order to measure "annual yearly progress" (one of the criteria used to determine if parents had the right to trigger reforms), so that "progress" was measured not by the scores the students were getting on the proficiency tests, but merely by what percentage of the students took the test.[5] Suddenly schools with dismal, backward progress in student achievement were turning in excellent improvements, avoiding implementation of the law. The deliberate circumventing of the Parent Accountability System was complete by 2017 when the State Board of Education adopted a "new state accountability system" that "provides a fuller picture of how districts and schools are addressing the needs of their students while also identifying the specific strengths and areas in need of improvement." Under this new system, as disclosed on the Board of Education website, "Due to the transition to the 'Dashboard,' the CDE can no longer identify those schools who are subject to the Parent Empowerment provisions."[6]

We must bring back the Parent Trigger Law, basing it again on objective data from completed academic achievement tests, and restore the capacity of the law to force a broad assortment of tough remedies. If anything, we need to give it even more teeth than it had originally. If a school fails to meet basic standards, if it gets a D grade year after year, why on earth should that school, or its district, be allowed to carry on with business as usual, condemning students to a lifetime of lost opportunity?

A new, easily accessible, and transparent grading system should also, obviously, be accompanied by open enrollment where, within an existing school district, parents would have the right to enroll their children based on what school best matches their child's needs instead of having the school automatically designated by the district based on zip code.

There are other public school reforms that candidates and activists can promote that have universal, bipartisan urgency. We have to eliminate ideologically driven curricula and restore an emphasis on teaching academic fundamentals, for example, with classical education.[7] The debate on how to teach children to read is over: the "phonics" method won. Yet this approach is still not universal in California's government-run schools. There should be zero tolerance for anti-learning practices in our schools, yet a bill to mandate effective techniques was killed in 2024 by the teachers union. Because of course it was.

Another aspect of the school-operating framework that needs serious change is how to handle discipline. In keeping with the ideology of Compassionism outlined in part I, recent approaches to disruptive students have moved away from holding them accountable for their behavior. Punishment is out; "restorative justice" is in.

We need to carefully evaluate the balance between the new practices of restorative justice and the traditional methods of classroom discipline. Restorative justice, when implemented well, can be effective and help stop the school-to-prison pipeline. But taken too far, or when implemented poorly, restorative justice makes things worse. It fails to remove disruptive students from the classroom and therefore intimidates and damages the education of students who do want to learn. In matters of discipline, as well as academic standards, real accountability must be the aim.

IMPROVE SCHOOL CHOICE OPTIONS FOR PARENTS

The central principle underlying structural reform of the education system in California is clear: parents should be able to send their children to the school that best suits their needs and circumstances. When so much in our modern world has progressed, why are we still stuck with the one-size-fits-all "factory" model for schools developed in nineteenth-century Germany? We can imagine—and call into being—a system where parents have multiple school options for their children. The near monopoly held by traditional union-run government schools needs to be broken, and healthy competition needs to be established between a variety of educational models. Parents should be able to choose between traditional public schools, private schools, charter schools, and parochial schools, as well as have the option to homeschool or participate in hybrid programs that blend on-site and homeschool instruction. Schools established under these various models need to be held accountable for the academic achievement of their students, and parents should have the right to enroll or withdraw their children in order to maintain the best individual results.

Charter schools are considered public schools, but they are governed according to a charter developed by the operators of the schools, and are not forced to adhere to the work rules and curricular requirements largely determined by the teachers unions. There are hundreds of successful examples of charter schools in California. Yet the laws (written by politicians funded by the teachers unions) are currently rigged to make it hard to open charter schools. There are caps on how many charter schools, and how many charter school students, are allowed in the state. Those caps have to be lifted.

Here are policy recommendations that candidates who aim to protect and grow charter schools in California should advocate:

1. Charter schools can be approved by the following entities: the State Board of Education, any county board of education, any school district school board, and any public or private accredited university.
2. The renewal operating permits for charter schools shall be subject to achieving and maintaining competitive standards of academic achievement.
3. There shall be no cap established by the state or any public agency on the number of charter schools or the number of charter school students.
4. Virtual charter schools that support "pod schooling" or "microschools" shall not have their applications denied on that basis.

5. No charter school application or renewal shall be denied on the basis of the financial impact it will have on the school district in which it is located.

Of course, charter schools should be subject to the same transparency and accountability requirements as other public schools. A charter school that gets a D grade two years in a row should face severe consequences, in the same way as a failing government-run school would.

It should be noted that almost every organization that is fighting the good fight to restore quality education, along with reducing crime and lowering the cost of living—all the big trade associations—are fighting incremental defensive battles because they can't take the risk of really fighting for what they need. We see that in water, energy, education, construction, and almost every issue where there is a trade association involved. They are fighting incremental defensive battles, which means it is up to new candidates to go on offense, come up with big solutions, and promote them. Nowhere is this more true than in education.

EDUCATION SAVINGS ACCOUNTS

With that in mind, here is another way to restore quality education: education savings accounts. ESAs are implemented by granting an annual credit to parents based on the amount of funding that goes into public schools. These parents can use the credit to pay tuition to the school of their choice. In 2021, this amount was about $14,000 per student. The average cost of K–12 private school tuition in California is much less than that, barely over $10,000. There are private schools that charge a lot more, but there are also much less expensive parochial schools and other types of private schools. There are now online options as well as in-person/online hybrids. There are a lot of ways to deliver quality education in California.

This solution preserves public funding for education but puts the choice of what school to attend in the hands of parents. ESAs are viewed by opponents as a radical solution, which is true for one overwhelmingly good reason: it will break the monopoly that union-run government schools currently wield over public education in California.

Here are policy recommendations that candidates who want to break the unionized public school monopoly in California should advocate:

1. Educational savings accounts should be created for K–12 students but will be restricted to students who are either in low-income households or are special education students. The purpose of this restriction is to deliver these options to the communities most able to benefit from better educational choices, as well as to prevent existing alternative school capacity from being initially overwhelmed. As the number of alternative schools increases and capacity grows, ESAs can be phased in to benefit progressively larger percentages of California's total K–12 student population.

2. These ESA accounts shall be credited annually with each student's pro rata share of K–12 education funding.

3. The parents of K–12 students shall be able to direct that money to a participating school, whether it is a public, charter, or accredited private or parochial school.

4. The money, if unspent, shall accumulate to be used for college, vocational, or any other accredited educational expense.

ESAs have already been adopted in several states. Having them in California would be a vast improvement in helping our students get a better education. They should be seen as part of a broader movement to give parents more power in the school system—power that should also be accompanied by responsibility. It is not good enough for parents to just hand over their children to a school and expect them to do all the work. We need all parents to behave as the majority do: understanding that education begins at home, and that it is up to parents to set an expectation of learning, discipline, and diligence.

Most of the organizations that support education reform in California are playing very conservative baseball. In general they are not willing to aggressively promote big solutions because they see it as too much of a risk. They are worried about being targeted by the teachers unions, and that is a rational concern. So it is up to new candidates and reenergized grassroots activists to advocate these big solutions and bring them to the voters.

Californians know their education system is failing. And the way the system is set up today, these failures are disproportionately affecting schools and students in low-income neighborhoods. When it comes to fixing education, Republican candidates don't have to get dragged into polarizing battles. Their message can stick to topics that will resonate with every parent in the state. California's public schools need reform to deliver higher standards, and structural change because they are not providing a quality education to the students who need it the most.

CHAPTER 15

A GUARANTEE OF SECURITY

Californians deserve the basic services that we expect of our government, and without the government ensuring our safety and security, none of the other basic services matter. As we have seen, our state government has enacted legislation that has compromised its ability to deliver this most basic of services. To turn around California's rising rates of crime and disorder, we need a new approach.

We may acknowledge that the contributory factors to criminal behavior can sometimes be complex. Nobody chooses their parents, their genes, or the society they're born into. Early childhood trauma can damage a developing brain for life.[1] One of the reasons crime-friendly district attorneys have been able to attract major donations and win elections is that they have seized the rhetorical high ground of compassion. It's necessary to expose the hideous results of progressive "compassion," yet measures to reduce crime in California will find broader support if proponents emphasize that they also have compassion, but that compassion comes with obligations. Sometimes genuine compassion seems cruel, but results matter.

Another key principle that must inform new measures to reduce crime is that deterrence matters. This fact comes with a crucial nuance. It turns out that criminals are not deterred by the severity of punishment nearly as much as they are deterred by the certainty of punishment.[2] In California today, criminals have almost no fear of punishment. The laws aren't in place to make it likely they will ever be held accountable, and either there aren't enough police to arrest them anyway or police who operate on limited resources are unwilling to spend time on yet another "catch and release" case. If California's laws and prosecutors were reoriented to a high probability of convictions with sentencing or other certain consequences, crime rates would drop overnight.

Finally, the entire concept of incarceration needs to be revisited. A retired sheriff we interviewed shared a story about an encounter he had with an ex-con who had recently been released. The ex-con confronted the sheriff who had made the original arrest that sent him to prison. But then something unexpected happened. The ex-con explained that while in prison, he earned a high school diploma, learned a vocation that accounted for his current employment, and had been cured of his drug addiction. Prison was the best thing that ever happened to this young man.

A related story came from someone who spent most of his career helping homeless people. He operated a private shelter that put conditions on entry. To get admitted, the homeless person had to commit to sobriety, counseling, and job training. This man and every other professional homeless advocate operating privately funded shelters that we interviewed have shared the same conclusion—homeless people are almost all substance abusers, mentally ill, or both. Whether that's the cause or the effect of their homeless status is irrelevant. They need to be compelled into shelters where they can get treatment and recover their dignity.

These positive outcomes accentuate an often-unrecognized upside to restoring harsher penalties and higher probability of conviction for criminal offenses. Not only would this reform deter crime, but incarcerated individuals might finally have a chance to turn their lives around. This reasoning helped make the case for repealing many of the provisions of Proposition 47, which California's voters had the chance to decide in November 2024. The new ballot initiative, Proposition 36, was passed with over 70 percent support and is called the Homelessness, Drug Addiction and Theft Reduction Act. From the initiative itself, here is a summary of its provisions:[3]

1. Provide drug and mental health treatment for people who are addicted to hard drugs such as fentanyl, cocaine, heroin, and methamphetamine.
2. Add fentanyl to existing laws that prohibit the possession of hard drugs while armed with a loaded firearm.
3. Add fentanyl to existing laws that prohibit the trafficking of large quantities of hard drugs.
4. Permit judges to use their discretion to sentence drug dealers to state prison instead of county jail when they are convicted of trafficking hard drugs in large quantities or are armed with a firearm while engaging in drug trafficking.
5. Warn convicted hard-drug dealers and manufacturers that they can be charged with murder if they continue to traffic in hard drugs and someone dies as a result.
6. Reinstate penalties for hard-drug dealers whose trafficking kills or seriously injures a drug user.
7. Increase penalties for people who repeatedly engage in theft.
8. Add new laws to address the increasing problem of "smash-and-grab" thefts that result in significant losses and damage, or that are committed by multiple thieves working together.

Most Democrat politicians, including Governor Gavin Newsom, fiercely opposed Proposition 36. They seemed to believe that the initiative would cause an unsustainable, unnecessarily harsh, and unaffordable increase in California's prison population. But will it, or will introducing more robust deterrence result in a manageable, more marginal increase in sentencing into California's most expensive high-security prisons? And what if incarceration, in both high-security and in minimum-security environments, while harsh, may also be a realistic opportunity—and perhaps the only remaining opportunity—for criminals to turn their lives around?

Incarceration keeps law-abiding citizens safe and offers justice for the victims. But in many cases, rehabilitation is possible. When it is achieved it not only offers the offender a second chance, but also the burden on taxpayers is reduced as there is one less inmate and one more productive member of society.

If we are able to reform the pro-crime laws that have incentivized criminals and if we can vote out of office our crime-friendly DAs like LA's George Gascón, then the overwhelming question going forward is how to ensure effective incarceration. The number of incarcerated individuals may not go up as much as statistics currently indicate. Crime is deterred by the certainty of punishment, not by the severity of the sentence. California's homeless population includes a high percentage of individuals who would find housing with family or friends if they knew they were going to have to go to a shelter and stay sober.

This very likely possibility—that crime rates will drop if the ratio of convictions for criminal behavior goes up—suggests that California's prison population may not have to increase significantly in order to get crime back under control in the state. This in turn suggests that while there is an intense debate over the level of state funding for prisons and law enforcement in the current fiscal climate, with the right policy changes the long-term trend may actually see improvement in public safety without having to increase spending or build new prisons.

Ultimately what is required is a strategy that accounts for all types of incarceration. Over time, policies that deter crime may reduce the need for maximum-security prisons. On the other hand, while changing the policies affecting California's homeless population will reduce their numbers by a significant percentage, and while resuming effective enforcement will reduce the incidence of misdemeanor crimes such as petty theft and public intoxication, California nonetheless must increase its congregate shelter and minimum-security detention capacity. Much of the funding to accomplish this can come by re-allocating the tens of billions being wasted every year on the failed Housing First programs.

A PRAGMATIC STRATEGY TO FIGHT CRIME

Any strategy to fight crime has to start with a transformation in our support for law enforcement. The untold damage of the "Defund the Police" movement is still being felt. We need to reverse the demoralization of our police officers and ensure that police and sheriff's departments are fully staffed, well led, and well funded.

We must work to rid our state of the true evil embodied in the pro-criminal DA movement and its associated policies on bail and charging, which have led to the collapse of civilized life in many parts of California. Why would police officers put themselves at risk pursuing criminals if they know they will simply be released? Why wouldn't criminals commit crime if they know there won't be consequences? Californians must rise up and vote these far-left ideologues out of office. Thankfully, that has started to happen.

Where it is not happening, we need to explore creative new approaches for the state to step in and provide security and public safety if local politicians fail to do so. Residents should not have to suffer indefinitely. There must be no "no-go" areas in California.

Then we need to make sure that our systems of punishment deliver deterrence and accountability, as well as rehabilitation. This can and must be achieved without increasing budgets. For example, we will need to expand California's capacity to absorb minimum-security inmates and recovering substance abusers: that could mean equipping new facilities with the latest robotic and surveillance technologies. The amount of money that is currently spent on failing programs to help the homeless in California could easily pay for shelters—voluntary and involuntary—established in less expensive parts of the state, with plenty of money left over for counseling, job training, and treatment.

Californians can reduce crime without having to invest hundreds of billions of dollars. It can be done by redirecting money that is currently wasted and by legislative, judicial, and prosecutorial reforms that change the rules, deter crime, and better reintegrate former inmates.

It can be done with compassion for everyone concerned and deliver results everyone wants.

Solutions to Restoring Law and Order

1. Fully implement 2024's Proposition 36, with prosecutors charging repeat offenders with felonies.
2. Impose mandatory prison sentences for anyone convicted of three or more felonies.
3. Impose mandatory jail terms for anyone convicted of three or more misdemeanors within a five-year period.
4. Require that anyone released pretrial without posting bail wear a remote monitoring device such as an ankle bracelet. Equip monitor to transmit alarm if disabled and mandate immediate apprehension and remand if monitor is disabled or removed.
5. Current proposal to save $1 billion per year out of a $14 billion annual corrections budget by closing five prisons does not save enough money to be worth the loss of high capacity. Retain prison capacity.
6. Require inmates to have arranged for a place to live before releasing them from prison.
7. Address the need for low-security custody options that target low-level offenders and substance abusers. Develop a continuum of facilities ranging from low-cost congregate shelters for the unhoused to minimum-security work camps for low-level offenders and substance abusers.
8. Compel the unhoused to stay in congregate shelters and require sobriety, counseling, and job training. Redirect the billions currently used to build permanent supportive housing to fund construction and operation of these shelters.
9. End the Housing First approach to helping the unhoused—building expensive permanent housing—in favor of low-cost shelters.
10. Empower the state attorney general to overrule county prose-

cutors who decline to prosecute criminals and try them in state courts.

11. Empower city prosecutors to try criminals in municipal courts if their county prosecutors decline to prosecute criminals arrested by the local police force.

Crime can never be completely eliminated, but with an improved system of incentives and deterrents, it can be minimized.

EARLY CHILDHOOD INTERVENTION

Frederick Douglass, one of the most influential civil rights leaders in American history, famously said, "It is easier to build strong children than to repair broken men." This expresses in simple and evocative terms the benefit of early childhood intervention. If we can help children avoid the adverse impacts of poverty and insecurity, they will be far more likely to become flourishing and productive members of society. In turn, that means they will be far less likely to require remedial or corrective intervention by the state. So whether our goal is expressed in terms favored by liberals ("a more just society") or conservatives ("more limited government"), addressing and solving social problems confronting children can move us forward together.

As we now know from the latest advances in neuroscience, developmental health care, and other fields, the root causes of criminal behavior and other costly social problems are often found in the family, and especially the early years of life.

Here in California, we have an opportunity to bring together the best of what has been tried around the world, and the lessons learned, in a globally pioneering program to strengthen families, enhance life chances, and abolish generational poverty by empowering every parent, regardless of economic circumstance or family structure, to raise their children in a stable, loving home. As we propose ways to enhance the safety and security of all Californians, programs of early childhood intervention can play a vital role.

It is easy to dismiss programs designed to help families, especially when they are government-administered. The legacy of failed programs and government bloat that typifies all too many social programs can give rise to cynicism. Much of this is warranted. Many publicly funded social programs have turned out to be mainly beneficial to the bureaucracies that run them, and instead of preventing poverty have perpetuated it.

These criticisms, however, ignore the potential for innovation to deliver different and better results. They ignore the fact that while many social programs are dismal failures, others are success stories that can be built upon. Most of all, they ignore the fact that as a society, especially one as wealthy as California, where we boast about being the world's fifth-largest economy, we have a moral obligation to address the poverty in our midst that shames us every day.

We have to tackle the causes of poverty as well as its symptoms. And as we investigate those causes, we inevitably come to the conclusion that what happens in those early and fragile first days, weeks, months, and years of a child's life can set the course for the rest of it.

Are we content to leave those lives to chance? To ignore the obvious truth that poverty, whether at the individual or neighborhood level, can make it almost impossible for parents, on their own, to create the kind of environment that will help their children flourish and thrive? Do we ignore the obvious truth that every parent, regardless of economic status or family structure, could do with some help every now and again?

That would be an abdication of responsibility and a denial of opportunity.

Why don't we design a new and effective way to empower parents by moving beyond traditional government interventions, replacing bureaucracy with humanity? The core of such a service would be home visiting, a trusted professional making regular visits to a new parent's home to give hands-on, practical advice and to connect the parents with other local services and networks. The visitor could be a trained nurse (one of the most successful examples of home visiting programs is the Nurse Family Partnership, established decades ago). Or it could be someone from a local faith organization or other community-based group. Here are some of the steps that would make a difference.

1. The governor of California, in partnership with relevant executive branch agencies, should establish a vision and year-by-year goals for the achievement of universally accessible parent empowerment and home visiting services for every family in California, starting with those at or under the California Poverty Measure.

2. The first step should be a feasibility and implementation study, including funding estimates and calculations of savings to other government programs as a result of the parent empowerment and home visiting programs at various levels of uptake.

3. Home visiting programs should be licensed under a decentralized system of quality certification, with authorization obtainable from a diverse list of qualified organizations, including cities, counties, state agencies, an accredited university, the State Board of Education, or local boards of education.

4. Similarly, home visiting program operation licenses should be available to a diverse range of organizations, including new and preexisting ones dedicated to providing home visiting services or under the management of public school districts, charter schools, parochial schools, private schools, hospitals and health clinics, faith-based organizations, community organizations, and government social service agencies.

5. The governor should specify the broad objectives of parent empowerment and home visiting programs and set specific guidelines for accountability. These criteria should measure the

collective progress of each organization against a baseline score assessed for each family prior to commencement of home visits.

6.   These standardized measuring criteria should be common to all participating organizations and would constitute the basis for funding and ongoing certification.

7.   Private funding of home visiting programs should be incentivized through performance-based awards of government matching funds.

8.   California parent empowerment and home visiting programs should be required to be universally available.

9.   Family participation in home visiting programs should be voluntary.

In this way, we can strengthen families, improve life chances, and finally break the cycle of generational poverty that is such a jarring repudiation of the California Dream. We can do this in a way that reduces overall government spending and enhances the security of every Californian.

SAVING RURAL CALIFORNIANS FROM WILDFIRE

Protecting lives and property from wildfires is an area where government regulations can ensure either good or bad outcomes. As we have seen, California's policies governing forest management have been mostly bad. The results are megafires that have devastated millions of acres in California over the past twenty years. They are an almost completely avoidable series of catastrophes. In just the last five years, nearly twenty-five thousand homes across the state have burned in wildfires, causing an estimated $18.7 billion in overall property damage.[4] More than one hundred Californians were killed in these fires.

Air quality has also suffered. Since 2000, according to the California Air Resources Board, wildfires have destroyed over 19 million acres, exposing millions of Californians to smoke so thick and toxic that people were advised to stay indoors for weeks.[5] Utility compa- nies, attempting to prevent fires from starting, cut power to millions more Californians during hot and windy summer days, sometimes for several days in a row. During one of the worst fire seasons in recent years, in the summer and fall of 2020, it is estimated that wildfire smoke released 127 million tons of CO_2 into the atmosphere, more than California's entire electricity, commercial, and residential sectors combined.[6]

Solving California's modern wildfire crisis requires a return to commonsense forest management. There is a set of new policies that if implemented over time would reduce regularly occurring wildfires to smaller, less intense, and more easily contained blazes. It would primarily engage the private sector, creating jobs and tax revenues. It would help revive California's timber industry, and in particular support one of the most exciting developments in construction: so-called mass timber, which is a transformationally stronger and more sustainable construction material than concrete and can be produced by combining previously unusable timber products. These modern ways to manage California's forests would restore them to health and introduce practices that guarantee California's forests are not only carbon-neutral but substantially carbon-negative.

Ways to Prevent Wildfires and Protect Homes and Property
1. Grant long-term logging rights. The California Board of Forestry should grant long-term rights for timber companies to harvest trees on state-owned land. This will attract private investment in timber company expansion.
2. Eliminate counterproductive bureaucracy. Logging companies currently have to submit timber harvest plans every five years. Each of these plans is costly, consuming thousands of pages and requiring significant forestry staff and outside consultant time to prepare. Requirements for plans should be consolidated to

encompass an entire parcel or an entire watershed within a large parcel. And instead of expiring every five years, timber harvest plans should be granted in perpetuity, with monitoring. Major revisions should be required only if there is "significant new information" affecting the plan area.

3. Streamline the process for smallholders of forest land to harvest their timber. Most timber harvested in California comes from large industrial holdings that account for around one-sixth of the total acreage in the state that contains marketable timber. But a further one-sixth is in the hands of private, nonindustrial owners. Many of these owners are deterred from participating in a modern system of forest management and timber harvesting because of the bureaucracy involved. The expense of repeatedly submitting plans, instead of being able to have a long-term plan approved, makes it economically impossible for small parcel owners to engage in logging. If this process were streamlined for nonindustrial owners of timberland, the quantity of harvestable timber in California could potentially double.

4. Establish state-government revolving loan funds for investors to build sawmills, as well as biomass energy facilities, chippers, and other equipment that would allow the industry to quickly expand operations and capacity.

5. The California Air Resources Board should modify the application process and time allowed for controlled burns to thin overgrown forests.

6. The state should develop an accreditation, incentive, and awareness campaign for in-state sourcing of timber for construction projects. Such action would help stimulate greater recognition of how California has to import lumber because its own timber industry has been unduly stifled. This would also raise awareness of California logging practices, which are more environmentally responsible than those in effect in the out-of-state areas where timber is currently sourced.

7. California's building codes were updated in 2023 to allow the wider application of mass timber construction by permitting timber towers to be built up to eighteen stories high.[7] But California's building codes still incorporate fire safety standards that are outdated with respect to mass timber. Current codes require layers of encapsulation around mass-timber structural beams that are already sufficiently fire-resistant to be fire safe with fewer layers. It would reduce costs and accelerate adoption of mass timber if these codes were revised. Regulatory agencies should use the most relevant and up-to-date testing data to adopt modern and appropriate codes for mass timber.

8. In 2022, Assembly Bill 2446 directed the California Air Resources Board to develop a framework for "measuring and reducing embodied carbon in buildings."[8] As the final rules to enforce AB 2446 are adopted and revised, they should provide for a streamlined compliance process if mass timber is used in construction, since it so clearly conforms to the intention of the law, which is to encourage use of construction materials with low carbon intensity. Mass timber produces minimal carbon emissions in its sourcing and manufacture while sequestering a tremendous amount of carbon in its structure.

9. End the private right of action under the California Environmental Quality Act (CEQA). Reforming CEQA by restricting the right to file lawsuits to district attorneys in California's counties and the state attorney general would deter what are now countless lawsuits that constitute a significant impediment to modern forest management. This reform would also go a long way toward streamlining the construction of housing in California, solving a chronic housing shortage, and creating in-state markets for its timber products.

10. The state should invest in workforce development that will enhance the management of our forests. This requires a political

commitment to expand the logging industry instead of shrinking it, which will help attract people to enter the workforce and commit to a career in the forests and sawmills.

11. The Department of Forestry, the California Air Resources Board, Cal EPA, Cal Fire, and every other state agency involved in managing California's forests should rebalance their staffing from bureaucrats to foresters, and make sure they spend a significant amount of time actually in the forests. California's colleges and universities that offer degrees in forestry should revisit their curricula to ensure sufficient coursework emphasizes modern forest management.

In addition to taking these steps, California should pressure the federal government to implement the following changes to its forest management policies:

1. Revise the EPA's "no-action" restrictions, usually based on the "single-species management" practice, which have led to more than half of California's national forests being off-limits to tree thinning, brush removal, or any other sort of active management.

2. Change the U.S. Forest Service guidelines that only permit active forest management, even in the areas that are not off-limits, for as little as six weeks per year. Restrictions on when and where forests can be thinned are making it impossible to adequately thin the forests and manage them responsibly. To be effective, thinning operations need to be allowed to run for several months each year, instead of several weeks each year.

3. Streamline the application process for the National Environmental Policy Act (NEPA) so it is less expensive and time-consuming for qualified companies to get permits to extract

timber from federal lands. Grant waivers to allow thinning projects to bypass NEPA, or at the least broaden the allowable exemptions.

4. Speed up Forest Service permitting. In the ten national forests within California, the U.S. Forest Service has over one hundred vacancies. This staffing shortage is slowing the process for qualified licensed timber operators to get permits to extract wood products. For a start, rebalance staffing, with more qualified foresters who will actually spend time in the forests, instead of bureaucrats. And make the whole process of granting permits faster, easier, and better.

5. Fast-track the granting of long-term stewardship contracts whereby qualified companies acquire a minimum twenty-year right to extract wood products from federal lands. This would guarantee a steady supply of wood products, which in turn would make new investment viable in logging equipment, mills, and biomass energy facilities.

6. Revise rules and conditions governing timber exports. The export of raw logs from federal lands in the western United States is currently prohibited. Lifting this prohibition is vital for restoring the health of our forests, especially while sawmill capacity remains below the level needed to process the necessary increase in volume of harvested timber.

Modern forest management is an enormous opportunity to develop positive, practical policies to protect Californians' security in a way that brings people together around commonsense solutions, moving beyond polarized and divisive ideological extremes.

Guaranteeing security to Californians can be achieved through these measures. A pragmatic strategy toward law enforcement and rehabilitation. A focus on early life and programs to reduce the childhood trauma that can lead to crime and other dangerous behaviors later in life. And an approach to forest management that will safe-guard the lives and property of millions of Californians living in rural and forested areas.

But beyond restoring public safety and reviving a healthy business environment, there is the quality of life we envision for ourselves and our children. Here, then, are some ideas for helping to make the California Dream a reality again, for all.

CHAPTER 16

THE CALIFORNIA DREAM

It is only in the last few decades that California became truly unafford-able, starting with housing. Housing affordability is the foundation of the California Dream. It is the prerequisite for equal opportunity, quality of life, and economic growth. We've already discussed the many ways in which the dream of owning a home became out of reach for most Californians. But there are solutions.

California's housing crisis is not some natural disaster or unavoid-able accident. It is the direct result of policy choices, many of them well intended, that have nevertheless combined over the years to make it almost impossible to build homes on the scale we need. But these policies can be changed. We can change the abuse of environmen-tal regulations artificially restricting the supply of housing. We can change the excessive taxes on house building artificially inflating the price of housing. We can move beyond the outdated "infill ideology" that prevents housing being built in the places people want and at the scale we need.

Instead of scarcity, we can have abundance. Instead of politicians telling people where and how to live, we can move into a new era of housing choice and homeowner autonomy. We can solve our debili-tating housing crisis with a new approach that is modern, sustainable, and more human. We must plan for, and achieve, universal housing affordability. Here's how we can do it.

To address the growing challenges in California's housing devel-opment landscape, we need a series of strategic reforms aimed at streamlining the process, reducing unnecessary delays, and ensuring that resources are used effectively. A key aspect of this reform is to end the private right of action under the California Environmental Quality Act (CEQA). Originally designed to inform government decision-makers and the public about potential environmental impacts of proposed activities, CEQA has become a complex and often obstructive system. Over decades, legislative updates and court rulings have transformed it into a tool that frequently hinders development, creating costly delays and uncertainty for developers.

To mitigate these issues, the right to file lawsuits under CEQA should be restricted to California's district attorneys and the state attorney general. This change would help reduce the excessive litigation that currently impedes housing projects.

In addition to reforming CEQA, lawsuits pursuant to CEQA should be required to be filed within ninety days of a project application's being received by the permitting agency. This would ensure that legal challenges are timely and do not become a prolonged barrier to development.

Another cause of scarce, expensive housing is the vehicle-miles-traveled analysis that the state currently requires for all land use projects. It was implemented supposedly to stop suburban sprawl that leads to more traffic. But this requirement often complicates and delays the approval process without significant environmental benefits, and should be abolished.

We must also restructure "impact fees." These fees, which developers are required to pay and which as we saw in part I, can often run well over $100,000 per home, should be placed in specific "impact accounts" to prevent their misuse for unrelated budget items. If the fees are not spent on their intended purpose within a specified time frame, they should be returned to the developers.

It would also be useful to eliminate so-called discretionary permitting, which currently allows bureaucrats to deny permit applications even if they comply with existing building codes and zoning regulations. Instead, building permits for compliant projects should be issued automatically. To further ensure an expansion in construction, changes to building codes or environmental regulations should not apply retroactively to projects that have already been approved, and these codes and regulations should not be revised more than once every five years.

Another way to reduce home prices would be to eliminate affordable-housing set-asides, which often force developers to raise prices for other buyers to offset the cost of below-market units. Instead, the market should dictate pricing and availability. There's more.

Revisions to the California Building Code should make the installation of certain equipment and systems driven by alleged "climate" benefits optional rather than mandatory, thereby allowing market demand to guide their adoption.

On top of that, a major reform enabling California's supply of homes to rapidly increase, thereby lowering prices, would be to repeal laws that discourage the construction of water and energy supply infrastructure, ensuring that the state's housing supply can again meet demand.

These policies will create the conditions where the private sector can again build affordable homes while still making a profit. The innovations that have occurred in the past few years as well as those that are just around the corner promise to deliver a future where urban centers and suburbs both experience a spectacular renaissance.

If we loosen the restrictions on land development, as well as the restrictions on development of energy, water, and building materials, and if we can significantly reduce the cost and the time required to get building permits, affordable market housing will be just one major dividend of these reforms. We can re-create the optimism and dynamism of California's golden age of building in the 1950s and '60s while incorporating the enormous innovation we've seen since then—

creating new cities and upgrading our existing cities and suburbs in positive, sustainable ways that we can only begin to imagine.

Californians should be creating new cities, built for the twenty-first century, offering an opportunity to incorporate the best new technologies and ideas, free of restrictions that inhibit innovation. New cities can incorporate everything we have learned over the past half century to engage in mindful development, with thoughtful urban design that always prioritizes its impact on the human experience.

There is plenty of room to build in California while protecting our precious natural heritage. We can give people housing choice and homeowner autonomy, reviving upward mobility for the working class and restoring the California Dream for everyone.

Cities can be revived. New, sustainable suburbs can be built—when thoughtfully conceived, they embody the finest aspirations of the garden city concept, an idealized vision of town planning where people live in healthy, spacious communities in proximity to open space and wildlife. Building new cities in California that meld garden city ideals with the latest innovations in architecture and sustainability is the antithesis of much-maligned "sprawl."

When it comes to housing and urban development, California can break out of its scarcity mindset, building new cities that embrace both new technologies along with a next-generation cultural identity that is both authentic and unique. This is how California can once again realize its potential, a place where people can live well, an example to the rest of the world.

Previous sections included specific components of some reforms we need. But we also have to change the vision of our leadership. Affordable housing does not have to be high-density. Cities should not be prevented from expanding outward. Infill and high density can make good sense economically and aesthetically, but only if the city can expand on its periphery at the same time.

Here are visions for how we build new cities and make the cities we already have truly great.

BUILD AND UPGRADE INFRASTRUCTURE

A fundamental obstacle to making housing affordable in California is that our state needs more energy, water, and transportation infrastructure. Even if private investors were not operating in a hyper-regulated environment, it is beyond their capacity to upgrade and expand the public infrastructure that supports their projects.

The economic argument goes something like this: The cost to build, for example, an aqueduct to transport winter floodwater from the Sacramento–San Joaquin Delta to quick-charging storage aquifers in the San Joaquin Valley is enormous. If 100 percent of the construction costs were paid for by a private company, the ratepayers who eventually consumed that stored water would pay a price too high for most households to afford.

Agricultural clients might be able to grow pistachios and almonds, which fetch a high price per pound, but tomatoes, which bring in less revenue by weight, would disappear from California's fields. The principle expressed by these examples extends to all enabling infrastructure. When end users have to pay too much for energy and water, the standard of living goes down, the cost of living goes up, and economic activity falters.

Californians thus have to answer a tough question: Do we want businesses to leave and residents to struggle financially, or do we want to subsidize the cost of public works in order to bring down the amount that private partners have to recoup from ratepayers? In the 1950s and '60s, so-called Pat Brown Democrats answered this question unequivocally.[1]

The state of California built the most magnificent system of water storage and interbasin transfers in the world.[2] It built the best network of universities in the world.[3] And it built freeways and expressways that connected every corner of the state and facilitated an era of spectacular growth.[4] There was surplus energy and water, the state was affordable, and millions of people moved here to follow their dreams.

What's changed? Californians remain willing to support the idea of serious investment in infrastructure. But the choices the state is making are terrible. Elected officials are not pouring billions of dollars into enabling infrastructure, but rather into *disabling* infrastructure. Instead of upgrading our natural gas pipelines, the legislature has declared war on natural gas and is spending tens of billions of dollars to subsidize solar farms, battery farms, and offshore wind.[5] These technologies remain unproven at scale and may be obsolete within a few decades.

Instead of permitting desalination plants on the Southern California coast—plants that could be built with a minimal infusion of public funds—or developing creative ways to divert floodwaters from the Sacramento–San Joaquin Delta, California's legislature is building a forty-five-mile-long tunnel under the delta to transport water from just one river, the Sacramento, to southbound aqueducts.[6]

This brings to mind a third example of hideous waste: California's high-speed rail project. As detailed previously, it was sold to voters as a way to move passengers from San Francisco to Los Angeles in two hours, at a cost of $30 billion to build.[7] Estimated travel time has expanded to four hours, and the estimated cost is now over $130 billion.[8] Pat Brown Democrats would have upgraded our railroads, widened and resurfaced our freeways, and built a few more freeways—and spent a fraction as much doing it.

The problem isn't just that leaving projects to public agencies breeds inefficiency. It does. But in the 1950s and '60s there was a consensus that California needed to grow. The state had a positive, practical, can-do approach. Back then we built energy, water, and transportation infrastructure that made everything else possible. The farm economy grew. Suburbs expanded around the cities, and homes were affordable. The state thrived.

That is the spirit we must recover in this age.

The results of practical infrastructure investment embrace all the human values that California's elites purport to cherish. When the government invests in sensible and practical transportation and water infrastructure and deregulates energy and land development, it delivers long-term economic dividends, realized for generations. These dividends enable more decentralized private ownership of homes and businesses, because the overhead payments for the basics—real estate, water, and energy—are affordable to working families along with small and emerging companies. When infrastructure is inadequate and prices soar, the only winners are the largest corporations and rentier class, who invest in artificially inflated assets and artificially overvalued commodities, making excessive profits as consumers struggle.

Imagine California with uncrowded freeways, inexpensive and abundant energy and water, and affordable homes, including beautiful, spacious single-family homes on large lots, if that's what people want. We had this before. We can have it again.

REINVENTING THE ECONOMIC MODEL OF OUR CITIES

As the virulence of the Covid pandemic subsided in 2020, a new phrase, "urban doom loop," became a common way to describe the failure of America's downtowns to recover economically.[9] The concept is simple enough. As occupancy in downtown buildings declines, businesses that service those occupants decline, tax revenues decline, and services are cut, thus causing still more businesses and commuters to relocate. This leads to a downward spiral.

A common solution proposed, which on the surface makes compelling sense, is to convert empty commercial space into apartments. Why not? We have vacant space and we have a housing shortage. But it's harder than it sounds. It isn't enough to urgently lift regulatory obstacles and rezone. The conversions have to make financial sense, and in most cases they don't. Commercial offices, for example, typically only have one restroom per floor. This means that converting a high-rise or midrise into a residential tower will require drilling holes for the bathroom plumbing through every floor in multiple places, from top to bottom—an extremely expensive job.

Notwithstanding the hard construction costs involved in conversion, which must be amortized, is the hard reality that except in the most high-end, gentrified echelons of urban residential real estate, the market price per square foot of leased commercial space greatly exceeds what the market will bear for residential space. Putting people into converted office buildings is a process that will require billions in government subsidies, if it is to happen at all. It's a good idea, but it might not be economically feasible except in limited circumstances.

We've already seen what billions in misguided subsidies have done to our cities. Just in 2023, total spending on homeless programs in Los Angeles County exceeded $3 billion.[10] Massive spending pursuant to the Housing First ideology, whereby the "unhoused" must be offered "permanent supportive housing" before they can be treated for addiction or trained for jobs, has turned the Southern California coast into a magnet for America's homeless.[11]

You cannot create a chic, culturally rich downtown while at the same time filling your hotels and formerly commercial high-rises with people who don't work and aren't sober. You will bankrupt your civic budget and you will scare away anyone with money and options. Successful downtowns, because they are beautiful and culturally rich, and because they host fabulously expensive buildings on the most expensive class of real estate there is, are by definition exclusive.

Despite these daunting reality checks, the preference for density over suburban expansion has become a quasi-religion among urban planners. One of the central tenets supporting this religion is the conventional wisdom, allegedly beyond all debate, that higher-density cities have less impact on the environment. But is the primary urban planning objective of higher density truly justifiable? Does it truly conform to the realities of economic geography and the obligations of environmental responsibility?

According to a recent and exhilaratingly contrarian study, *The Next American Cities*, published by the Urban Reform Institute, the answer to that question is emphatically no.[12] In a thorough discussion of every possible objection to urban expansion, coauthors Joel Kotkin and Wendell Cox take to pieces the density ideology. Some of their arguments should be self-evident by now.

For example, work-from-home technology has matured, with the pandemic constituting its shakedown cruise. Over 50 percent of the entire U.S. workforce was able to work remotely during the pandemic, up from only 7 percent prepandemic, and it is currently estimated that even with the pandemic over, the at-home workforce may not shrink below one-third of the total workforce.[13] This is a seismic shift. Downtown commercial real estate cannot recover from this unless either the overall metropolitan population of potential downtown commuters increases enough to make up for the loss, or something lures people back into the office. It also means that pressure on access roads will be permanently reduced, as there are fewer commuters.

There's another trend, however, decades in the making, that will not abate, which is the fact that jobs and people are migrating to suburbs. That was probably the most significant finding reported in the Urban Reform Institute's study: the clear preference of families, seniors, Latinos, Asian and Black Americans, as well as the foreign-born, to live in single-family detached homes, located in suburbs and exurbs.

Arguments in favor of more suburban development are comprehensive. There is plenty of available land. The transportation impact is overstated due to remote work and jobs following people to suburbs. Cars are becoming emissions-free and autonomous, greatly reducing their impact on the environment. The cost per square foot to construct housing in the urban core is far greater than in suburbs both because the real estate is more costly and because multistory residential structures have a much higher per-square-foot construction cost than wood-framed or prefab single- and two-story single-family homes.

Low-density, leafy suburbs have a lower per capita heat island impact than dense cities. Energy and water efficiency can be practiced in single-family homes just as effectively as they can be practiced in urban high-rises. Irrigated residential landscaping can be an ecologically healthy asset, beneficial for the environment. And the vast majority of Americans, certainly once they are planning to start a family, prefer living in detached homes in suburban communities. Higher density is fine to the degree that people want it and the market creates it—but it shouldn't be the goal of policymakers to force it.

Instead of rescuing our downtowns through further densification, why not de-densify them? Clear the streets and make them safe again by giving homeless people shelter in cheap-to-produce accommodation on inexpensive unused industrial land, and put lawbreakers in jail. In both cases, it may be the first chance they've ever had to recover their dignity and restart their lives. This will save billions of dollars when compared to the "permanent supportive housing" scam.

Create new spaces and new opportunities in the middle of central downtowns by demolishing commercial and residential buildings that are no longer economically viable. Central downtowns cannot be re-created as they were. They are not doomed, but they are morphing again, and reinventing them must accept the overall reality of decentralization. By embracing a strategy of decentralization, ironically, downtown real estate may come down enough in value that downtowns can once again become cultural magnets, if not commercial magnets, because the so-called bohemian cultural creatives will once again be able to afford to live and spend time there. More density and less density can actually coexist at the same time.

To make it all work, the trend in state infrastructure policies must be reversed, to deregulate energy and water development so private companies can afford to build new supply infrastructure, with public investment making up any shortfall. At the same time, the state must reverse course and deregulate and encourage new suburbs on the open periphery of urban areas, so as to vastly increase the supply of homes, which will make them as affordable today as they were in the 1950s. It can be done. Housing markets are regional, so home values won't moderate unless the state allows suburban construction as well as urban projects.

This is a more human, people-centric urban vision that defies the "progressive" orthodoxy. It is needed now more than ever. It will usher in the shared prosperity of a metropolitan megaboom that benefits everyone.

THE CITY OF THE FUTURE

Imagine California's cities a century from now. Imagine them as spectacular examples of a future that exceeds our wildest and most optimistic dreams. Imagine them with dazzling new buildings pushing skyward, with subways, transportation conduits, and physical infrastructure mostly underground, and penumbras of lower-density residential suburbs stretching outward from the city centers.

Getting from here to there won't be easy, but, to reiterate one of the primary themes of this book, if there's one place on earth where the best, most exciting and innovative version of human living and working, and the most positive urban future would be possible, it should be in California. Here are some of the things we might expect.

Growing Up, Down, and Outward
Ever since humans invented the built environment, and cities developed along major crossroads and on the forks of navigable rivers, meeting the challenge of providing adequate transportation has been a nonnegotiable prerequisite to continued growth and prosperity.

But how will cities remain inviting if most transportation conduits remain on surface streets and railways, at the same time as spectacular growth could mean the suburban and urban population density rising from 2,000 or 3,000 per square mile to 20,000 or 30,000 per square mile?[14] How will these cities retain the ability to offer sufficient pedestrian space and park space if the surface transportation arteries are required to handle an order-of-magnitude increase in traffic?

First, as the population density and absolute size of cities increase, the need for commensurate growth in transportation capacity will not be proportional. Some of the burden that might have traditionally required transportation capacity in past decades will go away. Growing percentages of workers will be working from home.[15] For better or for worse, additional millions of residents who might have used road and rail to travel to recreational destinations might be finding their tourism and social entertainment using stay-at-home video and virtual reality devices.[16]

An equally significant way that transportation capacity will not completely have to keep pace with the growth in urban populations is through rapid advances in the ways that cities, on-site, will be able to harvest rainwater and recycle wastewater, grow food, generate and store energy, and process garbage.[17] High-rise residential and commercial buildings will be designed to harvest rainwater, reuse their wastewater, and generate energy from the sun and wind. Innovations, for example, in photovoltaic technology will allow buildings to use their windows as solar panels to convert sunlight into electricity.[18] Indoor agriculture will include aquaponic, hydroponic, and aeroponic systems.[19] Presumably the emerging technologies of factory-produced high-protein products will also be sited within high-density urban neighborhoods.[20] Cities will not become entirely self-sufficient, but they will become far more so than ever before in history.

Nonetheless, as megacities grow, building new infrastructure and refining existing infrastructure, their need for rapid and uncongested transportation conduits will grow well beyond what exists today. But to solve this by relying solely on ground-based road and rail is no longer necessary. Precious and limited surface space can be preserved for human enjoyment by finding transportation solutions in the air and underground. This may sound fanciful, but it is nothing of the sort. At this moment, and for many years, virtually all major automotive and aerospace companies, along with dozens of high-tech companies, have been developing prototype passenger drones.

Already we are seeing freight drones being used by Amazon in two small U.S. cities: one in Northern California, the other in Texas.[21] The company intends to roll out delivery-drone service—to be called Prime Air—nationwide.[22] Amazon is not alone. At least twelve companies are developing drone delivery vehicles.[23]

But that is just the beginning of a revolution in air transportation.

As reported by *Air Mobility News*, there are five passenger drone companies now listed with a market value over $1 billion: Aero-Vironment, Joby, Vertical Aerospace, Archer Aviation, and Lilium. An additional seven companies are publicly listed with a market capitalization over $100 million: Ehang, ACSL, Parrot, AgEagle, Drone Delivery Canada, ONDAS, and Red Cat.[24]

Joby Aviation's eVTOL (electronic vertical takeoff and landing) "taxi drone" prototype has demonstrated a range of over 150 miles.[25] Its drone's range is extended because, while it takes off like a helicopter, in level flight it has a wing that provides lift. The six rotors on Joby's eVTOL point straight up to provide vertical lift during takeoff, then rotate 90 degrees to function as conventional propellers during flight. What the V-12 Osprey does for the military with turbojet-powered rotors, Joby does with electric motors and a battery.

But most passenger drone duty cycles will not require a range in excess of twenty miles, which is the range of the Ehang 216, a fully autonomous taxi drone that can transport two passengers and has already carried out over one thousand test flights.[26] Dozens of emerging companies are testing passenger drone prototypes.[27] One of them, based in Sweden, is leaning into the novelty of it all by naming its company Jetson Aero.[28] But the biggest companies on earth are also involved in the race to make drone transportation ubiquitous.

Among aerospace companies, these would include Boeing, Airbus, and Raytheon.[29] Every major airline is investing in passenger drone service, including Delta Air Lines, American Airlines, United Airlines, and Lufthansa.[30] Major automakers are deeply involved in the race to the air; entrants include Volkswagen, Honda, Toyota, and, of course, Tesla.[31] Not to be outdone, Apple is rumored to be working on a flying car, as is Microsoft in partnership with Hyundai.[32]

If, sooner or later, urban residents may count on seeing delivery drones, then passenger drones, making the skyline more interesting, a parallel revolution is happening out of sight. The revolution in underground tunneling technology has been quietly advancing for several years.

The global leader in tunneling systems is Herrenknecht AG, founded in 1975 and lead contractor on thousands of tunnel-boring projects around the world.[33] The company's projects range from digging underground metro systems in cities on every continent, to the Gotthard Base Tunnel in Switzerland, which at thirty-five miles is the longest tunnel in the world.[34] Leave it to the Germans to design machines several hundred feet long, and up to sixty feet in diameter, engineered to delve through the earth like a Sandworm out of Frank Herbert's novel *Dune*.[35]

But where the Germans lead, innovators nip at their heels. The Boring Company, founded by (who else?) Elon Musk, claims that the field of tunneling has not taken advantage of new technologies.[36] He proposes to lower the cost of tunneling by a factor of between 4 and 10 by: 1) tripling the power output of the tunnel boring machine's cutting unit, 2) continuously tunneling instead of alternating between boring and installing supporting walls, 3) automating the tunnel-boring machine, eliminating most human operators, and 4) replacing diesel motors with electric.

Musk has said, "The construction industry is one of the only sectors in our economy that has not improved its productivity in the last 50 years."[37] The Boring Company has already begun construction on the Vegas Loop, underground service extensions that will deliver passengers from the Las Vegas airport to destinations on the famed Vegas strip in three minutes instead of the typical thirty minutes required using aboveground transportation.[38] Beneath Los Angeles, the Boring Company has already completed and is testing a prototype tunnel that is 1.14 miles long and is claimed to have been built at a cost of only $10 million. If the Boring Company revolutionizes tunneling the way SpaceX revolutionized access to low earth orbit, the functions of the vertical city will indeed expand down into the earth as well as up into the sky.[39]

As the Herrenknecht website puts it, "Our high-tech machines enable high advance rates in any geology with maximum safety for buildings, infrastructures and personnel . . . modern, integrated tunnel systems for metro, road, railway, passenger, supply and disposal tunnels are the result."

The technologies needed to deliver flying cars are arriving fast, as are cost-effective tools to build bigger and upgraded underground transportation conduits. Above the skyline and under the streets, expect cities in the future to expand vertically, relieving congestion at the same time as more people live better lives on the same footprint of land.

Vertical Farms: Indoor Agriculture

Over 4 billion people have joined the global population in the last fifty years, putting stress on available farmland, water, and fertilizer. At the same time, the capacity of the planet to absorb farm waste—toxic farm runoff contaminating aquifers and rivers—has stretched the limit. Nearly 8 billion people now depend on 5.5 million square miles of water-guzzling farmland for their food.

California, global leader in outdoor agriculture, is now well positioned to become a global leader in the technology-driven future of indoor agriculture.

Vertical farms only require somewhere between 1 percent and 5 percent of the water required by outdoor farming. They also operate in a completely controlled environment, which eliminates the need for pesticides and herbicides.

They can be located anywhere. By siting them within urban areas, the transportation and refrigeration costs necessary to get the crops to market are largely eliminated.

An interesting 2021 study published in the *Rutgers Business Review* attempts to quantify these cost variables to compare traditional farming to vertical farming.[40] The authors found that vertical farming was at a huge disadvantage to traditional farming with respect to energy cost and labor cost while enjoying a decisive advantage in terms of water cost. The analysis was an oversimplification, since these costs vary greatly, depending on what crop is being compared, but overall it found vertical farming currently to run about 2.5 times more expensive per unit than traditional farming.

Apparently investors consider this cost disadvantage to be temporary. According to the Food and Agricultural Organization of the United Nations, farming worldwide is a $3.4 trillion industry, constituting 4 percent of total global GDP.[41] The vertical farming market, already worth an estimated $3.3 billion in 2020, is projected to grow to $24 billion by 2030.[42]

At that size, it will still represent a fraction of the total global farming economy. Its growth prospects—assuming the cost constraints can be overcome—are stunning.

In San Francisco, a company aptly named Plenty has already received nearly $1 billion in venture financing, with investors including Amazon's Jeff Bezos, Google's Eric Schmidt, and SoftBank's Masayoshi Son.[43] Plenty's CEO, Matt Barnard, intends to build five hundred farms in major cities around the world. Barnard was born into a seventh-generation Wisconsin farm family, but his vision for agritech is quintessential Silicon Valley.

Plenty's approach to achieving cost parity with traditional agriculture mirrors the leading vertical farming companies. It is attacking the labor disadvantage with robotics, with the goal of having a mostly automated vertical farm that remains safe and ergonomic for the remaining human workers. The challenge of energy to heat vertical farms and apply artificial sunlight to the plants is harder. Every serious contender in the large-scale vertical farming market considers its technological solutions and internal costs to be trade secrets.

Along with Plenty, another U.S.-based player is Bowery Farms in New Jersey, founded by Kimball Musk (yes, Kimball has a famous brother).[44] Bowery Farms, already valued at an estimated $2.3 billion, has two operating "warehouse farms" and is currently constructing three more. As reported in Bloomberg in 2022, it just acquired a robotics company, Traptic, which makes "artificial-intelligence-enabled robotic arms that pick strawberries."[45]

Outside the United States, Sky Green Farms in Singapore offers a look at how the challenges of artificial lighting and heating are minimized in a tropical climate.[46] With equatorial sunlight delivering roughly twelve hours of daylight year-round, Sky Green Farms claims to have no need for artificial lighting.

According to its website, it automatically moves the vertical towers of plant trays in and out of the sunlight coming into the periphery of the glass-clad building: "Rotation is powered by a unique patented hydraulic water-driven system which utilizes the momentum of flowing water and gravity to rotate the troughs. Only 40 watts of electricity (equivalent to one light bulb) is needed to power one 9 meter tall tower."

Skeptics may be forgiven for questioning the bold renewable-energy claim. The real question is: How much electricity does it take to grow a kilogram of food? Nonproprietary estimates that might answer this question are scarce. An in-depth 2012 study published by the National Center for Biotechnology Information evaluated hydroponic farming and concluded that most of the energy consumed by vertical farms is for heating and cooling, and transportation fuel to bring the produce to market.[47]

As for electricity for lighting, advances in LED technology, to the point where the spectral characteristics of the lights are tailored to each plant physiology, will bring down this cost. On the other hand, humanity is going to have to crack the challenge of abundant energy with or without the added demands of indoor farming, and if global food shortages become acute enough, it won't matter how much energy these farms require—they will still get built.

It may be profitable, or nearly so, to grow leafy greens and strawberries and wine grapes in your vertical farm, but what about wheat, corn, rice, soybeans, barley, sorghum, cotton, rapeseed, millet, and dry beans? These are the top ten crops by acreage in the world, and together these crops consume over 90 percent of all arable farmland.[48] Apart from the fact that tackling the chronic disease epidemic means we should be eating less of these corruptly subsidized crops anyway, solutions may be in the works.

Dickson Despommier, professor emeritus at Columbia University, is considered the father of vertical farming.[49] As he explained in a 2020 paper, "Wheat grown on a single hectare of land in a 10-layer indoor vertical facility could produce from . . . 220 to 600 times the current world average annual wheat yield."[50]

Imagine wheat, currently consuming nearly 25 percent of all farmland in the world, suddenly requiring a fraction of 1 percent of farmland. If Despommier's vision were actually implemented, and all the wheat in the world were grown this way, it could require buildings that altogether would have a footprint of only 1,500 square miles. Put another way, the space necessary to produce the world's wheat crop would shrink from 3,200 square feet per person to only 5 square feet per person.

As the world population passes the 8 billion mark, the ongoing innovations of the vertical farmers will play a growing role in feeding humanity—and could even boost the economies of cities.

Renewable Skyscrapers

Every so often a product comes along that presents itself as a "sustainable" innovation yet has compelling appeal even if sustainability isn't someone's top priority. Of course, *sustainability* has become something of an overused buzzword, but it generally refers to a production process that doesn't deplete natural resources or damage the environment.[51]

So-called mass timber, briefly described in the earlier section on wildfires, is such an innovation.[52] Able to replace reinforced concrete as a building material, it is economically competitive and aesthetically superior. It is perhaps the most profound innovation in building materials since the invention of reinforced concrete over 150 years ago—and it has the power to transform urban development.[53]

By every measure of sustainability, mass timber beats concrete. As a forest product, it is genuinely renewable. Since smaller trees can be used for mass timber rather than for conventional lumber, more comprehensive forest thinning and fire prevention operations are commercially viable and larger trees can remain untouched.[54]

For those who prioritize these variables, it is also an excellent way to permanently sequester carbon.[55] Manufacturing concrete, by contrast, is a far more energy-intensive process, and each year utilizes millions of tons of sand, which is, surprisingly, a dwindling and nonrenewable resource.[56]

Laminated veneer, commonly known as plywood, has been around for decades. Mass timber (also referred to by the more descriptive term *cross-laminated timber*) is where strips of wood are pressed together into large beams and panels, with each layer of grain running perpendicular to the layer above and below it. It has been around only since the 1990s.[57]

The products available today are amazing: structural pillars with cross sections 60 inches on a side; lateral beams; floor panels 8 inches thick, 10 feet wide, and 40 feet long.[58]

The specifications defining cross-laminated timber should silence the skeptics. They weigh about one-fifth as much as similar-sized structural materials made of reinforced concrete while offering the same strength.[59] They are not combustible. In hot structure fires, only the outer skin of the beams are charred. They are aesthetically pleasing and, unlike concrete, do not require surface treatments to soften their appearance.

This characteristic allows, for example, the floor panel in a high-rise unit to constitute the ceiling panel for the unit underneath. They have better thermal characteristics than concrete, meaning less additional insulation is required. And they can be manufactured to precise sizes and delivered ready for assembly, a tremendous time-saver.

You can't research the product without coming across endless computations of how much carbon mass timber will sequester, or horror stories about the amount of carbon emissions caused by the manufacture of concrete. But is mass timber renewable at scale? Could it replace reinforced concrete? The short answer is yes.

In the United States in 2020, about 370 million cubic yards of concrete were produced.[60] About 40 percent of that went for commercial real estate construction. If we assume half of that can be replaced by mass timber, that would mean our forests would need to replace 74 million cubic yards of concrete, which equates to 24 billion board-feet of timber. That sounds like a lot, but compared to the annual timber harvest in the United States, it's not.

According to the U.S. Forest Service, there are 12 trillion board-feet of timber volume in the United States and about 186 billion board-feet were harvested in 2018.[61] That is, the U.S. timber harvest each year represents about 2 percent of U.S. timber by volume. In the United States, forest growth has outpaced harvesting for many decades.[62] For mass timber to replace half the concrete used in commercial construction, the nation's forest harvest would have to increase by only 13 percent.

Increasing the timber harvest would certainly make sense in California, where the timber industry has been reduced from annual harvests of up to 6 billion board-feet as recently as the 1990s to only

1.5 billion board-feet in recent years.[63] The result has been over-crowding, with dense stands of unhealthy trees. In dry years, these trees drink up most of California's precipitation before it can percolate or run off, exacerbating the state's water shortage.

Also, as we have seen, the main reason for catastrophic forest fires in California is the combination of fire suppression and unreasonable restrictions on controlled burns or mechanical thinning, combined with the near destruction of the timber industry. So mass timber offers a public safety advantage too.

Despite some official resistance to increasing the harvest and man-ufacture of mass timber in-state, these products are catching on as a building material. California building codes have been updated to allow for construction of mass timber buildings up to eighteen stories tall.[64] Midrise buildings using mass timber are opening or under con-struction in Los Angeles, San Jose, San Francisco, Sacramento, and elsewhere across California.[65] One of the pioneers is Oakland-based start-up oWow.[66] The range of its projects shows the scale of the mass timber opportunity.

It's not always easy to know which technologies will gain the imprimatur of today's green clerisy; even advanced hybrid vehicles that provide versatility and economy are on the outs as extreme environmentalists promote purely electric vehicles. But advancements in mass timber should tick everyone's boxes—and it might soon transform our cities' skylines.

DRIVERLESS VEHICLES: ON LAND AND IN THE AIR

To enlighten those who have not watched the movie *2001: A Space Odyssey*, and to refresh the memories of those who have, the onboard computer named Hal did *not* malfunction. It was programmed by the designers of the spacecraft to consider the human crew expendable if their actions might jeopardize the mission.

To think that turning over control of transportation appliances to AI programs in the present day might lead to a human catastrophe at the hands of malevolent machines is paranoid. But to think that programs sophisticated enough to drive or fly us anywhere will not have *agency* is a failure of the imagination. Once they are here, self-driving cars won't just drive. They will also be our companionable chauffeurs, perhaps even offering stimulating conversation. Even if they're just "share cars," they will still know you intimately, because your psychographics are in the cloud.[67]

There is no place on earth better suited to bring these wonders to humanity than California, with our aerospace engineers, AI developers, and an ecosystem of venture investors that is second to none.

The reality of rapidly maturing AI technology is a necessary prerequisite context in which to frame the dawn of transportation free of drivers and pilots. How we are going to build the next generation of transportation hardware is a fascinating story. But it's the software inside that is a part of something much bigger. The internet-enabled—or is it Skynet?—algorithmic management of all things big and small.

The transformative impact of turning the management of all infrastructure, from the biggest hydroelectric plants or pipelines to the billions of household thermostats and water meters—along with every transportation asset we've ever invented—to automated mode is something to watch with eyes wide-open.

On the other hand, the benefits of automated vehicles are as dazzling as the dystopian scenarios are cautionary. New vehicle technologies offer improvements in safety, speed, convenience, fuel efficiency, cost, traffic congestion, and the environment. For example, the level of driving precision enabled by automation will permit vehicles to safely convoy on freeways at high speeds.[68] Bumper to bumper, these pelotons will achieve better fuel efficiency at the same time as their tight formations permit more congestion-free traffic per lane-mile of road.

Inside the urban core, automated vehicles will relieve traffic congestion in several ways. They will be able to gauge their speed to take into account the timing of traffic lights along the entire intended route. To the extent that shared cars are being used, fewer cars will be needed on the urban boulevards, since the incoming vehicles can drop off their passengers and then be used by someone else who is seeking an outgoing vehicle.[69]

This means urban traffic planners will have the welcome new ability to either do more with the same, or the same with less. That is, shared vehicles will allow either more traffic capacity with the existing urban network, or they will facilitate a stable capacity even while some urban lanes are transitioned into space for bicycles, scooters, or pedestrians.

Even these benefits don't fully describe how smart vehicles will relieve traffic congestion in cities. By the time vehicles are sophisticated enough to be fully autonomous, they will have total situational awareness—that is, each vehicle will know the location and destination of every other vehicle in the vicinity, and all of them will automatically swarm into routes that optimize the use of every street.[70] It will be as if human drivers were making perfect use of the Waze app.[71]

In the immediate future, the prototype application that is already here are self-driving taxis and buses. This makes sense, since they are perhaps the most efficient mass-transit applications possible. Unlike trains, they can go anywhere there is a flat surface. Also unlike trains, they're capable of far greater variation in configurations. At one extreme, a massive fleet of minibuses that only carry a few people can offer on-demand, point-to-point transportation covering an entire city. At the other, large buses each carrying one hundred people or more can convoy in and out of cities, offering the capacity of trains while retaining the route flexibility of cars.

Once the development costs of self-driving vehicles are amortized, the expectation is that they will deliver mass transit for far less, since labor remains the highest cost of transit operation—in high-income nations, around 70 percent of operating expenses.[72] But not so fast.

In the news site Streetsblog USA, which covers "the movement to end car dependence," the dawn of autonomous mass transit is being positioned as follows: "Will 'Autonomous' Buses Force Drivers Out of a Job—Or Make Them More Important Than Ever?"[73] As the blog put it, "The rise in vehicle automation technology—at least in the imperfect form in which it's expected to exist for the next few decades—may actually make trained transit professionals more important than ever before, and possibly even elevate their societal status and pay to a level similar to commercial airline pilots as the two jobs become more and more similar."

We may expect a fascinating tug-of-war between labor interests who will claim "transit professionals" will now have to be paid *more* as they drive less, versus public and private transportation innovators who will argue that we cannot afford to deliver universal "mobility alternatives" and end car dominance if we don't reduce the role of paid human operators. This controversy will likely drive innovation toward more microsolutions, shared cars, and minibuses where the presence of a human operator is obviously impractical.

The future of cars is inseparable from the future of AI and robotics; a future of total information awareness and algorithmic management with all the attendant ramifications. This may be a benevolent future of abundance and freedom from toil, as imagined (most of the time) by Robert Heinlein and Isaac Asimov, or it may bring with it the malign hellscape as imagined in the *Terminator* movies.[74]

Whatever the outcome, it won't be boring, as we flit from rooftop to rooftop in our passenger drones, from city to city in our high-speed convoys of driverless buses, and from address to address down on the streets, courtesy of cars that talk to us like long-lost friends.

CONCLUSION:
THE DREAM IS ALIVE

Restoring the California Dream involves practical policy solutions that can seem small-bore and mundane. Yet the compelling appeal of these solutions is not the grinding detail but the outcome they will collectively deliver, and in the fact that the problems they will solve—as well as the dreams they will fulfill—have universal appeal. These solutions, and the future vision they point toward, will captivate everyone, young and old, rich and poor, regardless of ethnicity or ideology or lifestyle. Prosperity and freedom have no identity. Realizing them is a goal shared by all.

We can move from defense to offense and change our policy environment. We can enact reforms to labor laws that will have what to some may be a surprising benefit of helping lift up all workers by creating more jobs and more opportunities. We can enact reforms to environmental regulations—again, in what will to some be a big surprise—that will benefit the environment while also lowering the cost of living. We can lower taxes and fees, especially on the basic essentials that form the building blocks of our economy, such as housing and energy. And we can reduce the size and complexity of government.

All of these reforms will help businesses stay in California and grow, as well as attract new businesses to relocate to the Golden State. At the same time, we will redirect public money away from failed programs and invest it in practical infrastructure that yields generational economic benefits, while returning to taxpayers whatever savings remain.

We will restore public safety with new laws that are tough but compassionate, with an emphasis on deterrence through certainty of accountability, combined with an emphasis on developing effective rehabilitation programs. We will develop programs to help and support young families, particularly those living in poverty, and by improving conditions during early childhood, we will rescue a generation while saving taxpayers money in the long run.

We will save K–12 education in California by insisting on higher standards, demanding transparency and accountability, introducing school choice, expanding charter schools, and protecting the public schools from the teachers unions. And we will manage our forests according to time-tested best practices instead of misguided environmental extremism, creating healthy forests and thousands of jobs, and generating tax revenues.

We can once again be a land of plenty, a place of unlimited possibility, abundance in place of scarcity. We can once again be that home for doers and dreamers, rebels and creators, visionaries and builders. That is the spirit of California, and it's time to reignite it.

These are ideas with power that transcend campaign financing. These are arguments that counter and overcome millions in opposition political spending. These policies represent a transformative, optimistic agenda to which politicians afflicted with "progressive" pathologies have no answer. The vision of the future that will come when these policies are realized is one that every Californian will want to leave for their children and grandchildren.

This is the positive Califuture we deserve, the antidote to Califailure. And it belongs to everyone.

ACKNOWLEDGMENTS

These sections tend to go on and on forever, so I would like to keep this one brief. Keith Urbahn was the instigator of this book, and I am immeasurably grateful to him for doing so, as well as for all his friendship and guidance over the years. Ed Ring was the essential ingredient in making this book happen. It literally would not exist without him. I am so thrilled to have found a policy, research and writing partner who is such a joy to work with. Eric Nelson, my brilliant editor at HarperCollins, was entirely responsible for transforming my idea for this book from a pedestrian recitation of issues-based grievances into something that I hope is more interesting and significant. Eric's challenges and provocations were indispensable. Of course the real work is turning a book from error and typo-ridden manuscript into finished product: James Neidhardt and all the production team at HarperCollins made that process perfectly smooth and easy—for me, at least! And finally I would like to put on record my immense gratitude to Rupert Murdoch, for giving me the extraordinary privilege of a platform at Fox News; to Lachlan Murdoch and Suzanne Scott for their years of friendship and support; and to every single friend and colleague in our warm, beautiful Fox News family. I am so proud and happy to have been part of it.

NOTES

Introduction

1. https://unitedwaysca.org/wp-content/uploads/2023/10/2023-ExecutiveSummary.pdf.
2. https://www.theguardian.com/us-news/2023/aug/23/california-firefighter-super-commuters-traveling-work.
3. https://www.cde.ca.gov/nr/ne/yr22/yr22rel50.asp.
4. https://ballotpedia.org/California_Proposition_47,_Reduced_Penalties_for_Some_Crimes_Initiative_(2014).
5. https://www.ocregister.com/2023/05/27/where-do-people-go-when-they-leave-california-and-why/.

Chapter 1: One-Party Rule

1. https://capitalresearch.org/article/big-labors-golden-state-part-3/.
2. https://showmeinstitute.org/blog/government-unions/what-was-fdrs-stance-on-government-unions/.
3. https://www.ed-data.org/article/Negotiating-Teachers'-Contracts-in-California. See also https://lao.ca.gov/1995/010195_calguide/cgsgov2.html.
4. https://californiaglobe.com/fr/the-financial-power-of-californias-government-unions/.
5. https://ballotpedia.org/California_State_Legislature.
6. https://ballotpedia.org/California_Proposition_25,_Simple_Majority_Vote_to_Enact_State_Budget_Amendment_(2010).
7. https://wedrawthelines.ca.gov/.
8. https://wedrawthelines.ca.gov/transition/index/.
9. https://wedrawthelines.ca.gov/final-maps/.
10. https://ballotpedia.org/California_state_executive_official_elections,_2022.

Chapter 2: Elitism

1. https://health.sccgov.org/news/story/meet-doctor-who-ordered-bay-areas-coronavirus-lockdown.
2. https://www.latimes.com/food/story/2021-03-18/timeline-los-angeles-dining-culture-march-2021-covid-19.
3. https://thepineapplehill.com/menu.
4. https://abc7news.com/los-angeles-country-restaurant-owner-viral-video-coronavirus-restrictions-covid-rates-cases/8530341/.
5. https://calmatters.org/politics/2020/03/gavin-newsom-california-coronavirus-shutdown-order/.
6. https://www.latimes.com/business/story/2020-04-02/la-fi-coronavirus-california-unemployed-mother.
7. https://www.latimes.com/business/story/2020-04-02/la-fi-coronavirus-california-unemployed-mother.

8. https://www.latimes.com/business/story/2022-01-06/blood-and-maggots-how
    -the-pandemic-made-hotel-housekeeper-more-difficult-and-disgusting.

9. https://www.dailynews.com/2020/04/08/la-hotel-rooms-come-online-to
    -quarantine-homeless-people-amid-coronavirus-outbreak/.

10. https://www.foxla.com/news/fox-11-obtains-exclusive-photos-of-gov-newsom-at
    -french-restaurant-allegedly-not-following-covid-19-protocols.

11. https://www.politico.com/states/california/story/2020/11/13/west-coast-states
    -issue-travel-advisory-ahead-of-thanksgiving-week-1336371.

12. https://www.chronline.com/stories/newsom-garcetti-get-blowback-for-maskless
    -photos-with-magic-johnson-at-rams-49ers-game,283705.

13. https://www.newsweek.com/gavin-newsom-mask-california-sofi-magic-johnson
    -1674517.

14. https://www.latimes.com/california/story/2021-09-21/sf-mayor-under-fire-for
    -going-maskless-attacks-fun-police.

15. https://nypost.com/2022/02/02/la-mayor-eric-garcetti-held-breath-for-maskless
    -photo-with-magic-johnson/.

16. https://nypost.com/2022/02/14/la-mayor-eric-garcetti-celebs-called-out-for
    -maskless-super-bowl/.

17. https://www.ksby.com/calif-senate-passes-bill-to-stop-employees-confronting
    -shoplifters.

18. https://www.washingtontimes.com/news/2024/feb/1/target-employee-blames
    -gavin-newsom-for-brazen-sho/.

19. https://www.politico.com/states/california/story/2020/10/30/newsom-sends-his
    -children-back-to-school-classrooms-in-california-1332811.

20. https://calmatters.org/commentary/2019/01/gavin-newsoms-keeping-it-all-in-the
    -family/.

21. https://www.britannica.com/money/J-Paul-Getty.

22. https://sjvsun.com/california/sour-grapes-emerge-as-most-calif-wineries-close
    -while-newsoms-winery-remains-open/.

23. https://www.snopes.com/fact-check/california-wineries-newsom/.

24. https://www.city-journal.org/article/californias-looming-crime-catastrophe.

25. https://www.foxla.com/news/new-california-bill-would-make-illegal-immigrants
    -eligible-for-first-time-homebuyer-loans.

26. https://www.opportunitynowsv.org/blog/mom-and-pop-property-owners-blast
    -city-scheme-to-favor-non-profits-in-housing-market.

27. https://www.collinsdictionary.com/us/dictionary/english/masters-of-the
    -universe.

Chapter 3: Narcissism

1. https://medium.com/@GavinNewsom/the-california-dream-starts-at-home
    -9dbb38c51cae.

2. https://calmatters.org/housing/2022/10/newsom-california-housing-crisis/.

3. https://www.sfgate.com/politics/article/Newsom-details-plan-for-homeless
    -Mayor-elect-2509363.php.

4. https://www.politico.com/story/2013/10/bob-filner-charged-san-diego-098329.

5. https://abc7news.com/charles-barkley-san-francisco-homeless-crooks-nba-all-star
    -game-sf-dirty/14447012/.

6. https://www.psychologytoday.com/us/blog/insight-is-2020/202306/the
   -narcissists-empathy-for-the-underdog-explained.
7. https://www.telegraph.co.uk/world-news/2023/08/30/homeless-attack-telegraph
   -reader-bay-area-san-francisco/.
8. https://www.kron4.com/news/bay-area/94-year-old-man-attacked-killed-by
   -homeless-man-in-san-francisco/.
9. https://sfpublicdefender.org/news/2022/06/sf-jury-acquits-man-of-murder-in
   -accidental-death-of-glen-park-resident/.
10. https://www.sf.gov/sites/default/files/2023-03/Mental%20Health%20SF%20
    Population%20Summary.pdf.
11. https://www.sfchronicle.com/sf/article/sf-homeless-hotels-costs-18659297.php.
12. https://sfethics.org/commission/budget.
13. https://www.dailysignal.com/2024/02/14/san-francisco-spent-massive-amount
    -of-taxpayer-dollars-to-house-homeless-during-pandemic/.
14. https://missionlocal.org/2018/10/the-complex-legacy-of-george-gascon/.
15. https://www.kqed.org/news/11765010/timeline-the-frustrating-political-history
    -of-homelessness-in-san-francisco.
16. https://www.macrotrends.net/global-metrics/cities/us/ca/san-francisco/property
    -crime-rate-statistics.
17. https://web.archive.org/web/20081031121928/http://foia.fbi.gov/weather
    /weath2a.pdf.
18. https://www.latimes.com/opinion/story/2022-06-01/chesa-boudin-recall
    -criminal-justice-reform-san-francisco.
19. https://www.public.news/p/narcissism-of-the-apocalypse.
20. https://www.history.com/this-day-in-history/marx-publishes-manifesto.
21. https://www.goodreads.com/book/show/170448.Animal_Farm.
22. https://a17.asmdc.org/press-releases/20240401-california-introduces-bill-give
    -workers-right-disconnect-non-emergency.
23. https://news.bloomberglaw.com/daily-labor-report/right-to-disconnect-plan-in
    -california-hits-employer-backlash.
24. https://www.fisherphillips.com/en/news-insights/california-bill-right-to
    -disconnect-could-impact-your-business.html.
25. https://www.pewresearch.org/race-and-ethnicity/2020/08/11/about-one-in-four
    -u-s-hispanics-have-heard-of-latinx-but-just-3-use-it/.
26. https://www.documentcloud.org/documents/6276132-EthnicStudies-Draft
    -Glossary.html.
27. https://www.spanishdict.com/conjugate/comer.
28. https://en.wikipedia.org/wiki/Pedro_Infante.
29. https://www.aei.org/op-eds/theres-some-truth-in-those-bizarre-charts-about
    -whiteness/.

Chapter 4: Maoism

1. https://s.wsj.net/public/resources/documents/stanfordlanguage.pdf.
2. https://www.insidehighered.com/news/2023/01/11/amid-backlash-stanford
   -removes-harmful-language-list.
3. https://www.thefp.com/p/why-i-am-suing-ucla.
4. https://www.change.org/p/ucla-fire-ucla-professor-gordon-klein.

5. https://www.aei.org/carpe-diem/ucla-lecturer-gordon-klein-fights-back-against-higher-educations-diversity-inclusion-equity-die-industrial-complex-and-a-woke-mob/.
6. https://bariweiss.substack.com/f/c4a8f715-54fd-4496-a661-909808caf480.pdf.
7. https://www.thefp.com/p/why-i-am-suing-ucla.
8. https://www.cal-catholic.com/ucla-prof-gordon-klein-holds-the-line-after-george-floyd-will-get-day-in-court-soon/.
9. https://whyevolutionistrue.com/2023/06/29/professor-lost-job-offer-at-ucla-after-grad-students-object-to-his-views-about-dei-statements/.
10. https://www.nytimes.com/2023/09/08/us/ucla-dei-statement.html.
11. https://unherd.com/newsroom/ucla-decides-against-hiring-professor-after-student-backlash/.
12. https://career.ucla.edu/resources/diversity-statements/.
13. https://www.nytimes.com/2023/09/08/us/ucla-dei-statement.html.
14. https://reason.org/commentary/californias-schools-are-failing-black-students/.
15. https://americanmind.org/salvo/the-peoples-republic-of-campus/.
16. https://www.opportunitynowsv.org/blog/sfsu-hedges-on-upholding-free-speech-following-assault-of-guest-speaker.
17. https://www.usnews.com/best-graduate-schools/top-law-schools/law-rankings?_sort=my_rankings-asc.
18. https://law.stanford.edu/wp-content/uploads/2023/03/Next-Steps-on-Protests-and-Free-Speech.pdf.
19. https://www.palladiummag.com/2022/06/13/stanfords-war-on-social-life/.
20. https://x.com/WillSwaim/status/1785013708714074117.
21. https://www.cta.org/our-advocacy/social-justice.
22. https://www.cta.org/hrprogramming.
23. https://dictionary.cambridge.org/us/dictionary/english/folx.
24. https://www.whitesupremacyculture.info/what-is-it.html.
25. https://www.scribd.com/document/468654458/SameStormDIffBoats-FINAL. See also https://californiaglobe.com/articles/l-a-teachers-union-says-schools-cant-reopen-unless-charter-schools-shut-down-and-police-are-defunded/.
26. https://stophate.calcivilrights.ca.gov/s/.
27. https://stophate.calcivilrights.ca.gov/s/.
28. https://stophate.calcivilrights.ca.gov/s/.

Chapter 5: Climatism

1. https://www.statista.com/statistics/942842/largest-california-wildfires-acres-burned/.
2. https://www.sacbee.com/news/politics-government/capitol-alert/article2459 48120.html.
3. https://calmatters.org/environment/2020/09/california-governor-climate-emergency/.
4. https://www.statista.com/statistics/1010152/transportation-sector-co2-emissions-us-by-state/. See also https://fred.stlouisfed.org/series/EMISSCO2TOTVTTTOCAA#:~:text=Download,2023%201:55%20PM%20CDT.
5. https://www.aclu.org/documents/brief-history-california-marriage-cases. See also https://www.history.com/this-day-in-history/obergefell-v-hodges-ruling-same-sex-marriage-legalized-nationwide.

6. https://ielc.libguides.com/sdzg/factsheets/californiacondor/population.
7. https://governors.library.ca.gov/addresses/s_34-JBrown1.html.
8. https://calmatters.org/commentary/2019/05/newsom-shrinks-brown-bullet-train-delta-tunnels/.
9. https://www.eia.gov/dnav/pet/hist/LeafHandler.ashx?n=PET&s=MCRFPCA2&f=M.
10. https://www.energy.ca.gov/data-reports/energy-almanac/californias-petroleum-market/foreign-sources-crude-oil-imports.
11. https://clkrep.lacity.org/onlinedocs/2017/17-0447_misc_71_07-29-2019.pdf.
12. https://www.eia.gov/analysis/studies/usshalegas/pdf/usshaleplays.pdf.
13. https://www.eia.gov/analysis/studies/usshalegas/pdf/usshaleplays.pdf.
14. https://williamliggett.com/2018/05/28/bunker-fuel-sounds-bad-its-worse-than-it-sounds/.
15. https://legiscan.com/CA/text/SB12/id/2615884.
16. https://www.gov.ca.gov/2022/11/30/governor-newsom-convenes-special-session-to-hold-oil-industry-accountable-for-price-gouging-keep-money-in-californians-pockets/.
17. https://www.gov.ca.gov/2023/03/28/governor-newsom-signs-gas-price-gouging-law-california-took-on-big-oil-and-won/.
18. https://gasprices.aaa.com/?state=CO.
19. https://gasprices.aaa.com/?state=CA.
20. https://taxfoundation.org/data/all/state/state-gas-tax-rates-2023/.
21. https://www.kqed.org/science/1991432/california-releases-formal-proposal-to-end-fracking-in-the-state.
22. https://www.independent.com/2024/03/16/santa-barbara-environmental-groups-looks-to-expand-californias-proposed-fracking-ban/.
23. https://www.theguardian.com/environment/2024/apr/09/berkeley-natural-gas-ban-lawsuit-repeal.
24. https://www.kqed.org/science/1992085/san-francisco-will-continue-enforcing-gas-ban-in-new-buildings-despite-berkeleys-repeal-of-similar-rules.
25. https://www.cleanenergyconnection.org/article/how-prepare-gas-bans-when-planning-your-home-upgrades.
26. https://ww2.arb.ca.gov/sites/default/files/classic/cc/inventory/Wildfire%20Emission%20Estimates%20for%202022%20%28ADA%29.pdf.
27. https://www.sciencedirect.com/science/article/pii/S0269749122011022#bib1. See also https://ww2.arb.ca.gov/sites/default/files/classic/cc/inventory/2000-2020_ghg_inventory_trends.pdf.
28. https://www.sciencedirect.com/science/article/pii/S0269749122011022#:~:text=Wildfire%20emissions%20in%202020%20were,climate%20change%20is%20%247.1%20billion.
29. https://www.gov.ca.gov/2022/11/16/california-releases-worlds-first-plan-to-achieve-net-zero-carbon-pollution/.
30. https://calmatters.org/california-wildfire-map-tracker/. See also https://www.minneapolisfed.org/about-us/monetary-policy/inflation-calculator/consumer-price-index-1913-.
31. https://mcclintock.house.gov/newsroom/speeches/our-forests-tragedy. See also https://californiaglobe.com/fl/california-is-on-fire-again-and-it-was-preventable/.

32. https://www2.census.gov/geo/maps/cong_dist/cd113/cd_based/ST06/CD113
    _CA04.pdf.
33. https://www.fs.usda.gov/pnw/pubs/pnw_gtr908.pdf.
34. https://gvwire.com/2020/09/15/california-forests-80-600-denser-than-150-years
    -ago-uc-researcher-says-biomass-is-one-of-the-answers/.
35. For studies: https://www.pnas.org/doi/10.1073/pnas.1410186112. Testimony:
    https://goldrushcam.com/sierrasuntimes/index.php/news/local-news/38779
    -previous-tree-mortality-and-density-big-factors-in-the-devastating-2020-creek
    -fire-in-california. And journalistic investigations: https://www.latimes.com/local
    /lanow/la-me-ln-forest-study-20150119-story.html.
36. https://www.sciencedaily.com/releases/2018/04/180424160251.htm.
37. https://www.sfchronicle.com/politics/article/Kamala-Harris-sounds-climate
    -change-alarm-from-15570029.php.
38. https://www.gov.ca.gov/2020/09/23/governor-newsom-announces-california-will
    -phase-out-gasoline-powered-cars-drastically-reduce-demand-for-fossil-fuel-in
    -californias-fight-against-climate-change/.
39. https://www.science.org/content/article/save-forests-cut-some-trees-down-scientists
    -say. See also https://www.sciencedaily.com/releases/2018/04/180424160251.htm.
40. Peter Zeihan, *The End of the World is Just the Beginning* (New York: Harper-
    Collins, 2022), 268.
41. https://www.goodreads.com/book/show/60784614-cobalt-red.
42. https://www.pbs.org/newshour/show/california-sues-oil-companies-for
    -exacerbating-climate-change.
43. https://builtin.com/hardware/new-battery-technologies.
44. https://www.bankrate.com/real-estate/median-home-price/?tpt=b#how-much.
    See also https://www.census.gov/quickfacts/fact/table/CA/BZA210221.
45. https://www.theguardian.com/us-news/2023/jul/21/climate-crisis-cost-of-living
    -energy-water-california.
46. https://calmatters.org/environment/2024/06/california-drinking-water-failing
    -systems/.

Chapter 6: Socialism

1. https://www.potreroview.net/short-cuts-48/.
2. https://www.sf.gov/sites/default/files/2023-07/AARAC%20Reparations%20
   Final%20Report%20July%207%2C%202023.pdf.
3. https://www.urban.org/policy-centers/cross-center-initiatives/state-and-local
   -finance-initiative/projects/state-fiscal-briefs/california. See also https://www
   .statista.com/statistics/187834/gdp-of-the-us-federal-state-of-california-since
   -1997/.
4. https://lao.ca.gov/reports/2013/bud/spending-plan/spending-plan-073013.aspx.
5. https://calbudgetcenter.org/resources/a-guide-to-the-california-state-budget
   -process/.
6. https://www.macrotrends.net/global-metrics/states/california/population.
7. https://edsource.org/2022/california-community-colleges-eye-a-different-future
   -amid-pandemic-disruption/681483. See also https://www.ppic.org/publication
   /factors-and-future-projections-for-k-12-declining-enrollment/.

8. https://edsource.org/2023/cal-state-contends-with-unprecedented-enrollment-declines/684803.
9. https://www.ocregister.com/2022/12/24/as-prisons-close-can-we-save-their-host-communities/.
10. https://leginfo.legislature.ca.gov/faces/billNavClient.xhtml?bill_id=201320140AB1050.
11. https://californiapolicycenter.org/the-boondoggle-archipelago/.
12. https://calhps.com/wp-content/uploads/2023/03/policy-brief-unsheltered-homelessness-11.20.2018.pdf. See also https://www.huduser.gov/portal/sites/default/files/pdf/2023-AHAR-Part-1.pdf.
13. https://legiscan.com/CA/text/SB770/id/2844348.
14. https://datausa.io/profile/naics/restaurants-food-services.
15. https://www.fordharrison.com/california-serves-up-another-headache-for-the-restaurant-industry.
16. https://legalaidatwork.org/factsheet/meal-breaks-and-rest-breaks/.
17. https://www.abc.ca.gov/new-law-requiring-bars-serving-spirits-to-offer-drug-testing-devices-to-take-effect-july-1/.
18. https://www.callaborlaw.com/entry/california-reaches-a-fast-food-compromise-increasing-minimum-wage-for-workers.
19. https://abcnews.go.com/Business/fast-food-workers-california-earn-20-hour-workers/story?id=106097720.
20. https://www.paycom.com/resources/blog/minimum-wage-rate-by-state/.
21. https://advocacy.calchamber.com/policy/issues/private-attorneys-general-act/.
22. https://californiacala.org/cala-in-the-news-posts/victor-gomez-executive-director-of-ca-cala-sits-down-with-california-insider.
23. https://www.investopedia.com/california-assembly-bill-5-ab5-4773201.
24. https://mooreonhealth.com/2020/06/06/assembly-bill-5-limits-access-to-healthcare/.
25. https://travelingnp.com/2020/12/18/california-ab5-bill/.
26. https://landline.media/ab5-harms-small-business-truckers-ooida-says/.
27. https://www.foxbusiness.com/small-business/truck-driver-shares-painful-decision-leave-california-sake-business.
28. https://www.nationalreview.com/2022/12/california-destroys-its-independent-truckers/.
29. https://www.cpuc.ca.gov/-/media/cpuc-website/divisions/energy-division/documents/demand-response/demand-response-workshops/advanced-der---demand-flexibility-management/joint-ious-opening-testimony-exhibit-1.pdf.
30. https://www.cde.ca.gov/ds/ad/ceffingertipfacts.asp.
31. https://oag.ca.gov/system/files/media/ab3121-reparations-interim-report-2022.pdf.
32. https://calmatters.org/california-divide/2022/09/reparations-task-force/.
33. https://oag.ca.gov/ab3121/report.
34. https://oag.ca.gov/system/files/media/exec-summary-ca-reparations.pdf.
35. https://www.latimes.com/california/story/2022-09-25/california-reparations-task-force-hears-from-experts-as-it-starts-to-dig-in-on-specifics.
36. https://calmatters.org/education/k-12-education/2023/10/california-student-test-scores/.

Chapter 7: Bureaucratism

1. https://ww2.arb.ca.gov/news/carb-passes-new-use-locomotive-regulation-estimated-yield-over-32-billion-health-benefits-0.
2. https://govt.westlaw.com/calregs/AgencyList.
3. https://www.waterboards.ca.gov/water_issues/programs/stormwater/docs/sb205/sb205_cities_counties_faq_eg.pdf.
4. https://guides.loc.gov/industry-research/classification-sic.
5. https://www.waterboards.ca.gov/water_issues/programs/stormwater/sic.html.
6. https://www.usbr.gov/projects/pdf.php?id=55.
7. https://www.youtube.com/watch?v=oD0DkZ8p-pw.
8. https://transparentcalifornia.com/salaries/search/?q=Alice+Busching+Reynolds.
9. Karla Nemeth: https://transparentcalifornia.com/salaries/search/?q=Karla+Nemeth. Liane Randolph: https://transparentcalifornia.com/salaries/search/?q=Liane+M.+Randolph.
10. https://centerforjobs.org/califormers. See also https://centerforjobs.org/about.
11. https://www.nzredwood.co.nz/profile/. See also https://www.forestinvest.com/q4-newsletter-2020-2/.
12. https://www.wfaa.com/article/news/local/california-landsea-homes-homebuilder-company-hq-move-to-dallas-will-cut-costs-boost-texas-footprint-ceo-says/287-07eaa52a-2dc0-4ed6-9a80-6ccfe1707020.
13. https://avocadosfrommexico.com/. See also https://www.ers.usda.gov/data-products/chart-gallery/gallery/chart-detail/?chartId=103669.
14. https://advocacy.calchamber.com/2021/02/25/california-still-a-top-exporting-state/.
15. https://labormarketinfo.edd.ca.gov/cgi/databrowsing/localAreaProfileQSResults.asp?menuChoice=occExplorer&state=true&geogArea=0601000000&selectedArea=California.
16. https://www.bls.gov/news.release/laus.nr0.htm.
17. https://capitalresearch.org/article/big-labors-golden-state-part-3/.
18. https://californiapolicycenter.org/californias-public-sector-unions-rake-in-921-billion-in-annual-revenue/.
19. https://calmatters.org/commentary/2024/05/newsom-tax-increases-business-budget/.

Chapter 8: Compassionism

1. https://da.lacounty.gov/sites/default/files/pdf/DA-Bio_English_03_2022.pdf.
2. https://www.ojp.gov/pdffiles1/nij/247350.pdf.
3. https://engineering.osu.edu/quick-guide-isms-and-phobias.
4. https://www.georgegascon.org/wp-content/uploads/2020/12/SPECIAL-DIRECTIVE-20-06-.docx.pdf.
5. https://www.heritage.org/crime-and-justice/commentary/meet-george-gascon-the-rogue-prosecutor-whose-policies-are-wreaking.
6. https://www.latimes.com/california/story/2020-04-30/los-angeles-police-blame-zero-bail-rise-repeat-offenders.
7. https://ktla.com/news/local-news/gardena-plumber-who-lost-30000-worth-of-tools-frustrated-with-crime-laws/.

8. https://capitalresearch.org/article/living-room-pundits-updated-guide-to-soros
    -district-attorneys/.
9. https://www.washingtonpost.com/nation/2023/03/20/oakland-prosecutor-crime
    -prison/. See also https://www.pleasantonweekly.com/news/2023/02/15/new-district
    -attorney-under-fire-for-controversial-plea-deal/.
10. https://www.cnn.com/2024/02/06/business/oakland-crime-business/index.html.
11. https://abc7news.com/oakland-business-strike-businesses-close-tuesday-crime
    -robberies/13830589/.
12. https://x.com/sunrisebayarea/status/1274049700610617344.
13. https://www.latimes.com/local/la-me-teachers3-2009may03-story.html.
14. https://www.lausd.org/site/handlers/filedownload.ashx?moduleinstanceid=81764&
    dataid=135710&FileName=FINGERTIP_FACTS_23-24.pdf.
15. https://californiapolicycenter.org/vergara-ten-years-in-the-rearview/.
16. https://www.nbclosangeles.com/news/local/where-do-problem-teachers-go-the
    -rubber-room/1946484/.
17. https://californiapolicycenter.org/vergara-ten-years-in-the-rearview/.
18. https://s10294.pcdn.co/wp-content/uploads/2018/04/Spring2018_Vergara-v.-CA.pdf.
19. https://vimeo.com/90273109.
20. https://calmatters.org/education/2016/02/how-to-follow-vergara-v-california/.
21. https://edsource.org/2016/plaintiffs-appeal-vergara-decision-and-back-legislative
    -fix/564777.
22. https://voiceofsandiego.org/2019/08/15/how-do-misbehaving-teachers-keep-their
    -jobs-districts-unions-blame-each-other/.
23. https://californiaglobe.com/articles/gov-newsom-signs-bill-banning-public
    -school-suspensions-for-willful-defiance/.
24. https://www.sfchronicle.com/crime/article/oakland-car-thefts-rising-18453221
    .php.
25. https://www.oaklandedfund.org/projects/restorative-justice/.
26. https://www.oaklandedfund.org/projects/restorative-justice/.
27. https://catalog.results4america.org/case-studies/rj-in-schools-oakland. See also
    https://results4america.org/.
28. https://www.cbs8.com/article/news/politics/proposed-ca-bill-ab1840-undocumented
    -immigrants-homeownership/509-7ea14326-13d1-42c5-86e4-d3b39c1f92d7.
29. https://leginfo.legislature.ca.gov/faces/billNavClient.xhtml?bill_id=202120220
    SB960.
30. https://apnews.com/article/fact-checking-046640064186.
31. https://www.latimes.com/california/story/2022-10-27/mexican-mafia-money
    -making-operation-los-angeles-county-jails.
32. https://www.nytimes.com/2009/12/18/us/18corrupt.html.
33. https://ktla.com/news/local-news/deputy-caught-with-100-pounds-of-fentanyl
    -was-working-for-el-chapos-cartel-report-says/.
34. https://www.usatoday.com/in-depth/news/nation/2023/06/18/cartel-backed-pot
    -grows-linked-to-california-oregon-human-trafficking/70329795007/. See also
    https://www.ojp.gov/ncjrs/virtual-library/abstracts/heroin-trafficking-golden
    -triangle.
35. https://www.usatoday.com/in-depth/news/nation/2023/06/18/cartel-backed-pot
    -grows-linked-to-california-oregon-human-trafficking/70329795007/.

36. https://www.latimes.com/local/california/la-me-hmong-marijuana-siskiyou
-20170910-htmlstory.html.

37. https://www.bloomberg.com/news/newsletters/2023-05-08/california-s-illicit
-marijuana-is-making-water-shortages-worse.

38. https://www.hcn.org/articles/water-a-california-county-spars-over-water-scarcity
-illicity-marijuana-and-racism/.

39. https://apnews.com/article/lifestyle-environment-and-nature-california
-discrimination-marijuana-14b9dfb417c0c538d5f52ddad1cfa0cb.

40. https://www.siskiyou.news/2023/10/31/get-siskiyou-back-get-involved-larue/.

41. https://www.newsnationnow.com/us-news/immigration/border-coverage/cartels
/cartels-native-reservations-fentanyl/. See also https://www.usatoday.com/in-depth
/news/nation/2021/12/19/mexican-drug-cartels-move-in-on-californias-shadow
-marijuana-industry/8960873002/; https://nypost.com/2023/07/10/honduran
-migrants-mexican-cartels-overtaking-san-francisco/;https://www.youtube.com
/watch?v=PTmaUMmz-Dc.

42. https://ballotpedia.org/Shannon_Grove.

43. https://ballotpedia.org/Nancy_Skinner_(California).

44. https://ballotpedia.org/California_State_Senate_District_9.

Chapter 9: Cronyism

1. https://www.hcd.ca.gov/about-hcd/newsroom/las-largest-supportive-housing
-project-opens.

2. https://www.foxla.com/news/dtla-luxury-high-rise-homeless-shelter-opens.

3. https://www.hcd.ca.gov/about-hcd/newsroom/las-largest-supportive-housing
-project-opens.

4. https://www.dailynews.com/2024/06/19/las-latest-homeless-housing-project-at
-nearly-600k-a-unit-opens-in-skid-row/. See also https://www.weingart.org/.

5. https://www.youtube.com/watch?v=1_QvH4WLCRQ&t=622s.

6. https://www.youtube.com/watch?si=MGjP6W_WUjnizpDl&t=82&v=tbJ-yANJSo0
&feature=youtu.be.

7. https://spectrumnews1.com/ca/southern-california/homelessness/2021/09/28/la
-s-largest-homeless-housing-development-breaks-ground-in-skid-row.

8. https://www.latimes.com/california/story/2024-01-25/photos-2024-greater-los
-angeles-homeless-count.

9. https://housinginnovation.co/deal/a-bridge-home-venice-beach/.

10. https://ktla.com/news/los-angeles-is-spending-up-to-837000-to-house-a-single
-homeless-person/.

11. https://www.landsearch.com/vacant/venice-ca.

12. https://www.cnn.com/2023/07/11/us/california-homeless-spending/index.html.

13. https://pathseldomtravelled.medium.com/nonprofit-accountability-registry
-c41e648abd34.

14. https://destinationhomesv.org/news/2019/08/23/silicon-valley-leaders-celebrate
-opening-of-san-joses-first-100-permanent-supportive-housing-development/.

15. https://www.rentcafe.com/apartments-for-rent/us/ca/san-jose/downtown-san
-jose/.

16. https://www.opportunitynowsv.org/blog/local-non-profit-npo-mismanagement
-of-housing-fails-tenants-and-neighbors-alike.

17. https://sanjosespotlight.com/formerly-homeless-residents-fear-eviction-from-san-jose-affordable-housing-project/.
18. https://www.siliconvalley.com/2023/07/27/did-san-jose-give-a-26-million-bail-out-to-a-struggling-affordable-housing-developer/?ref=biztoc.com.
19. https://sfstandard.com/2023/05/30/san-francisco-mayor-to-increase-homelessness-spending-despite-budget-deficit/.
20. https://abc7news.com/sf-homeless-plan-housing-all-san-francisco-supervisor-rafael-mandelman/12760671/.
21. https://nypost.com/2024/05/11/us-news/san-francisco-slammed-for-5m-a-year-program-to-give-free-alcohol-to-the-homeless-this-isnt-working/.
22. https://amgreatness.com/2019/07/13/americas-homeless-industrial-complex/. See also https://calmatters.org/commentary/2023/07/something-clearly-off-homelessness-spending/.
23. https://pathseldomtravelled.medium.com/nonprofit-accountability-registry-c41e648abd34.
24. https://www.statista.com/statistics/204160/retail-prices-of-gasoline-in-the-united-states-by-state/.
25. https://californiaglobe.com/articles/ringside-sacramentos-war-on-water-and-energy/.
26. https://www.ocregister.com/2023/03/05/how-much-california-relies-on-imported-natural-gas-might-surprise-you/.
27. https://californiaglobe.com/fr/ringside-water-rationing-is-the-worst-way-to-build-resiliency/. See also https://www.yourcentralvalley.com/news/local-news/with-snowpack-at-normal-whats-the-hold-up-with-ag-water-allocation/.
28. https://amgreatness.com/2023/04/19/the-bullet-train-epitomizes-golden-state-corruption/.
29. https://www.newgeography.com/content/007707-california-most-urban-and-densest-urban-state.
30. https://data.census.gov/profile/California?g=040XX00US06.
31. https://californiaglobe.com/articles/tracking-political-spending-by-government-unions/.
32. https://www.gov.ca.gov/2022/11/16/california-releases-worlds-first-plan-to-achieve-net-zero-carbon-pollution/.
33. https://theregistrysocal.com/fraud-allegations-cast-shadow-over-californias-low-income-housing-initiatives/.
34. https://ballotpedia.org/California_Two-Thirds_Legislative_Vote_and_Voter_Approval_for_New_or_Increased_Taxes_Initiative_(2024).
35. https://www.kcra.com/article/california-supreme-court-taxpayer-protection-act-arguments/60702177.
36. https://ballotpedia.org/California_Proposition_5,_Lower_Supermajority_Requirement_to_55%25_for_Local_Bond_Measures_to_Fund_Housing_and_Public_Infrastructure_Amendment_(2024).
37. https://campaignfordemocracy.com/#mission.

Chapter 10: Incompetism

1. https://www.sacbee.com/news/politics-government/capitol-alert/article5519280.html.

2. https://thesource.metro.net/2015/01/06/groundbreaking-held-today-in-fresno-for-california-high-speed-rail-project/.
3. https://www.mercurynews.com/2015/01/03/california-bullet-train-getting-on-track/.
4. https://www.sacbee.com/news/politics-government/capitol-alert/article5519280.html.
5. https://hsr.ca.gov/2023/05/10/photo-release-high-speed-rails-signature-arched-cedar-viaduct-complete/.
6. https://abc7news.com/ca-high-speed-rail-federal-investment-la-to-sf-train-bullet/14155943/.
7. https://ballotpedia.org/California_Proposition_1A,_High-Speed_Rail_Bond_Measure_(2008).
8. https://hsr.ca.gov/wp-content/uploads/docs/about/business_plans/BPlan_2008_FullRpt.pdf.
9. https://www.thezebra.com/resources/driving/average-miles-driven-per-year/.
10. https://www.cnbc.com/2023/05/17/why-californias-high-speed-rail-is-taking-so-long-to-complete.html.
11. https://www.pleasantonweekly.com/news/2023/03/12/new-cost-estimate-for-high-speed-rail-puts-california-bullet-train-100-billion-in-the-red/.
12. https://enotrans.org/article/timeline-california-high-speed-rail-cost-estimates/.
13. https://www.nytimes.com/2022/10/09/us/california-high-speed-rail-politics.html?linked=google&auth=linked-google.
14. https://www.newsweek.com/california-high-speed-rail-map-project-delayed-1893828.
15. https://www.travelmath.com/flying-time/from/SFO/to/LAX.
16. https://www.bart.gov/about/financials/crisis.
17. https://www.cato.org/commentary/san-jose-bart-extensions-93-billion-cost-way-too-much.
18. https://www.justice.gov/usao-edca/pr/superseding-indictment-adds-defendants-25-million-prison-based-unemployment-insurance.
19. https://www.justice.gov/usao-edca/pr/former-gang-member-and-california-state-inmate-receives-over-five-years-federal-prison.
20. https://www.kcra.com/article/analysis-edd-fraud-326-billion-and-counting/41281662.
21. https://calmatters.org/explainers/california-edd-unemployment-crisis-explained/.
22. https://www.eia.gov/state/?sid=CA.
23. https://www.semrush.com/blog/google-search-statistics/.
24. https://legiscan.com/CA/text/SB1263/id/2930775. See also https://www.ctc.ca.gov/educator-prep/tpa.
25. https://www.ppic.org/publication/student-achievement-on-californias-k-12-assessments/.
26. https://freebeacon.com/campus/a-failed-medical-school-how-racial-preferences-supposedly-outlawed-in-california-have-persisted-at-ucla/.
27. https://www.uclahealth.org/news/release/national-ranking-places-david-geffen-school-of-medicine-at-ucla-6-in-research-11-in-primary-care; https://www.usnews.com/best-graduate-schools/top-medical-schools/university-of-california-los-angeles-04010#:~:text=University%20of%20California%2D%2DLos%20Angeles

%20(Geffen)%202023%2D2024,Medical%20Schools%3A%20Research%20 and%20No.

28. https://ballotpedia.org/California_Proposition_1,_Behavioral_Health_Services _Program_and_Bond_Measure_(March_2024).
29. https://elections.cdn.sos.ca.gov/ror/15day-presprim-2024/complete-ror.pdf.
30. https://cal-access.sos.ca.gov/Campaign/Committees/Detail.aspx?id=1380675&- session=2023&view=late1.
31. https://www.cbsnews.com/losangeles/news/proposition-1-vote-remains-too -close-to-call/. See also https://www.cbsnews.com/losangeles/news/california -voters-pass-proposition-requiring-counties-to-spend-on-programs-to-tackle -homelessness/.
32. https://www.kcra.com/article/california-prop-1-passes/60259887.
33. https://www.axios.com/local/san-diego/2024/01/05/california-leads-nation -unsheletered-homelessness.
34. https://www.sfexaminer.com/news/state/newsom-touts-california-as-national -model-on-homelessness/article_358f0ff8-9f4c-5ee9-a6af-48ec133d5517.html.
35. https://dailycaller.com/2024/08/22/newsom-says-state-policies-neglect-homeless -blame/.

Chapter 11: A Revolution Is Brewing

1. https://www.ppic.org/publication/race-and-voting-in-california/.
2. https://www.cde.ca.gov/ds/ad/ceffingertipfacts.asp.
3. https://thebreakthrough.org/journal/no-14-summer-2021/green-jim-crow.
4. https://law.justia.com/cases/federal/appellate-courts/ca9/15-35845/15-35845 -2018-09-04.html.
5. https://californiapolicycenter.org/california-bureaucrats-embrace-water -rationing/.
6. https://www.mesawater.org/sites/default/files/2021-01/Mesa%20Water%20 _SRIA%20Review_Tech%20Memo_Final_Sept%2028.2023.pdf.
7. https://abc7news.com/scott-wiener-speed-governors-pedestrian-safety-california -bills-streets-safer/14356386/.

Chapter 12: Restoring Political Balance

1. https://ballotpedia.org/California_State_Assembly; https://ballotpedia.org/California _State_Senate.
2. https://ballotpedia.org/California_gubernatorial_election,_2022.
3. https://ballotpedia.org/Josh_Hoover.
4. https://ballotpedia.org/California_Proposition_1,_Behavioral_Health_Services _Program_and_Bond_Measure_(March_2024).
5. https://ballotpedia.org/California_2020_ballot_propositions.
6. https://ballotpedia.org/California_Proposition_19,_Property_Tax_Transfers ,_Exemptions,_and_Revenue_for_Wildfire_Agencies_and_Counties_Amendment _(2020).
7. https://ballotpedia.org/California_Proposition_187,_Prohibit_Persons_in _Violation_of_Immigration_Law_from_Using_Public_Healthcare,_Schools ,_and_Social_Services_Initiative_(1994).

8. https://ballotpedia.org/California_Proposition_8,_Same-Sex_Marriage_Ban_Initiative_(2008).

Chapter 13: A Foundation of Prosperity and Abundance

1. https://advocacy.calchamber.com/policy/bill-tracking/2023-job-killers/.
2. https://capitalresearch.org/article/big-labors-golden-state-part-3/.
3. https://calmatters.org/commentary/2023/05/labor-law-paga-still-rages/.
4. https://goldentogether.com/wp-content/uploads/2024/03/Universal-Housing-Affordability.pdf.
5. https://leginfo.legislature.ca.gov/faces/codes.xhtml.
6. https://ciceroinstitute.org/wp-content/uploads/2023/12/Sunset-One-Pager-Fall-2023.pdf.
7. https://ciceroinstitute.org/wp-content/uploads/2023/12/CBA-One-Pager-Fall-2023.pdf.
8. https://ciceroinstitute.org/wp-content/uploads/2023/12/Regulatory-Court-Venue-One-Pager-Fall-2023.pdf/

Chapter 14: Rescuing K–12 Education

1. https://tntp.org/blog/case-closed-why-vergara-must-be-upheld-in-california/.
2. https://fordhaminstitute.org/national/commentary/bless-tests-three-reasons-standardized-testing.
3. https://wgetsnaps.github.io/cde.ca.gov--ds-sp-ai/ta/ac/pe/index.html.
4. https://wgetsnaps.github.io/cde.ca.gov--ds-sp-ai/ta/ac/pe/index.html.
5. https://pacificlegal.org/california-department-of-education-effectively-repeals-parent-trigger-law-for-2015/.
6. https://www.cde.ca.gov/re/pr/parentempowerment.asp.
7. https://californiaglobe.com/fr/the-orange-county-classical-academy-is-going-to-transform-education-in-california/.

Chapter 15: A Guarantee of Security

1. https://www.cdc.gov/aces/about/index.html; https://learnbehavioral.com/blog/brain-plasticity-2.
2. https://www.ojp.gov/pdffiles1/nij/247350.pdf.
3. https://oag.ca.gov/system/files/initiatives/pdfs/23-0017A1%20%28Drug%20Addiction%20%26amp%3B%20Theft%20Reform%29.pdf.
4. https://www.washingtonpost.com/nation/interactive/2023/california-fires-home-prices/. See also https://www.valuepenguin.com/homeowners-insurance/wildfire-statistics.
5. https://ww2.arb.ca.gov/sites/default/files/classic/cc/inventory/Wildfire%20Emission%20Estimates%20for%202022%20%28ADA%29.pdf.
6. https://www.sciencedirect.com/science/article/pii/S0269749122011022#bib1; https://ww2.arb.ca.gov/sites/default/files/classic/cc/inventory/2000-2020_ghg_inventory_trends.pdf.
7. https://www.tectonus.com/resources/blog/mass-timber-california.
8. https://ww2.arb.ca.gov/our-work/programs/sustainable-communities-program/project-solicitation/reducing-embodied-carbon.

Chapter 16: The California Dream

1. https://californiamuseum.org/inductee/edmund-g-pat-brown/.
2. https://www.watereducation.org/aquapedia/edmund-g-pat-brown.
3. https://www.ucop.edu/institutional-research-academic-planning/_files/California-master-pan-topic-brief.pdf.
4. https://www.zocalopublicsquare.org/2017/05/09/california-created-road-map-americas-interstate-system/ideas/nexus/.
5. https://www.latimes.com/environment/newsletter/2023-02-09/california-declared-war-on-natural-gas-now-the-fight-is-going-national-boiling-point. See also https://www.sandiegouniontribune.com/2015/09/19/california-energy-dreaming-costs-consumers-billions/.
6. https://calmatters.org/environment/2022/05/california-desalination-plant-coastal-commission/#:~:text=The%20California%20Coastal%20Commission%20tonight,than%2020%20years%20of%20debate. See also https://waterblueprintca.com/wp-content/uploads/2022/12/BP-1-Fish-Friendly-Diversions-12-17-22.pdf; https://www.latimes.com/environment/story/2023-12-09/newsom-administration-advances-delta-tunnel-project#:~:text=Gavin%20Newsom%20and%20his%20administration,the%20state's%20aging%20water%20system.
7. https://www.hoover.org/research/little-engine-couldnt-californias-high-speed-rail-costs-rise-200-million-mile#:~:text=The%20system%20was%20to%20be,Los%20Angeles%E2%80%93San%20Francisco%20leg.
8. https://www.linkedin.com/pulse/safety-financial-fiasco-haunts-california-high-speed-rail-webster/.
9. https://www.urbandictionary.com/define.php?term=doom%20loop.
10. https://www.city-journal.org/article/californias-homeless-problem-has-solutions.
11. https://www.hcd.ca.gov/sites/default/files/docs/grants-and-funding/homekey/Housing-First-Guidance-Checklist.pdf.
12. https://urbanreforminstitute.org/2022/01/the-next-american-cities/#:~:text=The%20Next%20American%20Cities%2C%20a%20New%20Report%20from%20Urban%20Reform%20Institute,-in%20Demographics%2C%20Housing&text=The%20urban%20form%20has%20shifted,accelerated%20by%20a%20devastating%20pandemic.
13. https://www.pewresearch.org/short-reads/2023/03/30/about-a-third-of-us-workers-who-can-work-from-home-do-so-all-the-time/.
14. https://maps.latimes.com/neighborhoods/population/density/neighborhood/list/; https://worldpopulationreview.com/us-cities/new-york/new-york.
15. https://www.census.gov/newsroom/press-releases/2022/people-working-from-home.html.
16. https://www.tandfonline.com/doi/abs/10.1080/14616689908721293.
17. Harvest rainwater: https://www.smartcitiesdive.com/ex/sustainablecitiescollective/capturing-rainwater-rooftops-report-spotlights-practical-green-infrastructure-solutio/35605/; recycle wastewater: https://www.sciencedirect.com/topics/earth-and-planetary-sciences/urban-wastewater; grow food: https://www.usda.gov/media/blog/2018/08/14/vertical-farming-future; generate and store energy: https://trellis.net/article/turning-skyscrapers-urban-energy-generators/; https://cleantechnica.com/2022/06/03/turning-high-rise-buildings-into-batteries/; process garbage: https://www.mdpi.com/2071-1050/12/13/5337.

18. https://www.weforum.org/agenda/2022/09/transparent-solar-panel-windows/.
19. Aquaponic: https://www.theaquaponicsource.com/what-is-aquaponics/; hydroponic: https://www.nal.usda.gov/farms-and-agricultural-production-systems/hydroponics; aeroponic: https://modernfarmer.com/2018/07/how-does-aeroponics-work/.
20. https://www.forbes.com/sites/jamesconca/2020/07/10/feeding-the-planet-isnt -science-fictionits-cultivated-meat/?sh=338118d46c5b.
21. https://thehill.com/homenews/3786630-amazon-begins-drone-deliveries-in-2-u -s-cities/.
22. https://www.aboutamazon.com/news/transportation/amazon-prime-air-delivery -drone-reveal-photos.
23. https://builtin.com/articles/drone-delivery-companies.
24. https://www.urbanairmobilitynews.com/air-taxis/five-evtol-companies-valued-at -more-than-usd1-billion-drone-industry-insights/?utm_source=rss&utm_medium =rss&utm_campaign=five-evtol-companies-valued-at-more-than-usd1-billion -drone-industry-insights.
25. https://www.jobyaviation.com/.
26. https://www.ehang.com/ehangaav/.
27. https://trellis.net/article/7-urban-air-mobility-companies-watch/.
28. https://jetson.com/.
29. Boeing: https://www.aurora.aero/urban-air-mobility/; Airbus: https://www.airbus .com/en/newsroom/press-releases/2021-09-airbus-reveals-the-next-generation -of-cityairbus; Raytheon: https://www.rtx.com/news/2020/07/14/the-future-of-air -travel.
30. Delta: https://www.freightwaves.com/news/delta-invests-in-joby-and-home-to-airport -drone-service; American Airlines: https://www.businessinsider.com/american-airlines -flying-taxis-vx4-evtol-2022-7; United Airlines: https://dronexl.co/2022/09/14 /united-airlines-drone-taxis-transport/; Lufthansa: https://www.volocopter.com/en /newsroom/volocopter-and-lufthansa-industry-solutions-cooperate-to-build -voloiq-on-microsoft-azure.
31. Volkswagen: https://insideevs.com/news/601732/volkswagen-group-unveils-its -first-electric-flying-taxi-prototype/; Honda: https://www.youtube.com/watch?app =desktop&v=32mNTUrSeac; Toyota: https://dronelife.com/2020/01/21/the -model-for-urban-air-mobility-that-big-money-is-backing-toyotas-394-m-invest ment-in-passenger-drones/; Tesla: https://www.youtube.com/watch?v=avbX0 iQLrgQ.
32. Apple: https://www.macworld.com/article/671532/icar-why-apple-is-more-likely -to-make-a-flying-car-than-take-on-bmw.html; Microsoft: https://www.youtube .com/watch?v=F0ku1av1obQ.
33. https://www.herrenknecht.com/en/.
34. https://www.bbc.com/news/world-europe-36423250.
35. https://www.herrenknecht.com/en/products/tunnelling/.
36. https://www.boringcompany.com/.
37. https://californiapolicycenter.org/californias-transportation-future-part-four-the -common-road/.
38. https://www.boringcompany.com/projects#vl.
39. https://theconversation.com/how-spacex-lowered-costs-and-reduced-barriers-to -space-112586.

40. https://rbr.business.rutgers.edu/article/vertical-farming-economics-10-minutes.
41. https://openknowledge.fao.org/server/api/core/bitstreams/76b45dc9-c646-46fe -9b2b-52fcb06fe10a/content/CB1329EN.html.
42. https://www.alliedmarketresearch.com/vertical-farming-market.
43. https://forgeglobal.com/plenty_ipo/. See also https://www.plenty.ag/.
44. https://boweryfarming.com/.
45. https://www.bloomberg.com/news/articles/2022-03-15/vertical-farming-takes -on-strawberries.
46. https://www.skygreens.com/.
47. https://pmc.ncbi.nlm.nih.gov/articles/PMC3394405/.
48. https://www.keygene.com/wp-content/uploads/2017/12/shaping-wheat-for-the -future.pdf/.
49. https://www.publichealth.columbia.edu/profile/dickson-d-despommier-phd.
50. https://pubmed.ncbi.nlm.nih.gov/32719119/.
51. https://www.sustain.ucla.edu/what-is-sustainability/.
52. https://www.thinkwood.com/mass-timber?.
53. https://link.springer.com/chapter/10.1007/978-3-319-59471-2_316.
54. https://www.sustainalytics.com/esg-research/resource/investors-esg-blog/mass -timber-in-construction.
55. https://research.fs.usda.gov/centers/ccrc.
56. https://www.eia.gov/todayinenergy/detail.php?id=11911. See also https://www .cnbc.com/2021/03/05/sand-shortage-the-world-is-running-out-of-a-crucial -commodity.html.
57. https://sites.cnr.ncsu.edu/clt-panels/history-of-cross-laminated-timber/.
58. https://www.drjwoodinnovations.com/clt-machinery-price-reduction/.
59. https://www.structurlam.com/whats-new/news/concrete-vs-cross-laminated -timber/.
60. https://www.nytimes.com/2020/08/11/business/concrete-cement-manufacturing -green-emissions.html.
61. https://www.forest2market.com/blog/how-much-timber-does-the-us-harvest -and-how-is-it-used.
62. https://northamericanforestfoundation.org/tree-wood-facts/.
63. https://www.fs.usda.gov/pnw/pubs/pnw_gtr908.pdf.
64. https://archinect.com/news/article/150319903/new-california-building-codes -allow-for-high-rise-mass-timber-buildings.
65. https://dieselcommercialgroup.com/how-are-low-mid-and-high-rise-buildings -classified/; Los Angeles: https://www.archpaper.com/2021/08/lever-architectures -mass-timber-office-building-in-chinatown-will-be-l-a-s-largest/; San Jose: https:// www.bdcnetwork.com/san-jose-affordable-housing-project-will-feature-mass -timber-frame; San Francisco: https://www.sfchronicle.com/sf/article/s-f-s-first -clt-building-is-online-will-this-16777027.php; Sacramento: https://www.sansin .com/aia-first-wood-laminated-timber-building-in-sacramento/.
66. https://www.owow.com/projects.
67. https://www.aclu.org/news/privacy-technology/our-cars-are-now-roving -computers-fourth-amendment.
68. https://spectrum.ieee.org/autonomous-vehicles-traveling-in-convoys-will-run-into -this-inevitable-tradeoff.

69. https://www.aljazeera.com/news/2022/12/27/on-the-road-in-san-francisco-riding
    -in-a-driverless-taxi.
70. https://bgr.com/tech/waze-just-launched-its-first-dedicated-app-for-cars/.
71. https://www.youtube.com/watch?v=K6ZxC2ETRZs.
72. https://humantransit.org/2011/07/02box.html.
73. https://usa.streetsblog.org/2022/05/31/will-autonomous-buses-force-drivers-out
    -of-a-job-or-make-them-more-important-than-ever. See also https://usa.streetsblog
    .org/about.
74. http://www.technovelgy.com/ct/Science-Fiction-News.asp?NewsNum=472;
    https://webhome.auburn.edu/~vestmon/robotics.html.

INDEX

ABOUT THE AUTHOR

Steve Hilton is the founder of Golden Together, an independent, non-partisan organization whose aim is to develop positive, practical, and commonsense policy ideas that will help restore the California Dream.

Steve is a Fox News contributor and the host of the *Steve Hilton Show* podcast; he was previously host of *The Next Revolution* with Steve Hilton on Fox News. He is the author of *Positive Populism: Revolutionary Ideas to Rebuild Economic Security, Family, and Community in America* and the UK *Sunday Times* bestseller *More Human: Designing a World Where People Come First*. He has been a teacher, lecturer, and visiting scholar at Stanford University's Institute of Design (d.school), the Freeman Spogli Institute for International Studies, and at the Hoover Institution.

Steve was previously the CEO of Crowdpac, the political crowdfunding platform he cofounded in 2014, and before that he was a senior adviser to former prime minister David Cameron, with whom he helped lead the implementation of the British government's domestic reform program. Prior to the 2010 general election, as David Cameron's head of strategy, Steve is credited with helping to develop the ideas associated with the modernization of the British Conservative Party.

Before working in politics, Steve was a cofounder of Good Business, a corporate responsibility consulting firm, and the Good Cook, an award-winning London restaurant. He moved to the United States in 2012, became an American citizen in May 2021, and lives in the San Francisco Bay Area with his wife and two sons. Plus two dogs. And eight chickens.